THE REVOLT OF
THE CONSERVATIVES

A HISTORY OF

THE AMERICAN LIBERTY LEAGUE

1934-1940

THE REVOLT OF
THE CONSERVATIVES

A HISTORY OF
THE AMERICAN LIBERTY LEAGUE

1934-1940

George Wolfskill

HOUGHTON MIFFLIN COMPANY BOSTON

The Riverside Press Cambridge

1962

for Walter Prescott Webb

PREFACE

I REMEMBER the day very well. I was aboard a troopship anchored at Pearl Harbor musing over the hellish days so recently endured on that miserable, misbegotten island in the Pacific; Iwo Jima was a geological miscarriage that only war could make important. The day was April 12, 1945, the day Franklin Roosevelt died.

I had finished high school and college, done graduate work, left home, taught school, married, become a parent, joined the Marine Corps; and he was President the whole time. I was one of that generation who really could remember no other President. Now he was gone; and I sensed even then that this was more than the inevitable passing of a mortal man. An era had ended. Elected during the worst of depressions, Roosevelt had died during the worst of wars. In between were twelve fateful years, years that had changed the face of America and maybe its body chemistry.

He had been the symbol of those years, the Roosevelt years. Maybe there had been other symbols in other years; I vaguely recalled my professors talking about the Jeffersonian Era and the Age of Jackson. But few men had dominated an era as Roosevelt did; still fewer had aroused the passionate feelings of so many as he did. Many loved him with an uncomplicated love that approached idolatry; others disliked him; a few hated him; no one could ignore him.

The early Roosevelt years are the setting for this book, the years before the war. It is a book about the American Liberty League, about people who feared and distrusted Roosevelt, disliked him, about some who doubtlessly hated him. It is a book about people who shared the desire to be rid of him and his short-cuts to the New Jerusalem.

This story of the American Liberty League is not one of strange and furtive people, hiding out in dank cellars, haranguing one another with some alien plan of salvation, and passing out shoddy handbills with counterfeit union labels to Bowery bums. It is a story of respectable people, people of character, education, breeding, people whose roots were deep. The American Liberty League attracted to its ranks a substantial cross section of the leaders of American business, industry, finance, law, and the professions. It is perhaps no exaggeration to say that not in the history of the country did one organization marshal so much prestige, wealth, and managerial skill to undo a President as the Liberty League did in the fight against Roosevelt and the New Deal.

At the time, the 1930's, the Liberty League was the most articulate spokesman of what (for lack of a better term) may be called political conservatism. It was a time-honored creed, a creed with impressive credentials, one that needed no apologies. Yet the Liberty League probably did the cause of conservatism a disservice. Almost from the outset (with no little help from the Administration), it was made to look ridiculous or dangerous, and sometimes both.

In the first place, the organization was too rich. The resentment of the have-nots toward the haves lurks just below the surface anytime; in the 1930's, for rich men to insist that Roosevelt was not the Word made flesh, that the New Deal was a snare and a deception seemed the crowning touch of irony to those many people who were innocent victims of depression. The purist will observe that most of the thousands of members of the League were not rich, and that is true. But its leaders were. Its spokesmen were. These were the people that the man in the street thought of when he heard or read about the League. These were the people the Administration made synonymous with the League. New Deal spokesmen did not have to refute the views of the League; they had only to call the roll.

A few of the people identified with the Liberty League behaved badly. They said things and they did things that appeared inexcusable no matter what the provocation. Someone will probably raise the point that the League could not be responsible for the behavior of all its members, and this is also true. But the League, nonetheless, was held responsible; the behavior of the few hurt the cause for which it stood. They embarrassed the League — embarrassed it to death.

Now, a quarter of a century later, it is apparent that the Liberty League was doomed from the start. Everything, the temper of the people, the mood of the country, pointed to defeat; the wrong people were espousing the wrong philosophy at the wrong time. Yet, strangely, it did not seem so to them then. With confidence they set for themselves a rock-pushing job that would have made Sisyphus throw up his hands in despair. They fought Roosevelt and lost.

It is impossible for me here to acknowledge my indebtedness to all the people, both friends and foes of the New Deal, with whom I have talked and corresponded. I am especially obligated, however, to Jouett Shouse and James A. Farley, both of whom occupy conspicuous places in this book. Generous help was extended me by the staffs at the Franklin D. Roosevelt Library, the National Archives, and the University of Texas Library. For many favors, large and small, I owe much to my colleague John A. Hudson, Head Librarian at Arlington State College, who also read the manuscript and criticized it as only he can. Miss Mary Swisher and Mrs. Lois Pool, members of the Arlington State College library staff, are entitled to special credit

for allowing me to impose upon their time and ingenuity. Mrs.
Mary Nicholson deserves stars in her crown for typing the manuscript as a labor of love. Craig Wylie, Managing Editor of
Houghton Mifflin Company, has saved me from innumerable
follies with a gentleness and warmth of understanding reserved,
I feel sure, only for invalids and beginning authors. Finally, I
wish to express my appreciation to Alberta, patient, tolerant,
good-humored, but bemused by the thought that shuffling note
cards and gazing out of the window are forms of work.

G. W.

Arlington State College
January 15, 1961

CONTENTS

ILLUSTRATIONS
FOLLOWING PAGE 176

THE REVOLT OF
THE CONSERVATIVES

A HISTORY OF

THE AMERICAN LIBERTY LEAGUE

1934-1940

PROLOGUE: SUMMER 1934

THE OCCASIONAL CLANG of streetcar bells echoed mournfully on the hot, humid air along Pennsylvania Avenue. On The Mall hardly a leaf stirred in the trees. Off a short distance to the south the majestic monuments to Washington and Lincoln shimmered in the bright sunshine like the pleasure domes of Kubla Khan. It seemed cooler under the trees of Lafayette Square and the White House; but to the tourist, armed with camera and guidebook, the winds sweeping across Capitol Plaza, raw and cold in winter but now hot and oppressive, might have been imported from the tropics. The evenings were not much better; and the long rides out to Great Falls or the concerts at the Watergate brought little relief. Summer had arrived early along the Potomac. The year was 1934.

Congress adjourned in mid-June. With elections coming in the fall, the servants of the people needed an early start at the business of pointing with pride and viewing with alarm. On July 1, President Roosevelt cleared his desk of work left in the wake of the Seventy-third Congress and boarded the U.S.S. *Houston* for a leisurely trip to Hawaii by way of the Panama Canal. With Capitol Hill deserted and the Chief Executive about to depart on vacation, the city seemed to lose its vitality.

But while Washington was subsiding into the lethargy of summer routine a great drama was unfolding in Europe. In the fretful summer of 1934, "Nazi" became a household word.

II

On January 30, 1933, Adolf Hitler became Chancellor of Germany. "I want," he said, "precisely the same power as Mussolini exercised after the March on Rome." Eight weeks later he got it.

Germany's defeat in World War I ruined the engineering career of Gottfried Feder. Turning to politics after the war, Feder was one of the half-dozen original colleagues of Hitler and eventually became the closest economic adviser to Der Führer. It was Feder who, in 1920, wrote the National Socialist party platform of "Twenty-five Points" later expanded by Hitler into a volume of memoirs, *Mein Kampf*. In the lean years, when National Socialism was struggling for survival and respectability, he was quietly working to gain the confidence of German businessmen. National Socialism, he assured them, was not aimed "at the real creators of our heavy industry — the Krupps, Kirdorfs, Thyssens, Mannesmanns, and Siemens." Fearing communism more than they approved of National Socialism, Germany's leading industrialists took Feder at his word; and their support was Hitler's salvation.

The National Socialist movement appeared to have reached floodtide in the summer of 1932. In the short interval between the Reichstag elections of July and November 1932, popular support of the Nazis fell off by nearly two million votes. In the same period the Communists, who had polled nearly two million votes in 1924, four and a half million in 1930, and almost five million in the presidential election of 1932, added another seven hundred thousand votes. By 1933 the Communists had become the third-largest party in Germany.

Despite the waning popularity of National Socialism, Hitler still controlled the largest party bloc in the Reichstag. When in January 1933, the government of Kurt von Schleicher collapsed over the issue of land redistribution (after only fifty-seven days in power), German business leaders panicked. Bold action, they insisted, was the only alternative to Communist violence. President Hindenburg, although already suspicious of Hitler's intentions, had nowhere else to turn for a chancellor.

The new Chancellor, needing a subservient legislature that could give an air of legality to his grab for power, called for new Reichstag elections in March 1933.

The Nazis took no chances. With government approval they commandeered radio, press, and platform. While denying police protection to the opposition parties, roving detachments of Sturmabteilungen and Schutzstaffeln, armed with clubs and rubber truncheons, savagely subdued rival electioneering.

The climax to this shameful farce came just one week before the election. The Reichstag building was gutted by fire, an act of arson which the Nazis very promptly and conveniently blamed on their strongest rivals, the Communists.

The election was an indecisive victory for the National Socialists; Nazi Reichstag candidates garnered only 44 per cent of the vote. Unless they counted the 52 members of their allies, the Nationalists, the Nazis lacked a majority. But Hitler knew how to cope with the situation. Surrounding the Reichstag with his brown-shirted Storm Troops, he excluded the Communists from their seats and intimidated other opposition members. By an overwhelming majority, 441 to 94, the Reichstag voted to suspend the constitution of 1919 and to give the Chancellor dictatorial powers for four years. Hitler had "the same power as Mussolini," and the Weimar Republic was dead.

III

On July 13, 1934, Chancellor Hitler addressed the Reichstag. "In this hour," he shouted, "I was responsible for the fate of the German nation. . . . I gave the order to shoot the ring-leaders of this treasonable plot. . . . I am fully prepared to assume before history the responsibility. . . ." In Hitler's twisted reasoning willingness to assume the responsibility was sufficient justification for dismissing the Blood Purge of June 30.

Early in 1934 it became evident that there was dissatisfaction within National Socialist ranks. Since gaining power the Chancellor had deliberately ignored the socialistic side of the party program, a loss of memory which many rank-and-file Nazis regarded as a flagrant betrayal of their interests. More ominous than the civilian discontent was the mounting unrest between the Reichswehr, or regular army, and the Brown Shirts, the Sturmabteilungen. Ernst Röhm, an associate of Hitler for many years and chief of staff of the Brown Shirts, demanded that he be promoted to Minister of Defense, the post held by Reichswehr general, Werner von Blomberg. Had Röhm's demand been met, he would have controlled the armed forces and through them the government as well.

Both Hitler and Blomberg rejected the plan; and Hitler was correct in suspecting that Röhm's keen disappointment would result in surreptitious plans for revolt. The intrigue came to a head on the night of June 30, 1934, when, on signal from Wilhelm Göring, Hitler raced to Röhm's headquarters and personally arrested him. The Blood Purge had begun.

Outstanding among the victims of the purge were Röhm, Gregor Strasser, one of Hitler's earliest associates in the Nazi movement, Karl Ernst, commandant of the Berlin Storm Troops, Kurt von Schleicher, whom Hitler had succeeded as Chancellor, Schleicher's wife, and Dr. Erich Klausener, leader of the Catholic Action group. These and some seventy other alleged conspirators were murdered or executed. It was for these acts during the twenty-four hours "in which I came to the bitterest decisions of my life" that Hitler assumed responsibility before the Reichstag. And in a formal resolution the Reichstag thanked the Chancellor for his vigorous forestalling "of civil war and chaos."

That dictators were not ordinary mortals was a lesson that the world of the 1930's was slow to learn. In Germany, Hitler had crushed an incipient revolution with cruel efficiency and dispatch. Such an experience, which might have made lesser men wary, seemed to stimulate Hitler to bolder action. Having successfully met the challenge bolstered his confidence, inflated his ego, sent him off in pursuit of more elusive goals. The Blood Purge had scarcely ended when he instigated a premature and ill-conceived revolt in Austria.

On July 25, Nazi assassins murdered the Austrian chancellor, Engelbert Dollfuss, in an abortive putsch that exposed Hitler's plan to bring about by violence a union of Germany and Austria. Alarmed by Hitler's boldness, Mussolini, whose plans for invading Ethiopia were already complete, massed troops at the Brenner Pass. Il Duce's saber-rattling frustrated German designs on Austria at least for the moment.

A week later, President Hindenburg died. In the plebiscite that followed, 88 per cent of the electorate voted *Ja* to the proposition that Hitler be given sole executive authority in Germany. Hitler was now Chancellor and President of the German Reich; but he declined both titles, preferring the more meaningful salutation, Der Führer.

So ended the summer of 1934 in Germany. And Europe would never be the same.

IV

On the continent there were signs that at least some recognized the menace of National Socialism. At The Hague, Queen Wilhelmina's government adopted measures that debarred Nazis from holding public office; and in Belgium, by royal decree,

Leopold III prohibited the formation of quasi-military units or the wearing of uniforms by political organizations. Bearded Foreign Minister Louis Barthou toured France's eastern and central European allies with a view of strengthening existing bonds of friendship. With a complex system of alliances and rapprochements that included Bulgaria, Poland, Greece, Turkey, and the Little Entente, Barthou was singularly successful in isolating Germany. Before he and Alexander I of Yugoslavia were cut down at Marseilles by the Macedonian assassin Vlado Chernozemsky, Barthou figured prominently in the preliminary negotiations that led to the admission of the Soviet Union into the League of Nations, another move calculated to maintain the status quo in Europe.

But this was the sort of political intrigue that baffled Americans and left them suspicious and confused. They did not understand what was happening in Europe, and what they did not understand they tried to ignore. A whole flood of material began to appear that was anti-war, anti-European, and pacifist in tone. And always the theme was the same. By staying aloof from Europe's troubles and strengthening democracy at home the American people could make their best contribution to the cause of world peace, ran the argument. What went on in Europe was none of their affair. The United States had made a mistake in becoming involved in Europe in 1917 and that mistake must not be repeated.

In the summer of 1934, the temper of the American people was more persistently isolationist than ever before. Students joined pacifist movements like the Fellowship of Reconciliation; a strong wave of pacifism swept through the ranks of Protestant churchmen; "No War" parades with their lines of silent marchers were held in New York and elsewhere. This was a time of apprenticeship for the isolationist America First movement that mushroomed in 1940.

By the fall of 1934, when Senator Gerald P. Nye began to

capture daily headlines with his munitions investigation, leaders of the peace movement were certain that Americans were too sophisticated to be led down the international garden path again. Neither were they disturbed that native fascists applauded their noninterventionist stand.

V

Summer was also a time for matters less complicated than international politics, for familiar and long remembered things, things that were somehow distinctly American. Summer was a time for baseball, and in 1934, baseball meant the St. Louis Cardinals' Gas House Gang and the irrepressible Dean brothers, Dizzy and Paul. The Deans missed trains, refused to appear for exhibitions, tore up uniforms, quit the team, went on strike. They built bonfires at third base, made home runs on bunts, hurled no-hit games. They badgered manager Frank Frisch and made the Old Puritan, Branch Rickey, mutter "Judas Priest!" oftener than at any other time in his life.

But "Me and Paul" won forty-nine games between them; and when the stands at Sportsman's Park rocked to the chant "We want Dean!" there they were, all arms and legs, with a blazing fastball to snuff out an enemy rally. The Cardinals caught the New York Giants in the last week of the season and went on to beat the Detroit Tigers in the most riotous seven games ever played in a World Series.

Americans were fascinated that summer by another kind of hero, the federal agent. In the year that elapsed between the convict break from the Indiana State Prison which he engineered until the "Lady in Red" led him into a trap at a Chicago moviehouse, John Dillinger was the most hunted man in the history of American crime.

Shortly after the break, Dillinger was captured but broke

jail at Lima, Ohio, killing the jailer in the escape. Recaptured in Tucson early in 1934, he was taken to Indiana and jailed at Crown Point. In a sensational escape, Dillinger bribed and bluffed his way to freedom with a wooden pistol that he had carved. For more than four months, despite numerous gun battles, he eluded police and FBI agents.

Thirteen lives had been lost before Melvin Purvis and the federal agents cornered him again. Late in July a tip brought Purvis and his men to Chicago's Biograph theater. After an agonizing two-hour wait, Dillinger walked into the ambush and was killed trying to escape. Unwittingly, Dillinger had made a national hero of Purvis, the slight, red-haired South Carolina lawyer. Later that fall, Purvis led the hunts that ended in similar deaths for "Pretty Boy" Floyd in Ohio, and "Baby Face" Nelson in Illinois. When the *Literary Digest* published its list of the ten outstanding persons for 1934, Melvin H. Purvis was eighth on the list.

In 1934 everyone read (or at least claimed to have read) Hervey Allen's novel *Anthony Adverse*. For months it led the bestseller lists until challenged in midsummer by another of the orange blossoms and magnolia stories of the ante-bellum South. In Stark Young's nostalgic story *So Red the Rose*, the reader could escape once more to Natchez, to the McGehees and Bedfords of Montrose and Portobello, to charming ladies and dashing young men who enjoyed the good life until Jeff Davis' call brought it all crashing down around their heads.

At the *Shubert* on Broadway, playgoers thrilled to the superb performances of Fay Bainter and Walter Huston in *Dodsworth*, the hit play of the season. And James Barton replaced Henry Hull as Jeeter Lester in *Tobacco Road* when it began the second year of its record run. The movie box-office favorites were still Will Rogers and Shirley Temple; but early in July patrons flocking to see *The Thin Man* were smitten by the spouse of detective Nick Charles, a charmer with turned-up nose and

sardonic smile named Myrna Loy. William Powell had a new
screen wife and Hollywood had a new star. In August, Aca-
demy Award winner Marie Dressler, of the raucous voice and
mobile face, died of cancer.

Led by ranking Protestant churchmen and the Catholic Legion of Decency, public indignation over vulgarity and immorality in motion pictures reached a peak that summer. The
industry received more unfavorable publicity than at any time
since the Fatty Arbuckle incident. Although film producers
(noting the financial success of the Mae West pictures) won-
dered whether the public really agreed with its spiritual leaders,
they accepted a code of ethics and the Breen Office went to
work policing movie morals.

Helen Jacobs dominated women's tennis, and Fred Perry, a
small, handsome Englishman, was unbeatable in the men's ranks.
An aging Glenn Cunningham battled Bill Bonthron for track
laurels; Max Baer clowned his way to the heavyweight title
with a knockout victory over the ponderous Primo Carnera;
and a youthful Lawson Little won every important amateur
golfing honor in sight. In the Sport of Kings, Mrs. Dodge
Sloan's Cavalcade made racing enthusiasts forget the comeback
attempt of the great Equipoise.

Understandably, young lovers preferred "Be Still My Heart"
or "June in January" to Shirley Temple's little ditty about a trip
to the candy shop "On the Good Ship Lollipop."

VI

Arriving on the West Coast from Hawaii early in August, the
President began the long trip back to Washington. He had been
gone more than five weeks and had covered nearly 18,000
miles when he arrived in Green Bay, Wisconsin, for his first
major speech of the congressional campaign.

"There is no lack of confidence," said the smiling, sun-tanned President, "on the part of those businessmen, farmers, and workers who clearly read the signs of the times." He said he saw no reason "to offer apologies" for his policies, and he offered none. On the contrary, the speech was a stirring defense of New Deal accomplishments, a ringing promise that new policies would be undertaken and old ones extended.

No one doubted that, once back in the capital, Roosevelt would resume the vigorous leadership that had marked his first year and a half in office. But everyone also recognized that the New Deal honeymoon was over. Despite definite and encouraging signs of recovery the country was still in trouble. Opposition, quieted at the outset by the flush of victory and a disposition to give Roosevelt a chance, was beginning to mount; and even a minor defection of the voters that fall would lend comfort to New Deal critics and slow down the Administration's program in the new Congress.

No one knew these things better than Roosevelt. In his Portland to Washington jaunt, he learned firsthand what Secretary of Agriculture Henry Wallace meant when he said that "never before in history has there been so little rain over so wide a territory during the growing season." The losses in twenty-four drought-stricken states were expected to run as high as five billion dollars, and the grain crops would be the smallest since 1893. While the critics of the President did not blame him because it did not rain, they were highly critical of his $525,000,000 agricultural relief program.

On the business front, the National Industrial Recovery Act (which Roosevelt had called "the most important and far-reaching legislation ever enacted by the American Congress") was being assailed on every side. All had gone smoothly at first until it became clear that the NRA codes had given bigger businesses an unfair advantage over their smaller competitors. Efforts to ameliorate the inequities raised a storm of protest from the other side. President Roosevelt, seeking to palliate the mounting discontent, appointed a committee headed by the famous criminal lawyer Clarence Darrow to investigate and make recommendations. Much to the embarrassment of the Administration, Darrow dealt with the NRA as though it were on trial for murder.

Labor likewise was becoming disenchanted with the NRA. The codes had gained objectives for labor which, in its weakened condition, it could not have gained for itself in such a short time. Labor leaders were particularly heartened by Section 7a, which gave workers the right to organize and bargain collectively. But industry leaders were for the most part as intransigent as ever toward unionization and fought it with every resource at their command. Section 7a seemed more a statement of hope than an accomplishment.

The result was a wave of strikes and bloody labor disorders. In July, San Francisco was tied up by a strike of longshoremen; textile workers walked out in Alabama; the National Guard was called up during the strike of truckers and taxi drivers in Minneapolis. The following month workers of the Aluminum Company of America walked out in four states; the Chicago stockyards were snarled for days by a strike of livestock handlers; and a general steel strike was only narrowly averted. Before the year was out, more than a million American workers were involved in strikes, blood and lives were expended, millions of dollars were lost from damages and work stoppages, and the worst was yet to come.

In the strange world of politics, the troubles besetting the Administration were a source of encouragement to the Republican party. Shamed into silence by the humiliation of 1932, Republican leaders breathed deep and dared to speak out against Roosevelt in the summer of 1934. Early in July, Senator Borah, in a radio address from Washington, denounced Roosevelt for attempting to "fasten a stranglehold system of bureaucracy upon the people" and for "fostering monopoly." The next day the Idaho senator departed for the West on a crusade against "New Deal waste, bureaucracy, and monopoly," a crusade which he hoped would advance him toward the Republican nomination in 1936.

Out in Jackson, Michigan, the Republican party faithful gathered about a bronze tablet to celebrate the eightieth anniversary of the party and to hear the new national chairman, Henry P. Fletcher, castigate the Administration. The New Deal, said Fletcher, is "government from above." It is predicated "on the proposition that the people cannot manage their own affairs and that a government bureaucracy must manage for them." Our national economy, he charged, is "being restricted . . . displaced, may ultimately be destroyed by . . . an all-directing State."

Meanwhile, others rallied to the attack. Standing at the graveside of Calvin Coolidge, James M. Beck, Solicitor General in the Harding Administration, charged that "no one who knows our history can justly claim that it [the New Deal] is American in spirit." Senators Reed, Robinson, Hatfield, and Fess took to the platform, while Herbert Hoover let it be known that he was writing a book.

The Republicans even stole a leaf from the New Deal book. They organized their version of the much maligned "brain trust." The idea began with Representative Robert Low Bacon of New York. With the help of Representatives Chester Bolton, Richard Wigglesworth, Edward Goss, and Charles Bakewell, and Senators Daniel Hastings, Charles McNary, Lester J. Dickinson, Wallace White, and Peter Norbeck, Bacon organized the Bureau of Economic Research to assist Republicans on Capitol Hill as well as the Republican National Committee.

Instead of college professors and academicians, the Republicans staffed their "brain trust" with business and industrial research experts. Sidney Brooks, for many years head of the research bureau of the International Telephone and Telegraph Company, was hired as director. F. Lawrence Babcock of the Institute of Politics, Edward L. Evensen, director of commercial and industrial research in Mount Vernon, New York, and Alice M. Dodd, consultant with the Brookings Institution and the United States Chamber of Commerce, were brought in as Brooks's principal assistants. From its offices in downtown Washington the bureau, by midsummer, had issued pamphlets critical of the Administration's recovery program, spending, home financing, relief, public power, monetary policies, and bureaucracy, and was busily preparing material for the congressional campaign.

VII

November 6, 1934. Election day, with all the moving drama of a people about to speak.

Vox populi, vox Dei. The voice of the people is the voice of God, Alcuin had said. And how they spoke that day! Where the Democrats had had 60 senators, they now had 69; and where they had had 309 representatives, they now had 322; 72 per cent of the voting strength in the Senate and 74 per cent in the House. Only once since the Civil War had a party in power gained seats in both houses in a midterm election; and not since Reconstruction days had one party achieved such overwhelming majorities in the Congress.

In the midst of the election jubilation there were some ominous overtones that did not escape the President's notice. "Is it not a warning to the victorious Democrats as well as the defeated Republicans," inquired the Salt Lake City *Evening News*, "that the people are impatient for relief from the stupidity of poverty?" Said the Philadelphia *Public Ledger* editorially, "If the Democrats fail now to bring back the prosperity so long promised, there can be no excuse for failure."

Roosevelt knew that if the election meant anything it meant he had to deliver. And soon.

The New Deal program had begun with a great and dramatic burst of speed and energy. With contagious smile, resonant, reassuring voice, and an unerring sense of the theatrical, the President radiated confidence. On that cold, bleak day in March 1933 he had told a demoralized nation, "The only thing we have to fear is fear itself — nameless, unreasoning, unjustified terror"; and those who heard, those shivering in the cold wind of Capitol Plaza and the countless millions across the country huddled around their radios, had awakened and responded. There had never been anything like the First Hundred Days, and Washington throbbed with all the excitement of a city preparing for a holy crusade against depression and privation.

But for all the speed and boldness of action, the New Deal was, in spirit, cautious progressivism, Wilsonianism executed with the flourish of a Theodore Roosevelt. The Administration counted on a coalition of farmers, workers, and businessmen for its support; and, save for some misgivings about the farm and relief program and some inflationary legerdemain, the recovery program, leaning neither toward the extreme Right nor Left, was conceived and executed within the framework of capitalism.

Roosevelt's first two years in office had by no means brought recovery; and by the spring of 1934 some of his favorite projects, notably the NRA, were in serious trouble. The worst phase of the depression over, the normally conservative business community, much of which had supported Roosevelt at the outset, found more and more reason to criticize the New Deal.

A large proportion of the criticism was coming from members of the President's own party. Among the first of the prominent Democrats to break rank was Alfred E. Smith. Despite the appearances of a warm and fast friendship between the two, Smith and Roosevelt had never really been very close. By 1932 Smith had grown to distrust Roosevelt. Although he campaigned for Roosevelt, the bitter contest for the nomination had severed whatever bonds of friendship still remained.

Shortly after the Chicago Democratic convention, Smith became editor of the *New Outlook,* a position occupied by such illustrious predecessors as Lyman Abbott and Theodore Roosevelt. From its editorial page Smith observed the progress of the New Deal, first benignly and then with increasing acidity. The effect of Roosevelt's monetary policies, said Smith, had been to produce "baloney dollars." He ridiculed the mushrooming bureaucracy, calling it "alphabet soup." And what, he asked editorially, had happened to the 1932 party platform?

Others were asking the same thing. The Democratic platform of 1932 was as uninspired as most party platforms. Among the more significant planks was a demand for the repeal of the Eighteenth Amendment; a promise to reform the banking system and to maintain a sound currency; a promise to balance the budget and cut federal spending by 25 per cent; the demand that the federal government withdraw from all fields of private enterprise, "except where necessary to develop public works and natural resources"; a pledge to lower tariffs and control crop surpluses; an offer to lend federal money to the states for unemployment relief; and an endorsement of old age and unemployment insurance "under state laws."

Referring to the platform as "that admirable document" in his acceptance speech at Chicago, Roosevelt had said, "I accept it one hundred per cent." But accepting and following were two different things, and Roosevelt did not think that party platforms were to be taken too seriously. To John W. Davis, the Democratic nominee in 1924, this cavalier attitude had been "a tragic disappointment." In a series of anti-New Deal speeches Davis criticized the administration for adopting a "dishonest currency," for introducing "a system of state capitalism" through an expanding bureaucracy, and for spending money with "unprecedented profligacy," all in defiance of the platform.

Both Bainbridge Colby, onetime Secretary of State in the Wilson Administration, and William R. Pattangall, Chief Justice of the Maine Supreme Court, campaigned vigorously against the New Deal in Maine, where elections were held in advance of the rest of the country. Colby's speech in Portland was the most comprehensive attack on the New Deal yet to come from one so conspicuously connected with the party; and Pattangall's speeches received wide circulation in conservative political circles. Demanding a halt in the march toward a bureaucratic, paternalistic state, Pattangall, who had led the fight for the anti-Ku Klux Klan plank in the 1924 Democratic convention, delivered the sternest rebuke to the Roosevelt program by one of judicial rank.

Roosevelt was well aware that the public attacks by these prominent Democrats were not isolated shots in the dark. Their purpose had been to sound the keynote and then watch the response; meanwhile, behind the scenes a movement was afoot to create a community of interests based on a "back-to-fundamentals" appeal within the Democratic party. The *Literary Digest* reported rumors that Senators Gore, Byrd, Glass, Bailey, and Clark of Missouri, despite protests of loyalty to the Administration, had had private conversations and exchanged correspondence with Colby and Pattangall. How successful was this movement to organize a bloc of conservative Democrats would not be known until the meeting of the Seventy-fourth Congress.

VIII

The overwhelming Democratic victory in November 1934 did not diminish the fact that the New Deal had done little to alleviate the condition of the tenant and marginal farmers, the unemployed, the pensioners, and the indigent aged. In their plight, these distressed and forgotten groups were easy prey to those with cure-all schemes ranging from the impractical and through the fantastic, to the corrupt.

The lugubrious climate of California seemed peculiarly adapted for such movements as End Poverty in California and the Old Age Revolving Pension. The former was the idea of the old muckraking novelist Upton Sinclair, and included the proposal of a monthly pension of $50 to everyone over sixty, to be financed by a program of high state income and inheritance taxes. His book *I, Governor of California* sold a million copies; and, to the consternation of everyone except the voters, Sinclair won the Democratic gubernatorial nomination in 1934. He lost the race for the governorship, and his EPIC movement quickly collapsed; but its temporary success was symptomatic of serious dissatisfaction.

A more important and lasting movement was the Old Age Revolving Pension, better known as the Townsend Plan. The idea began with Dr. Francis E. Townsend of Long Beach, California; by 1935 some five million people, organized into thousands of Townsend Clubs, were agitating for the federal government to pay $200 monthly to all unemployed persons over sixty.

More disquieting to the Administration were the obvious successes of the extremists. William Dudley Pelley and his Silver Shirts, the Reverend Gerald B. Winrod, and particularly the Reverend Charles E. Coughlin's National Union for Social Justice and Senator Huey P. Long's Share-Our-Wealth Society. Such schemes often crossed the line dividing fantastic economic programs from base appeals to racial and religious bigotry.

Long's share-the-wealth movement was a particularly real and present danger to Roosevelt. The Louisiana senator proposed to make "every man a king" by giving each family a homestead worth $5000 and a guaranteed annual income of

$2500. This happy state of affairs was to be accomplished by the confiscation of large American fortunes. Long had been one of the earliest and most ardent advocates of Roosevelt's nomination, had supported him in the Chicago convention, and campaigned for him against Hoover. But when Roosevelt refused to accede to his demands for expropriation of wealth and nationalization of the banks, or to approve his unconscionable grab for patronage, Long turned savagely against the Administration. Until he was cut down by an assassin in the fall of 1935, the share-the-wealth movement was only a thinly disguised attempt by Long to capture control of the Democratic party.

IX

Roosevelt pondered these signs in the summer of 1934. On the one hand was a growing conservative movement, castigating the Administration for its radicalism and claiming that recovery had been sidetracked because the New Deal had strayed too far from conservative capitalism, a movement being aided and abetted by a Republican party showing signs of recovery. On the other was a large segment of population, largely overlooked in recovery planning, that was urging more radical measures by the Administration, egged on by disgruntled reformers, crackpots, and demagogues. And from it all came the haunting, disturbing knowledge that had the New Deal program succeeded as Roosevelt had hoped, these discordant voices would never have been raised.

In the election post-mortem the Bangor *Daily News* editorialized with prophetic insight. "Now we shall see some super-New Dealing, and very likely it will astonish the natives." However, the editorial continued, "it is what the voters ordered so there is nothing to do but make the best of it."

What the editorialist foresaw as "super-New Dealing" was a definite shift leftward on Roosevelt's part in early 1935. With the mounting pressure of conservative and radical factions forcing the issue, Roosevelt made his choice. It was to try to alleviate the miseries of the masses through the most far-reaching program of economic and social legislation ever undertaken in the history of the Republic. Roosevelt had not foreseen this shift, nor had he planned it this way; but with his usual political agility, he moved swiftly to choke off the kind of lower-class discontent that had produced the Hitlers and Mussolinis in Europe.

That the President was already thinking along these lines was evident in his speech at Green Bay, en route home from Hawaii. He related how, before his departure, he had received letters from two prominent men. And to both he had replied, "What would you like to have me say?" One urged the President to demand the abolition of all government supervision over business. "My friends," said Roosevelt emphatically, "I told him and I tell you that the people of the United States will not restore that ancient order."

That was August 10, 1934. The defenders of the "ancient order" had also been reading the signs. Two weeks later, on August 23, the *New York Times* carried this headline on page one: "League Is Formed to Scan New Deal, 'Protect Rights.'"

I

A STRANGE POLITICAL NOSEGAY?

. . . a strange political nosegay.
Time

The Tories have come out of ambush.
Newsweek

OFF PENNSYLVANIA AVENUE, at the corner of 14th and F Streets, stands the National Press Building. On the top floor is the National Press Club, where Presidents, ambassadors, foreign statesmen, the great and the near-great vie for the honor of addressing luncheon meetings of that impressive fraternity of journalists and newsmen.

The usual business and professional enterprises occupy the lower floors, one of which is the law office of Jouett Shouse on the tenth floor. Walking down the long corridor from the elevator a visitor finds himself thinking about England, about William the Conqueror, and the Battle of Hastings. Shouse's office number is 1066.

On the afternoon of August 22, 1934, a hot, sultry day in Washington, newsmen gathered in this office to hear an important announcement. They had been here many times before to cover the activities of the Association Against the Prohibition Amendment. Certainly Jouett Shouse was no stranger. They had known him both as president of the Association and as former chairman of the executive committee of the Democratic party. A many-talented man, Shouse had been a newspaper editor in Kentucky, a stock-breeder, a legislator and congressman after moving to Kansas in 1911, and an Assistant Secretary of the Treasury during the waning months of the Wilson Administration. For years a power in Kansas politics, Shouse was one of William Gibbs McAdoo's floor leaders at the 1920 and 1924 Democratic conventions. A man in his fifties, charming, confident, eloquent, persuasive, Shouse was a born leader of men.

Between 1928 and 1932 Shouse was one of the most important men in the Democratic party. Yielding to the importuning of his friend Alfred E. Smith, John J. Raskob had retired from active directorship of General Motors in 1928 to become chairman of the Democratic National Committee and to direct the Smith campaign. A former Republican, Raskob was a novice with no particular taste for politics, and was handicapped by his limited acquaintance with Democratic party leaders. Recognizing his own shortcomings, and not wishing to see the National Committee lapse into the usual inactivity after the disastrous election, Raskob persuaded Shouse to assume active leadership of the committee as its executive chairman.

Shouse set up a permanent party headquarters in Washington, hired Charles Michelson, head of the Washington bureau of the New York *World*, as publicity director, and went to work to rebuild the party. With the operation financed largely out of Raskob's own pockets, Shouse breathed new life into the demoralized party, a party that made impressive gains in the congressional elections of 1930 and overwhelmed the Republicans in the presidential election of 1932.

But it was in a new role that Shouse faced the reporters that August afternoon. He had called them there to announce formally the creation of the American Liberty League.

Adjusting his glasses, Shouse began to read from a prepared

text: ". . . to defend and uphold the Constitution . . . to teach the necessity of respect for the rights of persons and property as fundamental to every successful form of government . . . to teach the duty of government, to encourage and protect individual and group initiative and enterprise, to foster the right to work, earn, save and acquire property, and to preserve the ownership and lawful use of property when acquired."

The reporters asked endless questions. No, the American Liberty League was "not inimical to the national administration." No, it was "definitely not anti-Roosevelt." No, it was not a movement "to stop Roosevelt in 1936." Yes, we "intend to try to help the administration." No, the Liberty League "would not actually participate in elections." Yes, the League "would take an active interest in and definite position on questions of legislation affecting economic and social problems," and would report to the public its conclusions "as a result of its research and studies." Yes, it "would appear before congressional committees, oppose legislation that appeared dangerous and conduct a thorough educational campaign through the press and radio." Yes, it was hoped that the American Liberty League would be "a real factor in assisting toward recovery." [1]

II

Newsman pressed around the long table in the Old Senate Office Building to catch the words of the senator. "These letters," Senator Gerald P. Nye was saying, "bear all the earmarks of having been the birth-place and the birth-time of the Liberty League." He was referring to an exchange of correspondence between John Raskob and R. R. M. Carpenter, brother-in-law of Irénée, Pierre, and Lammot du Pont, and a vice-president of the du Pont corporation.

In the spring of 1934, Nye, a congenitally isolationist Re-

publican from North Dakota, had succeeded in getting the
Senate to approve an investigation of the munitions industry, an
investigation which, under Nye's chairmanship, quickly turned
into a crusade to prove that wars are always inspired by the
insatiable greed of bankers and businessmen.

Included in the voluminous mass of evidence subpoenaed by
the committee were the Raskob-Carpenter letters written in
March 1934. The letters referred to an informal discussion of
the national political situation following a board meeting of the
du Pont corporation late in 1933. In the face of what apparently was a general feeling of dissatisfaction with the New
Deal among other board members, Raskob took an anomalous
stand, cautioning his associates that they should not "attack the
President without knowing what they are talking about." A
good example of this sort of thing, he said, was a recent statement from the United States Chamber of Commerce urging
Roosevelt to maintain a sound-money policy. The statement,
Raskob pointed out, had been couched in language that left
the impression that the President opposed such a policy, when
only a few days before he had declared that in planning the
Administration fiscal policy two things — sound money and
good credit — were paramount.

A few months later Carpenter wrote to Raskob. In his
letter Carpenter expressed approval of Raskob's earlier position
that the President should not be criticized without knowing all
the facts. But the Administration, he went on, was pursuing
some policies that were "a great mystery" to him. He won-
dered why the Administration was competing with industry for
labor, unless Roosevelt was simply using the CCC and CWA
to buy the votes of the country. Why, he asked, was Roosevelt
condemning businessmen and corporate wealth, and apparently
trying to set labor against capital?

Just recently, Carpenter complained, five Negroes in South
Carolina had refused his offer of employment on his property

because they had "easy jobs with the government." A cook on his houseboat at Fort Myers had quit because he had secured a job with the government as a painter for a dollar an hour although he was not a painter by trade. Planter friends in South Carolina had been unable to get harvest hands because they had all joined the Civilian Conservation Corps. "A man like yourself," wrote Carpenter, "a supporter of his [Roosevelt's] and persona grata in Washington could . . . set many minds at rest" by finding out what the government was trying to do.

Raskob replied four days later. In the months that had elapsed since the du Pont board meeting, Raskob had himself become alarmed over the leftist direction to which the New Deal seemed to be veering. He explained to Carpenter that he had been out of politics since 1932 and was "anxious to stay out." It was time, however, that "some organization" should come up with a plan for getting across to the people "the value of encouraging people to work; encouraging people to get rich; showing the fallacy of communism. . . ." Something had to be done, said Raskob, to counteract the idea that businessmen are crooks and that no one should be allowed to get rich. Why not get the du Pont and General Motors people to undertake such an organization? "You haven't much to do," wrote Raskob, half jokingly, "and I know of no one that could better take the lead in trying to induce the du Pont and General Motors groups . . . to definitely organize to protect society. . . . I, of course, know you won't do it, but I personally think you should. . . ." [2]

III

Raskob was never more serious about the idea of an organization to combat radicalism, and he was correct in assuming that Carpenter would be unwilling to undertake the task of promoting it. It was quite natural, then, that he should turn to Jouett Shouse, the one man that he knew could do the job.

Early in July 1934, Raskob called Shouse to New York to discuss "a matter of some urgency." At recent meetings of the du Pont and General Motors companies, explained Raskob, the subject of the New Deal had continually cropped up. At the last du Pont meeting Raskob had suggested that instead of merely wringing their hands and lamenting the excesses of the Administration something positive be done to curb it. What he wanted Shouse to do was to think it over and then they would go to John W. Davis with their ideas.

Sometime later, Shouse and Raskob met with Davis, Irénée du Pont, Al Smith, and James W. Wadsworth, Jr. This was the first of a series of meetings, some at Davis' offices, some in Al Smith's offices in the Empire State Building, others in the General Motors Company offices off Columbus Circle, and still others at various clubs and private dining places in New York. Attending the meetings, besides Raskob, Shouse, Smith, Davis, and Wadsworth, were Alfred P. Sloan, Jr., of General Motors, Irénée du Pont and his brothers, Lammot and Pierre, Ernest T. Weir, president of Weirton Steel, Earl F. Reed, chief counsel of Weirton Steel, Mike Benedum, the legendary oil wildcatter, and numerous other men prominent in business and industry.

From these meetings it was evident that there was enough sentiment to justify the creation of an organization to combat what seemed to these men the dangerous trends of the New Deal. To give the organization the proper bipartisan character, it was agreed that two prominent Democrats, Al Smith and John W. Davis, and two Republicans, James W. Wadsworth, Jr., and Nathan Miller, a director of U.S. Steel and former governor of New York, would serve as directors with Irénée du Pont. Du Pont had been a Republican but had supported Smith in 1928 and Roosevelt in 1932.

Shouse was asked to serve as president.[3]

IV

Shouse's August press conference was an unfortunate but un-avoidable piece of bad timing. The original plan had been to wait until after the November election before announcing the formation of the League.

The reason for this was twofold, psychological and financial. Had the announcement been withheld until later it would have obviated the charge that the American Liberty League was trying to influence the election. Moreover, Shouse wanted to wait until enough funds were forthcoming to carry the League financially for at least a year, or until public contributions could take up the slack. During August more than $40,000 was pledged by Raskob, Sloan, Irénée du Pont, and others; but this was hardly enough for the ambitious program Shouse had in mind.

Somehow Elliot Thurston of the Washington bureau of the New York *World* got wind of the plans. Thurston, who succeeded Charlie Michelson as head of the bureau (when Michelson went to work for the Democratic National Committee) and who later served with the Federal Reserve Board, told Shouse that because of its great news value he would have to run the story.

Shouse had either to announce the League prematurely or let the *World* publish a story based on rumor, a story that would probably be distorted and maybe even damaging. Left with less than no choice, Shouse elicited a promise from Thurston not to release the story if he would himself make the news public within a few days.

Working against time, Shouse completed the legal technicalities and the American Liberty League was incorporated in the District of Columbia on August 15, 1934.

The same afternoon Shouse kept a White House appointment with Franklin Roosevelt.[4]

v

Back at his office the next morning Shouse dictated an account of his visit with the President the previous afternoon.

The President was most "cordial and attractive," he reported, during an interview that lasted nearly an hour. Roosevelt talked pleasantly and informally of many things, particularly of his recent trip to Hawaii. Whatever misgivings Shouse might have had about walking into the enemy camp were quickly dispelled.

Eventually the conversation turned to the point of Shouse's visit. "Mr. President," he began, "there has recently been formed an organization behind which there is a very powerful group and I have been asked to take the Presidency. I feel that you are entitled to know of the organization . . . and I should be unwilling to enter upon active work in connection with it without first telling you of it." He went on to assure Roosevelt that despite whatever the newspapers might say about the League, it would be "absolutely non-partisan in character."

After listening quietly to the list of League aims, Roosevelt turned to Shouse and said, "I can subscribe to that one hundred per cent and so can you. I think it is fine." He heartily agreed that the League would be far more effective in combatting radicalism than the Chamber of Commerce or numerous other smaller groups with similar aims scattered throughout the country, adding that he might be able to use a committee from the League in an advisory capacity in preparing the new federal budget.

As he was about to leave, Shouse once more reassured the President that the League was just what the charter said it was.

At this point, Roosevelt did the unexpected. Ringing for his secretary, Marvin McIntyre, Shouse reported, the President said:

> Mac, Jouett has just told me of an Association which is being formed, an announcement of which will be shortly made. . . . If I should be away, or for any reason unavailable at the time this Association is made public, I want you to call in the newspaper men and tell them that the aims and purposes of the Association have been presented to me; that I approve them most heartily; that I approve the organization of such an Association and think it a valuable thing for the Country and that I am delighted that Jouett is to head the Association.

Wednesday afternoon, August 22, 1934. A week after his meeting with Roosevelt, Shouse kept his bargain with the New York *World*.[5]

VI

Shouse's protestations that the Liberty League was nonpartisan and not anti-Roosevelt fell on deaf ears. Those who castigated and the many who applauded did so on the assumption that the Liberty League would take up the role of Administration critic which a moribund Republican party was unable to fill.

Both *Collier's* and the *Commonweal* pointed out the improbability of known critics of the Administration remaining nonpartisan for long, and suggested that formation of the League might presage a realignment of parties along more definite "conservative" versus "liberal" lines. In any case, the *Collier's* editorial continued, "an opposition to a Democratic administration headed by conspicuous Democrats has obvious comic features."

Others were equally unimpressed with the nonpartisan posture of the League. Said the *Christian Century*, ". . . it would require an incredible degree of credulity to accept the fair words of the stated aims of the League as implying anything less than a concerted attack upon the main features of the President's policies." "The Tories," observed *Newsweek*, with whimsical abruptness, "have come out of ambush."

The *New York Times* predicted that many Wall Street leaders would "take an active part" in the League, that "most brokers and bankers will join," employees and workers in the financial district "will follow along," and corporation executives would apply pressure "by writing to their stockholders to point out the advantages of the League." "The financial community," said the *Times*, "sees in the movement the nucleus of a new force for conservatism."

The *Times* represented the view of a large and important segment of the press toward the Liberty League. In general sympathy with the aims of the League, it was not unaware of the problem inherent in trying to maintain a nonpartisan position. Admitting that the League was "hardly created by New Dealers or enthusiastic admirers of the Administration's trends," nonetheless, the reputation of its founders was "sufficient to acquit them of the suspicion of being 'anti-Roosevelt' and nothing else."

But the League must be scrupulously nonpartisan, warned the *Times*. There was a need for some check upon "certain of the New Deal theorists-in-office . . . certain trends and acts among the President's subordinates . . . and even upon occasional states of mind of the President himself"; but the League must prove that "it would not retrace all the steps taken since March, 1933; that it sympathizes with the broad Administration aim to improve the lot of the common man; that it seeks not to be the nucleus of a new party or a new political alignment. . . ."

It was left to the unsophisticated man in the street to put the matter bluntly. In a letter to the editor of the *New York Times*, one writer observed that in "the very essence of things, such a body cannot be non-partisan, it cannot help being against President Roosevelt. If it is not against him, why is it started?"

Others with special axes to grind leaped to the attack. Henry Goddard Leach, editor of the *Forum*, savagely contested the League's claim to having rediscovered the Constitution and the Bill of Rights. "Greed and selfishness had locked away these two charters of liberty," wrote Leach, "until Franklin D. Roosevelt brought them forth again from the vaults of bankrupt banks on March 4, 1933, and waved them courageously from the balcony of the Capitol." Professor John Dewey of Columbia University and head of the "people's lobby" dispatched to Shouse a letter asking, "Can you cite any instance in which property has been taken without 'due process of law'?" Through Arthur Garfield Hays, general counsel of the American Civil Liberties Union, Shouse was sent a list of nine questions to find out how far the League was prepared to go to protect the civil liberties of radicals and liberal minorities. "With the exception of Alfred E. Smith," wrote Hays, "there appear few names among your members of men who have been conspicuous in fighting for the rights of individuals, particularly workers." And in one of his weekly broadcasts from the Shrine of the Little Flower in Royal Oak, Michigan, the Reverend Charles E. Coughlin split the Sunday afternoon air with the charge that the League was "the mouthpiece" of the bankers through which they "voice the cowardly cry for the preservation of their bonds." [6]

VII

Democratic leaders also raked the League with verbal criticism; the more ardent New Dealers out of a sense of dedication to a cause, others, who had had their differences with Roosevelt, as a gesture of conciliation, a peace offering, or an act of contrition for prior sins.

"It looks to me as if the League was organized to stop the New Deal," said Senator James P. Pope of Idaho. Senator Elmer Thomas of Oklahoma was more positive. Thomas (whose amendment to the Agricultural Adjustment Act gave the President power to inflate the currency by at least six different methods) used his utmost term of contempt when he called the Liberty Leaguers "gold dollar men . . . die-hards and stand-patters who have always been opposed to the New Deal." "A humorous feature," observed Michigan's Senator James Couzens, "is the announcement that the league is non-partisan." What Couzens wanted to know was how an organization made up entirely of men of the same political persuasion could be called nonpartisan.

Representative Clifton A. Woodrum of Virginia attacked the League with an *argumentum ad hominem*. Of Al Smith he said "the Happy Warrior of old has joined the disgruntled and malcontents"; in his own language, "he just couldn't take it." John W. Davis, said Woodrum, led us "to about the worst beating we have ever had"; and of Wadsworth, "we recognize in him an aspirant for the Republican nomination in 1936." To Woodrum the Liberty League was "two has-beens" and "a would-be" trying to embarrass the Administration.

The Administration used the Liberty League announcement as the occasion for forcing recalcitrant Southern Democrats to a public pledge of New Deal fealty and constancy. Knowing that some Democratic senators had probably been in communication with Bainbridge Colby and other prominent conservatives, the rumor was started that Senators Glass and Byrd of Virginia, Tydings of Maryland, Gore of Oklahoma, and Bailey of North Carolina were about to join the League, in order to force them to a public denial.

The trick worked. "I have had no conferences with Republicans or Democrats about this matter," protested Carter Glass, "and I do not intend to hold any." Said Harry Byrd, I will not "join in any movement to obstruct or embarrass President Roosevelt in his efforts to end the deplorable conditions which resulted from twelve years of Republican misrule." Although each had from time to time been critical of the New Deal, all denied any intention of aligning themselves with the Liberty League. The purpose of this little drama, explained the *New York Times*, was to serve warning on Democratic politicians everywhere "to watch their step."

Senator Huey Long, no longer the hot-eyed Roosevelt man he had once been, denied that he was going to join the League because "someone else is president." James W. Gerard, Wilson's millionaire ambassador to Germany, a vigorous supporter of Smith in 1928, and a contributor to the Roosevelt campaign, wrote the *New York Times* denying an earlier report that he was a member of the League. "I have no connection whatever with this organization and am not supporting it," wrote Gerard. A few days after Shouse's announcement, Rudolph Spreckels of the West Coast family of sugar producers called on Roosevelt to suggest the possibility of creating a counterorganization. The same idea occurred to A. P. Giannini, founder of the Bank of America. On September 2, Giannini sent Roosevelt a telegram from San Francisco saying that if a counterorganization were formed, "count me in." Apparently the President thought the plan unwise, because nothing more came of it.

Even some prominent Republicans had unkind words for the League. Patrick J. Hurley, Hoover's Secretary of War, expressed regret that men like Smith, Davis, and Wadsworth were "taken in by the old smear brigade." "The Liberty League," he growled, "is financed by the same people and led by the same man [Shouse] who led the 'Smear-Hoover' campaign, and I have never joined a 'smear gang.' " In line with his own personal vendetta against the NRA, the irascible senator from Idaho, William Borah, said that "this move to preserve liberty is an important undertaking" and the American Liberty League "is not too early in the field"; but in its platform it should have included "economic freedom." Years later, Hoover was still shaking his head over the League: "Unbelievable as it may be, Raskob wrote asking me to join."

Harold Ickes thought the League was the best thing that could have happened to the country. Ickes, a Republican Progressive from Illinois who had breathed the same optimism as Theodore Roosevelt and Woodrow Wilson, saw in the New Deal a reincarnation of the New Freedom and the New Nationalism. Stubborn and untidy, the Old Curmudgeon of the Interior Department had made a career of being charmingly hard to get along with. "I've been hoping ever since 1912 that we'd have political parties divided on real issues. It looks as if it's working out that way at last." Ickes foresaw a realignment of political parties, with the League the nucleus around which the conservatives could rally. When that happened "you'd always be facing your enemy and not wondering about what is happening behind your back."

Harry Hopkins, the gaunt social worker turned relief administrator, was more cynical: "The League may be composed of right-thinking people but they are so far Right that no one will ever find them." [7]

VIII

Meanwhile, League spokesmen sought to stem the tide of criticism with reassuring words.

In Milwaukee, members of the legal profession were told that the Liberty League "was not opposed to the Roosevelt program" (Nathan Miller, at the annual meeting of the American Bar Association). "Its purpose is educational primarily" (James W. Wadsworth, addressing a New York audience). Newsmen were told that "every government needs intelligent criticism"

(Alfred Sloan, debarking from a vacation in Europe). "As a member of the American Liberty League I am most desirous of being of use to the administration, having voted for Mr. Roosevelt" (Irénée du Pont, in a press interview at Wilmington). "Thousands have sent in pledges of support and asked for further information" (Jouett Shouse, in a press conference). From all parts of the country the response had been "astounding," and the preponderance of small contributions, said Shouse, showed that "greatest interest comes from the mass of the people."

Despite their mild words of protest that their role was educational, that they wanted only to be helpful, that they were not opposed to the Administration, it was soon obvious the Administration would not allow the League to play that role even if it wanted to. Democratic critics had taken their cue from the President.

On August 19, 1934, Henry T. Rainey died quite suddenly in St. Louis. The next day, President Roosevelt and his party left by train to attend the funeral of the beloved Speaker of the House. It was an unhappy accident of history that had the President on his way to Carrollton, Illinois, when Shouse released to the press the story of the American Liberty League.

Shouse called the White House. Explaining to Presidential Secretary Steve Early (McIntyre was with Roosevelt in Illinois) that the President had promised an endorsement of the League, Shouse asked Early to get in touch with Roosevelt. Early, who was not present at the Roosevelt-Shouse interview the week before, obliged. From the noncommittal reply that Early relayed to him from the President, Shouse was reminded once more that in politics a week is a long time.

Roosevelt was back in Washington for his regular Friday morning press conference on August 24. The Liberty League, he told reporters, was like an organization founded "to uphold two of the Ten Commandments." It talked only of protecting property, but nothing was said of protecting the average citizen, of helping the unemployed, of aiding people to keep their homes, of providing facilities for education, or any of the other factors summed up in the commandment "Thou shalt love thy neighbor as thyself." The League was fine "as far as it goes," but it was "stopping short" instead of going "the whole hog."

When asked, Roosevelt admitted that Shouse had informed him in advance of the organization, and that he had voiced no objections because it was "none of my business." As the press conference broke up, one reporter was heard to wisecrack that the President had "praised it with faint damns."

Five days later, Ambassador William C. Bullitt in Moscow received a "Dear Bill" letter from Roosevelt, hidden from prying eyes in a diplomatic pouch. Bullitt, one of the bright young men of the Wilson Administration, had accompanied his chief to Versailles. Disgusted by the peace conference and disenchanted by the collapse of progressivism in the postwar decade, Bullitt had languished on the Riviera and along the Bosporus until the New Deal wooed him out of retirement and rekindled the fires of his Wilsonian idealism.

"All the big guns have started shooting," wrote the President; but their organization "has already been labeled the 'I can't take it club.' " [8]

IX

Everyone, it seemed, dismissed the nonpartisan claims of the Liberty League. The Administration from the President down had seen to that. No one, it seemed, doubted that its real purpose was to harass Roosevelt, embarrass the New Deal, and to get rid of both if it could.

But while observers were clear on the objective of the League, they were confused on motives. What manner of organization was it that could unite under the same banner an impressive array of American businessmen led by two former Democratic presidential candidates, a former Republican governor, a Republican senator turned representative, and a former chairman of the Democratic party's national executive committee?

A "strange political nosegay," *Time* Magazine had called the League; but this was distorting the truth for the sake of sounding clever. To those who knew the full background there was nothing at all strange about the association of these men in the Liberty League. Regardless of party labels, they were as one in their political conservatism; and not a few of them could readily oppose Roosevelt for reasons of personal revenge.

Roosevelt's refusal to endorse the League was regarded by them as another example of his perfidy, the latest in a long chain of deceits, doublecrosses, and broken pledges. But from a political standpoint an endorsement which would have wed Roosevelt to the forces of conservatism would have been sheer folly. Roosevelt had neither foreseen nor desired the realignment of political forces that were already apparent in the late summer of 1934. Yet the realignment was taking place and the President was forced to a choice — to improve the lot of the workers, farmers, and unemployed or be overwhelmed by the forces of mass political discontent. The New Deal program that unfolded after the election of 1934, a program of far-reaching social and economic welfarism, indicated that the Administration had chosen the former.

The founders of the American Liberty League anticipated this leftward shift. And many of them sincerely felt that it implied an attack on the bedrock principles of the Republic. Others had a mutual dislike and distrust of Roosevelt. The forces were sufficient to draw them together in such an organization.

Many of these same men had made common cause before; and the target then had been the Eighteenth Amendment.[9]

2

THE CONSTITUTION IN A BOTTLE

The reason I ask is that this Association was fighting primarily and wholly for a constitutional principle. Its aim and purpose was to take from the Constitution a police statute.

Jouett Shouse

I think Mr. Pierre du Pont's interest in this is greater than it is in anything else in the United States.

William H. Stayton

ON DECEMBER 31, 1933, the *New York Times*'s Arthur Krock began a feature story like this:

Washington, Dec. 30 — The Association Against the Prohibition Amendment went out of existence today. It quietly closed its offices in the National Press Building and sent its files to the Library of Congress as the record of a great adventure in sociological legislation. Having attained its objective — the repeal of national prohibition, the first amendment to the Constitution ever excised from that document — the association resisted the temptation to linger on as a "sentinel of American liberty."

The last sentence of Krock's opening paragraph was only technically correct.[1]

II

The Association Against the Prohibition Amendment had started quite inconspicuously a little more than fifteen years ment involved an improper delegation of power to the federal government. In effect, here was a constitutional amendment that was unconstitutional.

And what did the AAPA propose to do about it? According to its prospectus of 1919, the Association had two immediate aims: (1) to prevent the country from going on a bone-dry basis on July 1, and (2) to make the Eighteenth Amendment forever inoperative.[2]

IV

In 1930 the activities of the AAPA came under the scrutiny of a subcommittee of the Senate Judiciary Committee. Unraveling the story took weeks, filling more than five thousand pages of sworn testimony.

The investigation revealed that during the early years the association had struggled along, largely on money from Stayton's own pockets, making very little headway in the fight against prohibition. But in 1926 a great transformation had taken place. Stayton found himself titular head of an association that had been taken over by a group of multimillionaires, the actual management passing into the hands of Pierre, Irénée, and Lammot du Pont, John J. Raskob, and Charles H. Sabin. Pierre du Pont became chairman of the executive committee of the AAPA; Irénée became a member of the executive committee, and Lammot took over as chairman of the finance committee. Raskob, a business associate of the du Ponts, was also placed on the finance committee. Sabin, chairman of the board of the New York Guaranty Company, the Intercontinental Rubber Company, and the Mechanics and Metals National Bank, and a director of sixteen corporations, was added to both the executive and finance committees, and eventually became treasurer of the AAPA.

Funds for financing the prohibition fight were now practically unlimited. In 1928, Raskob and the three du Pont brothers contributed more than $130,000; in 1930 these same men with five business associates gave more than $200,000. Beginning in 1927, receipts of the AAPA began exceeding half a million dollars annually, and before the prohibition victory was achieved in 1933 the AAPA was funneling more than a million dollars a year into the cause. The source of these huge sums was of more than passing interest to the Senate investigating committee. In 1928 Captain Stayton was made chairman of the board and Major Henry H. Curran replaced him in the presidency. Curran was a New York native who had worked as a journalist and lawyer before entering upon a political career that spanned half a century and carried him from alderman, through the offices of Manhattan borough president, city magistrate, and deputy mayor, to commissioner of immigration and justice of the Court of Special Sessions.

On the witness stand, Major Curran admitted to the committee that of the more than $700,000 collected by the AAPA in 1929, 75 per cent had come from fifty-three men. The most generous were: Irénée du Pont, $30,000; Edward S. Harkness, $30,000; James Arthur Curtiss, $25,000; Eldridge Johnson, $25,-000; R. T. Crane, Jr., $25,000; Lammot du Pont, $17,500; Pierre du Pont, $17,500; John J. Raskob, $17,500; Samuel Mather, $10,-000; Thomas W. Phillips, Jr., $10,000; and Charles H. Sabin, $10,000.

Money was only one form of power which these men were able to wield. They had great influence, also, through newspapers and other widely read publications. For sheer power and professional efficiency the propaganda machine of the AAPA surpassed anything the country had ever seen. "A great debt is due to the liberal press of the nation," said the president of the AAPA in his final report, "which has been a factor of overwhelming importance in the accomplishment of repeal." Referring to a speech he had made in New York, he continued:

> As on no other question of modern times, without regard to partisan politics, a large proportion of the powerful and influential newspapers and periodicals of America have united in a program of education which has had profound effect. In season and out of season, by editorial and by cartoon, the press has brought home to the American people the fallacy of the Eighteenth Amendment. And with all due regard to the work done by this association . . . I do not hesitate to assert that save for what the press has done, we would not be celebrating victory tonight and the possibility of such a celebration might have been delayed many, many years.

The annual report for 1930 indicates the reason for such lavish praise of the press. The report contained these items:

> three times as many readers reached in 1930 as in 1928 . . . over 55 per cent more than in 1929 . . . six hundred millions of copies of newspapers, containing conspicuous publication of our news, were read . . . 153,617,704 copies of magazines and periodicals containing articles and editorials attacking prohibition have been read . . . seventy news stories were issued in the year . . . each of them reached an average of almost 9,000,000 readers . . . of the recent Senate investigation, more than 15,000 clippings "on our side of these hearings" had a combined circulation of nearly 200,000,000 . . . more than 4,000,000 copies of books, pamphlets, reports, reprints, letters and leaflets were distributed from our office in 1930 . . . with the cooperation and consent of the newspapers and artists concerned, a collection of cartoons attacking and ridiculing prohibition was published and widely distributed.[3]

V

After 1926 the Association was able to exert tremendous political pressure, particularly on the Democratic party. This was accomplished largely through the influence of Alfred E. Smith. Smith was a "wet" and a staunch supporter of the AAPA program. When he received the Democratic nomination in 1928, he made John Raskob, one of the most influential members of the AAPA, chairman of the Democratic National Committee.

With Smith and Raskob it was a case of love at first sight. Drawn to each other by their religion and by a wholesome regard for the success achieved by the other against tremendous odds, they developed a fondness for one another that lasted out their lives. Both men were of immigrant stock and piously devout Roman Catholics. Shy and retiring, with a barely audible speaking voice, Raskob had worked his way up in the business world from a lowly start as a stenographer. Smith, born literally in the shadow of the Brooklyn Bridge on New York's Lower East Side, had served a long apprenticeship in Tammany politics as borough alderman, county sheriff, state legislator, and finally as governor for four terms in the executive mansion at Albany. By 1928 he was in sight of the White House.

The brown derby, oversized cigar, and dapper dress were the symbols of the true American cockney personality that was a perfect complement to Raskob's self-effacing modesty. They could use each other, and did. For Smith the alliance presented the possibility of splitting off part of the business-minded Republican vote and of assuring the party adequate campaign funds for the first time in years. Raskob's appointment, although it alienated Southerners and progressives (Raskob had earlier expressed the hope of voting for Coolidge in 1928), brought peace of mind to the business community. It was an additional guarantee that if Smith were elected his humanitarian instincts would not be allowed to get out of hand.

Raskob saw little need for social changes except for the repeal of prohibition. On this public issue Smith and Raskob were as one. Both were determined to rid the country "of the damnable affliction of prohibition."

After the election of 1928, Raskob brought in Jouett Shouse as chairman of the Democratic national executive committee; and for the next four years this triumvirate — Smith, Raskob, and Shouse — guided the destinies of the Democratic party. After Franklin Roosevelt wrested control from Smith and Raskob at the 1932 convention, Shouse replaced Major Curran as president of the AAPA and led the Association in its final and victorious assault on the Eighteenth Amendment.

VI

Although the AAPA was never able to capture control of the Republican party in quite the same way as it had the Democratic party, it did have powerful friends in Republican ranks, notably James W. Wadsworth and James M. Beck.

Wadsworth, an uncompromising conservative, was a gentleman farmer and cattle breeder from upstate New York, where his family owned some 35,000 acres of fertile land in the Genesee Valley. The family had a long tradition of Republicanism. Wadsworth's grandfather had helped organize the Republican party and unsuccessfully opposed Horatio Seymour for the governorship of New York in 1862; his father had served ten terms as a Republican congressman.

After five years in the New York legislature, Wadsworth moved into national politics in 1914, when he defeated James W. Gerard for the United States Senate. A member of the AAPA executive committee for years, his antiprohibition stand cost him his Senate seat in the 1926 election. In spite of the Roosevelt sweep in 1932, Wadsworth was elected to the House of Representatives, where he was to serve for nine consecutive terms.

The tall and distinguished-looking senator-representative worked tirelessly on behalf of the AAPA, speaking at meetings of every description, and defending its views in the halls of Congress and before government agencies and investigating committees. One of the ways that Wadsworth aided the anti-prohibition cause is revealed in an exchange that took place during the Senate investigation of the AAPA. Montana's Senator Thomas Walsh was putting some embarrassing questions to Major Curran:

> Senator Walsh (Montana). And what magazines have you contributed articles to?
> Mr. Curran. Let us see. Senator Wadsworth contributed an article to the *North American Review* which was published about four or five months ago, and, oh — maybe this is what you have in mind, sir. . . .
> Senator Walsh. . . . Senator Wadsworth is one of your directors?
> Mr. Curran. Yes.
> Senator Walsh. What did your association have to do with the article?
> Mr. Curran. Why, we wrote it.
> Senator Walsh. Who was the author of it?
> Mr. Curran. Senator Wadsworth. We wrote it.
> Senator Walsh. What do you mean by saying, "We wrote it"?
> Mr. Curran. It was written by — this is a shame — it was written by Mr. Samuel Morse, who is of our organization, and it was corrected and revised and approved or disapproved by Senator Wadsworth and sent to the *North American Review*. . . .

Beck was useful to the AAPA because of his great reputation as a constitutional lawyer. His career was no less a success story in the American tradition than were Smith's and Raskob's. Studying law by night and working as a railway clerk by day, Beck went on to build no small clientele as a practicing lawyer before accepting appointments with the Attorney General's office during the Cleveland, McKinley, and T. Roosevelt Administrations. In 1914, he was elected a bencher of Gray's Inn, London, the first foreign lawyer so honored in over six hundred years.

Appointed Solicitor General by Harding, Beck stayed on in the job until 1925. Even the slight accretions of federal power under the studied indifference of Coolidge appeared ominous to Beck, a conservative among conservatives, who in 1926 could entitle his book *The Vanishing Rights of the States*. When Franklin Roosevelt became President, Beck had already served three terms as a Pennsylvania congressman.

Beck was a bitter critic of prohibition. To a man with his approach to federalism the Eighteenth Amendment was an unpardonable assault upon the rights of the states, and he never passed up an opportunity to say so. "Get Hon. James M. Beck to make speech in Congress in defense of Constitution," wired Henry B. Joy, head of Packard Motors and a director of the AAPA, to Captain Stayton in January 1930. "He can do it better than any other and carry tremendous weight." Stayton replied: "I had a talk with Mr. Beck yesterday and he is going to make the constitutional speech as per your suggestion."

A few days later Stayton sent telegrams to the New York *Evening Post* and the *New York Times:* "I have just read advance sheet Congressman Beck's speech to be delivered on Friday. . . . If your policy would permit an editorial on this matter it would greatly aid our plans."

Both papers obliged.[4]

VII

During the Senate investigation of the AAPA, Senator Robinson elicited from Stayton the information that, besides the many other financial and business leaders who were generous supporters of the cause, fifteen of the twenty-eight directors of the General Motors Corporation were members of the AAPA. The question arises why such men should have been so interested. There was, of course, the constitutional principle so frequently enunciated by the Association. In 1929 the executive committee of the Association was still resolving that the Eighteenth Amendment should be repealed because it was "misplaced in the federal Constitution, in violation of the fundamental American right of local self-government in local affairs, and in surrender to the federal authorities of police duties over the habits and the conduct of individuals which belong of right to the states. . . ." Many years later Shouse would write that the AAPA was fighting "primarily and wholly" for a constitutional principle. The aim of the AAPA was to take a "police statute" from the Constitution.

In addition to their concern for the constitutional question, a second, more "human" force may well have motivated business leaders as it did millions of less conspicuous Americans. For the first time in their lives, people who had always been law-abiding citizens found themselves unable to gratify what seemed a natural, more or less innocent, desire without breaking a law. Particularly to those whose worldly situation removed the temptation to violate most laws — to whom, in fact, the laws existed largely to protect people such as themselves from the depredations of what they readily considered the more criminally inclined elements of society. To such men it was a novel and displeasing situation that now confronted them. They had either to deny themselves or break the law. In short, when they were thirsty, they wanted a drink — legally.

Finally, if the leaders of the AAPA were motivated both by constitutional principles and natural desires, they were also, perhaps, not unaware that with the revocation of the amendment they could save money too. There are those, notably Fletcher Dobyns, who believe that this was the sole motive after 1926, and that the constitutional issue was only a smoke screen to obscure the fact.

Dobyns, an assistant United States Attorney General, wrote *The Amazing Story of Repeal* in 1940. Relying almost exclusively on the testimony of the Senate investigation of the liquor lobby in 1930, Dobyns came to the conclusion that the real motive of the AAPA leaders was "to get rid of their income taxes!"

Dobyns built a strong case. Even a casual reading of the voluminous testimony makes it clear that the tax issue was a conspicuous selling point in the AAPA propaganda campaign.

In a memorandum dated October 25, 1926, Captain Stayton wrote:

> I have selected by hand-picked method the names of about 2,000 men who pay income taxes on incomes of $100,000 or more each. . . .
> Whenever I have written . . . I have tried to lay the whole business out in advance . . . and let them know how their pocketbook and personal interests will be involved. . . .

To one of the "hand-picked" names went the following:

> For example, the treasury department figures show that there were nine individuals in Arizona who in 1925 had incomes of $90,000 and over. . . . Based on a modification of the Volstead Act and the adoption of the proposed beer or beer and natural wine tax, each of these individuals would be relieved of the payment of an average of more than $20,000 a year tax.

A memorandum of Captain Stayton's listed these ideas that might be used in form letters to the "hand-picked":

Irénée du Pont's statement that one of his companies would save $10,000,000 in corporation tax if we should have, say, the British tax on beer.

In 1914 the brewers paid taxes on 66,000,000 barrels of beer. If we should have back the right to manufacture beer, if we should manufacture just as much as we did in 1914, and if we should tax it at the British rate, the income would be $1,320,000,-000, or more than the net amount received from income and corporation taxes. Note too that this tax would be practically all net for it would be a stamp tax and there would be no scandals concerning rebates and no snoopers in business offices examining books.

I suppose we might want to say something to the effect that a man would save personal income taxes.

Do you realize that Congress has power to at once legalize a glass of mild, wholesome beer?   And, that the workingman and others would willingly pay a tax of three cents per glass and that that amount . . . would enable the federal government to get rid of the burdensome corporation taxes and income taxes and to take the snoopers and spies out of offices and homes . . . ?

An argument that might perhaps appeal to business men is that if we had wines the purchase of them would lead to revival of prosperity in Europe and lead to the payment of the debts due us and to an increase in our trade with Europe. . . .

In a letter sent to large taxpayers over his signature, Pierre du Pont made this point:

As our average tax collections for the years 1923-26 from individuals and corporations were $1,817,000,000, resulting in a considerable surplus, it is fair to say that the British liquor policy applied in the United States would permit of the total abolition of the income tax both personal and corporate. Or this liquor tax would be sufficient to pay off the entire debt of the United States, interest and principal, in a little less than fifteen years.

And Thomas W. Phillips, Jr., president of T. W. Phillips Gas and Oil Company, member of the AAPA board of directors, and repeal candidate for governor of Pennsylvania in 1930, complained bitterly:

> As I look upon this matter, I realize that prohibition has indirectly cost me already several hundred thousand dollars; and, of course, if it continues indefinitely, the amount that I will be assessed on account of this religious and reform fanaticism will mount into the seven-figure column. I do not know how this strikes other people, but it is very irritating to me.

Phillips believed that a propaganda program playing up the tax aspect of the prohibition issue ("featuring this point," he called it) was the most effective means of carrying on the fight.

He also called attention to another interesting possibility. "Perhaps the quickest and most effective way of bringing religious, not necessarily Christian, people to their senses," wrote Phillips, "is to stage a demonstration of what their attitude is doing and will do to the financial support of their work." He proposed that big income taxpayers let their churches understand that the amounts they were having to pay in taxes because of prohibition and the amounts which they were having to contribute to organizations fighting prohibition would leave "very little or nothing" for the support of the churches.[5]

VIII

The transfusion of corporate wealth after 1926 not only assured the AAPA of robust health but enabled the association to unite the support of various subsidiary organizations.

Early in 1932 there was created an organization known as the United Repeal Council. In addition to the AAPA, the organization included the Voluntary Committee of Lawyers, the Crusaders, the Women's Organization for National Prohibition Reform, and the American Hotel Association. With the AAPA providing the bankroll and the leadership, the wet forces were now capable of carrying on the fight against prohibition on virtually every front.

For several years prior to this amalgam of antiprohibition groups, the Authors and Artists Committee had been operating as an auxiliary of the AAPA. By 1930 the ranks of the committee had swelled to nearly six hundred members, and Major Curran boasted before the Senate investigating committee that it included "many of the most prominent and beloved authors, artists and cartoonists in the country." Of all its members, none was more "prominent and beloved" than the chairman, the Kentucky humorist Irvin S. Cobb, whose devastating wit and Old South charm added color and humor to the antiprohibition crusade.

The role of the Voluntary Committee of Lawyers was quite different. The lawyers needed none of the writers' tools, the analogy, the innuendo, the gentle persuasion of humor, the cap and bells. Singleness of purpose, reason, logic, surgical preciseness, facts were the way of the lawyers.

"The general purpose of the corporation is to preserve the spirit of the Constitution of the United States," ran the opening statement of the lawyers' committee. "Its immediate purpose is to bring about the repeal of the Eighteenth Amendment." That was January 23, 1929. Sometime during the nearly five years of its existence the committee apparently lost sight of its general purpose. On November 9, 1933, the executive committee of the lawyers' committee was to announce that it was disbanding, "repeal having fulfilled the purpose of the organization."

The lawyers' committee had quickly recruited an imposing array of the most eminent legal minds in the land. Heading the committee was Joseph H. Choate, Jr. (of the New York firm of Evarts, Choate, Sherman and Leon), a member of the board of directors of the AAPA, and son of the former ambassador to

England. Working closely with Choate was James H. Winston, senior member of the Chicago firm of Winston, Strawn and Shaw. Ralph Shaw was also a member of the board of directors of the AAPA and one of the most dedicated workers the Association had in the Midwest.

The program of the lawyers' committee was concise enough. The first objective was to recruit an impressive membership and get local bar associations to adopt antiprohibition resolutions. Considering the prestige of the men leading the organization this was not too difficult to accomplish. Effective spadework at the local level produced results at the national level. In 1930, the American Bar Association went on record as favoring repeal.

The next step was repeal. Working closely with the parent organization, the lawyers' committee kept up a constant pressure, first on the states, urging them to repeal their enforcement acts, and then upon the Congress to enact repeal resolutions.

Even the report of the Wickersham Commission did not cause the lawyers to break stride. Early in 1931 President Hoover submitted to the Congress the report of the National Commission on Law Observance and Law Enforcement, better known as the Wickersham Commission, a group of recognized experts whose assignment had included the making of a thorough study of the whole prohibition problem. The report could have been damaging to the cause of repeal had the lawyers' committee not brought to bear the full force of its legal skills to neutralize its effect.

When repeal was imminent the lawyers prepared a model legislative measure covering the legal steps involved in setting up special conventions in the states to consider the repeal amendment. Since this was the first time the convention method had ever been used to act upon a constitutional amendment, the model prepared by the lawyers' committee proved immensely helpful and was already in the hands of thirty-nine legislatures when Congress referred the repeal resolutions to the states in 1933.

After repeal had been accomplished, the *Literary Digest* wrote:

> The American public is entitled to know the extraordinary role in this accomplishment played by the Voluntary Committee of Lawyers. . . . To them belongs the credit for the amazing precision of the rapid series of explosions which has blasted prohibition from the Constitution within the year. . . .
>
> It advanced with signal success toward its original objective, the passage of repeal resolutions by the nation's bar associations. Then, with the imminence of congressional action, it turned its attention from the agitation to the mechanics of repeal. . . .
>
> But, as usual in such affairs, one man led the rest. He is Mr. Choate — tall, friendly, diffident, but immensely purposeful son of our former ambassador to the Court of St. James. He should take the final curtain.

And he did. In 1933, President Roosevelt appointed Choate chairman of the Federal Alcohol Control Administration.[6]

IX

The Crusaders and the Women's Organization for National Prohibition Reform were more than auxiliaries of the AAPA. They were blood relatives.

Both groups were formed in 1929. The founder and president of the WONPR was Mrs. Charles H. Sabin of New York, wife of the treasurer of the AAPA. Their son, Charles H. Sabin, Jr., was chairman of the executive committee of the Crusaders. For years Mrs. Sabin had been a prominent figure in New York Republican circles, a member of the state Republican executive committee, and after 1924, Republican national committee-woman until she resigned to organize the WONPR. Counted among her active associates were the ladies of many of America's most distinguished business and social leaders — Mrs. Pierre du Pont, Mrs. Henry B. Joy, Mrs. August Belmont, Mrs. Cornelius Bliss, Mrs. Courtlandt Nicoll, Mrs. J. Roland Harriman, and a hundred more of equal prominence. Working in close cooperation with the AAPA, Mrs. Sabin supervised the organization of WONPR chapters in forty-four states and the District of Columbia.

The Crusaders were young men, among whom were found Charles H. Sabin, Jr., Charles E. Otis, John Hay Whitney, Morton Banks, Avery Rockefeller, Lammot du Pont III, and numerous others who were scions of the wealthiest families in the land. In keeping with their name, the Crusaders organized along military lines, with a national commander and battalion commanders at the state and local levels. The national commander was a Cleveland oil man, Fred G. Clark.

x

It was a devastating combination of forces that accomplished repeal in 1933, the victory of the AAPA, WONPR, and Crusaders being almost as much a family effort as it was an organizational one. These were people who had unlimited money and the ability to use it effectively. They had motive. Sometimes, doubtless, the motive was patriotic, a fight to protect a constitutional principle; frequently it must have been a personal desire for freedom to take a drink; sometimes the motive was unquestionably what the dry forces contended it was, a fight to avoid paying taxes. The first was perhaps more noble than the others, but none was contemptible. There was brilliant and imaginative leadership. There was powerful influence with every means of mass communication and the ability to use that influence. Here were husbands, wives, and sons in tandem with their legal retainers, literary friends, and hotel allies working to convince the public of the desirability of repeal, a public that really did not need a whole lot of convincing.

It is little wonder that the combination was irresistible.

XI

Contrary to Krock's assertion that the AAPA "resisted the temptation to linger on," it did not go out of existence in December 1933. Like others, Krock confused mitosis with annihilation.

On December 6, 1933, the board of directors of the AAPA passed a double-barreled resolution:

> . . . that there be formed immediately a group to be known as Repeal Associates, charged with the duty of acting, in effect, as a sort of clearing-house to keep each of the 48 states advised as to the success or failure of liquor laws in the other 47 states. . . .

More significant was the second part:

> . . . that the individual members of the Executive Committee of the Association Against the Prohibition Amendment continue to meet from time to time and have in view the formation of a group, based on our old membership in the association, which would in the event of danger to the Federal Constitution, stand ready to defend the faith of the fathers.

Early in 1934, Repeal Associates opened headquarters in the Otis Building in Washington, began publishing the *Repeal Review*, and started a campaign to organize five hundred "listening posts" throughout the nation. To the venerable Captain

Stayton, then seventy-three years old, went the job of executive director. Pierre du Pont was chairman of the advisory committee, which included such AAPA veterans as Grayson Murphy, Ralph Shaw, and James W. Wadsworth.

Like the AAPA before it, Repeal Associates took as its fundamental purpose protection of the Constitution; Captain Stayton was more blunt when he said that "Repeal Associates, the successor to the Association Against the Prohibition Amendment, is keeping tab on what the drys are doing. . . ."

More important than Repeal Associates were those members of the AAPA executive committee — Pierre du Pont, Irénée du Pont, Grayson Murphy, William Stayton, James Wadsworth, and Jouett Shouse — who stood ready "to defend the faith of the fathers."

In the early summer of 1934, when John Raskob initiated the series of meetings that culminated in the formation of the American Liberty League, it was a simple matter to summon these men and other past members of the AAPA. The former executive committee of the AAPA was "unanimously of opinion" to assist in the new organization.

Shortly after, Captain Stayton began on his own initiative to alert the old membership of the AAPA. "At a recent meeting of a group of the former members of the Executive Committee of the Association Against the Prohibition Amendment," wrote Stayton, it was unanimously agreed that the radical drift of the New Deal justified the formation of "a patriotic organization to advocate the restoration and preservation of the fundamental principles of the Constitution." It was also their unanimous opinion that the "former members of the Association Against the Prohibition Amendment, together with former members of the Women's Organization for National Prohibition Reform, offer the best nucleus around which to build such a new organization."

The new organization was the American Liberty League.[7]

3

MARKETING A NEW PRODUCT

The American Liberty League will unite several millions
of people from all walks of life who are now without organized influence in legislative matters.

Jouett Shouse

The American Liberty League is a movement which will
not be stilled by the wise-cracks of politicians and partisans or
epithets that come from those who are unfamiliar with the
depth of conviction and solemnity of purpose which are the
heart and soul of a militant cause.

Jouett Shouse

THE AMERICAN LIBERTY LEAGUE was a sensation almost from
the beginning. Unlike the AAPA in its early years, there was
no grinding poverty, no flirting with obscurity, no quiescent
period. From the start the League was able to concentrate unlimited money, powerful organization, and superb propaganda
behind the fight to preserve the Constitution.

For more than two years it made headlines almost daily. The
President took it seriously; public figures both in and out of
government attacked or defended it with the zeal of medieval
crusaders; and Democrats campaigned against it rather than
against the Republican party. The American Liberty League
was potentially one of the most powerful pressure groups ever
seen in American politics. On paper, at least.

II

Under the expert guidance of Jouett Shouse the organization quickly began to take shape. League headquarters in the National Press Building occupied some thirty-one rooms, the entire tenth floor, and at full strength employed a staff of more than fifty persons.

Newsweek pointed out that Republican national headquarters had only twelve rooms and a staff of seventeen. But the Republicans were still in a state of shock. Shouse was going to try to block the New Deal's new turn to the Left, to organize the voters to support conservative candidates, to revive an order of things that had perished in one mad month in the fall of 1929, and all of this had to be done in the guise of nonpartisanship. In short, Shouse was going to attempt a miracle before 1936, and he would need all the expert assistance he could get.

The League assembled the finest staff that money could hire. Shouse's personal assistant was Ewing Laporte, a Yale man, slight, wiry and taciturn, who had worked with him off and on for more than fifteen years. Their association had begun while Shouse was Assistant Secretary of the Treasury. When he resigned, President Wilson replaced him with Laporte at Shouse's urging. After a short stint in the Harding Administration, a brief fling at the academic life with the University of Pittsburgh, and a short but successful private law practice, Laporte rejoined his former chief when Raskob brought in Shouse to rebuild the Democratic party. Long on ability but short on qualities of aggressive leadership, Laporte was the perfect example of the hardworking, behind-the-scenes assistant.

To head the League publicity corps Shouse would have preferred Charles Michelson. "Who in hell is Charley Michelson?" Raskob asked when Shouse had hired him as publicity director of the Democratic National Committee in 1929.

Raskob soon found out. Michelson was the kind of legendary newsman that Hollywood was fond of. A leathery, hard-bitten yet likable cynic who had peered in every dark doorway on each side of the political street, Michelson brought to his job a functional professionalism uncluttered by any illusions. A veteran of the Hearst chain and head of the Washington bureau of the New York *World* for a dozen years when Shouse hired him, Michelson more than any other person was responsible for creating the depression image of the Hoover Administration which plagued the Republican party for years afterward.

When the smoke cleared at the 1932 Democratic convention in Chicago, Michelson was on the Roosevelt bandwagon. Even though he realized that it would have "meant more money" for himself, Michelson declined Shouse's invitation to join "the new cabal." Shouse settled for the bespectacled William Murphy, head of the Washington bureau of the Philadelphia *Public Ledger* and president of the National Press Club when he took the publicity job with the Liberty League. To head the research division Shouse turned to Arthur W. Crawford of the Chicago *Journal of Commerce*.[1]

III

The officers and policy-makers of the League were all seasoned campaigners.

To Captain Stayton went the job of secretary. Another veteran of the prohibition fight, Grayson M.-P. Murphy, became treasurer. R. J. Dillon, comptroller of the AAPA, was given his old job; and Carey Jarman, treasurer of Repeal Associates, became Stayton's assistant secretary.

The Board of Directors was composed of John W. Davis, Alfred E. Smith, James W. Wadsworth, Nathan Miller, and Irénée du Pont. John Raskob, who was primarily responsible for starting the Liberty League, chose the role of unofficial adviser and generous contributor, but he would accept no office.

The plan of organization was to recruit a group of prominent persons, representing every state if possible, to serve on a national advisory council. From this group a number would be selected who (along with the Board of Directors) would make up the National Executive Committee.

The Executive Committee was expected to be the effective policy-making body of the Liberty League; but experience soon proved that it was too large and cumbersome. In January 1935 Shouse recommended that a small administrative committee be created with full authority to act on behalf of the Executive Committee. Throughout the life of the League the initiative for its activities came from the Administrative Committee.

The National Advisory Council consisted of about two hundred persons drawn from each section of the country to give the League "widespread appeal at the local level." This meant that the council was essentially window dressing. And impressive window dressing it was. Among the important persons agreeing to serve were Dr. Samuel Harden Church, head of the Carnegie Institute in Pittsburgh; David A. Reed, former Republican senator of Pennsylvania; Detroit industrialists Alvan Macauley and Henry B. Joy; Channing Pollock, Frederic R. Coudert, Jr., W. R. Perkins and George E. Roosevelt of New York; Robert Woods Bliss, former ambassador to Argentina; Richmond Pearson Hobson, the naval hero of the Spanish-American War; Henry P. DuBois of the J. G. White Companies; John J. Raskob; Alfred P. Sloan, Jr., of General Motors; E. T. Weir of Weirton Steel; and the motion picture producer Hal E. Roach.

Even more impressive was the membership of the National Executive Committee, a smaller group of about twenty-five. In addition to the original directors, the Executive Committee included men such as: Sewell L. Avery of Montgomery Ward;

H. B. Earhart of Detroit; J. Howard Pew of Sun Oil Company; General Foods Corporation president Colby M. Chester; Frank C. Rand of International Shoe Company; Colonel A. A. Sprague of Chicago; Judge Joseph M. Proskauer, former justice of the New York Supreme Court and counsel to the Consolidated Gas system; Raoul E. Desvernine, prominent New York attorney and president of Crucible Steel Company; former Secretary of War Dwight F. Davis; Pierre du Pont; James M. Beck; Joseph B. Ely, former Democratic governor of Massachusetts; Edward F. Hutton, chairman of the board of General Foods Corporation; Robert L. Lund of St. Louis, a past president of the National Association of Manufacturers; and William L. Clayton, the Houston cotton factor. Representing the distaff side were Mrs. Charles H. Sabin, Mrs. Henry B. Joy of Detroit, and Mrs. James Ross Todd of Louisville, each of whom had been national officers in the Women's Organization for National Prohibition Reform.

Jouett Shouse, Irénée du Pont, Mrs. Sabin, Alfred E. Smith, and Colby Chester made up the first Administrative Committee. When Governor Nathan Miller resigned from the Board of Directors in May 1935, Chester became also a director of the League. In June 1935 Captain Stayton was added to the committee. When Chester resigned to become president of the National Association of Manufacturers, Raoul Desvernine replaced him.

The task of actually running the Liberty League was entrusted to the Administrative Committee. Of its six members — Shouse, du Pont, Mrs. Sabin, Smith, Stayton, and Desvernine — all but Desvernine had been prominent in the work of the AAPA.[2]

IV

The buildup of organizational strength at the local level proceeded very rapidly. Membership in the League was of two classes, contributing and noncontributing. By 1936, the peak year of League strength, it could boast of contributing and noncontributing members in every state of the Union as well as the District of Columbia, Hawaii, Alaska, the Philippine Islands, and Puerto Rico.

This farflung membership was organized into state divisions. At the first meeting of the League's Board of Directors it was agreed to organize the first state division in Delaware to serve as a model for subsequent state divisions. The Delaware Liberty League was incorporated on September 1, 1934, only a week after Shouse's first press conference. Shortly after the election in November, the New York state division, headed by Henry P. DuBois, opened headquarters in the Empire State Building.

The organization of state divisions proceeded smoothly so that by 1936 the Liberty League had active headquarters in twenty states — New York, New Jersey, Massachusetts, Maryland, Delaware, Pennsylvania, Illinois, Indiana, Ohio, Minnesota, Wisconsin, Iowa, Nebraska, Missouri, Kentucky, Alabama, Georgia, South Carolina, Florida, California, and the District of Columbia. (The Liberty League organizations in Delaware and Pennsylvania were separately incorporated but operated as affiliates of the national organization.) The staggering blow dealt the League by the re-election of Roosevelt in 1936 halted plans for expansion into nine other states.

To coordinate the work of the state divisions, Liberty League field organizers established regional offices in New York City, Newark, Philadelphia, Wilmington, Baltimore, Chicago, St. Paul, Louisville and Atlanta. But despite impressive national and local machinery, the organization was never able to rally any significant popular support. By July 1935, eleven months after the formation of the League, there were only 36,055 members — 9730 contributing and 26,325 noncontributing. As late as January 1, 1936, the total membership was only 75,000. The League reached its maximum numerical strength, 124,856, during the summer of 1936, then tailed off badly after the presidential election.

Since membership involved no more than sending one's name and address to the headquarters in Washington (with or without a contribution) the Liberty League could hardly be regarded as a grass-roots movement. When finally the League was forced to a test of strength at the ballot box this lack of popular support was fatal.[3]

v

If the Liberty League lacked numbers it did not lack money. Twitting it for its paucity of members, *Time* observed that to start a political organization "takes only two members and a slogan, but to keep it healthy takes money." By this standard, said *Time*, the League was "really healthy."

Without a broad base of popular support, the League was thrown back upon the wealthy men of the country for financial backing, and of these it had its pick. Shouse very faithfully reported his receipts and expenditures to the Clerk of the House like the head of any other political organization, although he was not legally required to do so. Those reports revealed that during its six-year history the Liberty League collected and disbursed nearly $1,200,000, more than a million of which was spent in the twenty-six months between August 1934 and November 1936. This did not include funds collected and spent by the state and local units, which would drive the totals still higher. In the last four months of 1934 expenditures totaled a little more than $95,000; in 1935 the League raised nearly as much money as each of the national committees of the two major parties, and its expenditures fell only $26.08 short of $390,000; in the election year the League spent over half a million dollars ($518,123) trying to beat Roosevelt.

From time to time Shouse liked to announce that "several thousand" were contributing one to five dollars, which was true; but the large amounts that the League was spending were not being raised from the widow's mite. In a typical year, 1935, only $34,700 came from contributors who gave less than $100. But in that same year the League received contributions such as these: Irénée du Pont, $79,750; Charles C. Copeland, $15,000; Lammot du Pont, $10,000; Pierre du Pont, $10,000; S. Halleck du Pont, $10,000; William du Pont, $10,000; John J. Raskob, $10,000; Alfred P. Sloan, $10,000; H. B. Rust, $10,000; E. T. Weir, $10,000; William L. Clayton, $6500; Thomas L. Chadbourne, $6250; Edward F. Hutton, $5000; H. B. Earhart, $4000; and contributions of one to three thousand dollars from a score of other prominent men.

This meant that fewer than two dozen bankers, industrialists, and businessmen contributed over half the League's funds for 1935; and nearly 30 per cent of all League funds that year was from the du Pont family. In 1936, approximately two thirds of the money came from thirty men contributing $5,000 or more apiece; and one of every four dollars spent was from the pockets of the du Ponts.

After the 1936 election, contributions dwindled and the League had trouble collecting pledges. Hal Roach, who had been solicited by the board chairman of General Foods, Edward F. Hutton, indicated an intention to lend the League $20,000, but the loan was never made. Walter P. Chrysler, who proposed to give $5,000 in cash and a loan of $20,000, also reneged because of a disagreement over matters of policy. And there were others. For all the good it did, lamented one disappointed Liberty Leaguer, "I might just as well have sent the money to Farley." After 1936, the du Pont brothers, Irénée, Lammot and Pierre, put up practically all the money to carry on the League's curtailed activities.

The wealth of those backing the organization was at once a help and a hindrance. It meant that it could speak with a voice of authority not justified by its numbers. But it also meant that the League was invitingly vulnerable. With little effort and considerable justification its enemies could attack it as the tool of the warm, comfortable, well-fed rich, those who knew nothing firsthand about unemployment, foreclosed mortgages, vanishing savings, disconnected utilities, threadbare clothes, or the shame and indignity of being on relief. The opposition charged that the League spoke only for entrenched corporate wealth; and whether that was good or bad, dangerous or harmless, patriotic or conspiratorial, the charge was essentially true.[4]

VI

Most of the money was spent on salaries, bolstering the state organizations, and promoting the propaganda campaign. In exploiting the "rich-man, poor-man" theme, much was made of the lavish salaries paid League personnel. As its head, Shouse received $54,000 annually for salary and expenses. William C. Murphy, director of publicity, received $14,000, four others were paid $10,000 or more, and another four got from $5000 to $10,000. If the League had more high-priced help than either the Democratic or Republican national headquarters, it was at least in part because it was attempting more than either of them, certainly more than the Republicans.

An effective organization had to be built before 1936, and that did not leave much time by political reckoning. To make the drive at the top successful the state and local units had to be created carefully but with utmost speed. This took time, it took talent, and above all, money. In two years the League had active organizations in twenty states and the spadework completed in nine other states. Given perhaps another year it is quite likely that there would have been divisions in every state.

High-priced personnel and elaborate organization were only means to an end; the people would have the last word. Hence a favorable public opinion had to be molded, a "great moral issue" found, and the people rallied behind the cracked Liberty Bell emblem of the League. To accomplish this the League launched an educational campaign that surpassed even that waged against the Eighteenth Amendment.

VII

The League used much the same propaganda techniques that had been tried and tested by the Association Against the Prohibition Amendment. The most effective feature of the educational campaign was the Liberty League pamphlet series. Between August 1934 and September 1936 there were issued 135 pamphlets, a rate of better than one per week. Skillfully written and edited, expertly printed on high-quality paper of a size for easy mailing, the pamphlets represented perhaps the most concise and thorough summary of conservative political thought written in the United States since *The Federalist* papers. A little more than half of them were originally delivered as speeches and radio addresses by men like Shouse, Al Smith, James Wadsworth, John W. Davis, James Beck, and others. The remainder were prepared by the League research staff.

The responsibility for preparing the pamphlets rested with Shouse, Murphy, and Crawford, who each week decided on an appropriate subject, either editing a prepared speech or writing on a topic prepared by the research staff. Frequently Shouse consulted Wadsworth, Beck, or other important friends of the League in Washington about the tentative subject. The rough draft was then presented to the Administrative Committee, which met each Thursday in New York in rooms adjacent to Al Smith's offices in the Empire State Building. After Shouse relayed to Crawford in Washington any changes suggested by the committee, the pamphlet was ready for the printer.

The pamphlets were given the widest possible distribution. Copies were supplied in advance to the Washington bureaus of about 350 papers, all the press associations, and to well-known editors to facilitate timely editorial comment. The result was more than 200,000 individual items of varying length, innumerable editorial comments, and frequent feature stories — "altogether a publicity coverage," wrote Shouse, "such as probably never attached to any other organization aside from the two major political parties within the same length of time" — and since all of it was being passed off as "news" the publicity cost the League nothing.

Altogether the League sent out more than 5,000,000 pamphlets to members, newspapers, other political organizations and government agencies. More than 7500 public libraries and college and university libraries received them regularly; every member of the House and Senate was on the mailing list; and, with considerable delight, the League revealed that even some Cabinet members had requested copies.

As a supplement to the pamphlets the League distributed a monthly bulletin, a leaflet series, and the reports of its Lawyers' Committee. The leaflets, usually little two-page affairs, were mostly reprints of editorials and random items critical of the New Deal. Chosen for their shock effect (*Government by Busybodies; Will It Be Ave Caesar?; The Way Dictatorships Start; Abolishing the States*), and intended for a less sophisticated audience than the pamphlets, the twenty-four leaflets were given shotgun distribution, the last appearing in October 1936.

From August 1935 through October 1936 the monthly bulletin was published. The series was resumed early in 1937, and thirteen bulletins were issued that year but not on any regular schedule. Only one appeared in 1938, after which the League suspended all publications.

The bulletin series, the house organ of the Liberty League, received about the same distribution as the pamphlets. Mimeographed on multicolored paper, the bulletins featured articles on timely subjects (budget, executive reorganization, TVA, taxes, etc.), plus news of League activities, items about members, humorous notes and anecdotes about the Administration, and plugs for funds and support.

A selected distribution was given the five reports of the Lawyers' Committee on the constitutionality of the National Labor Relations Act, the Bituminous Coal Conservation Act, the Potato Control Act of 1935, the Social Security Act, and the Agricultural Adjustment Act.

In January 1936 the League began a special service for weekly and small daily papers. Through the Western Newspaper Union, editorials and canned news stories were distributed to papers in fourteen western, midwestern, and southern states. The purpose was to push conservative political principles rather than to publicize the League itself; and before the service was discontinued late in 1936, more than 1600 papers were subscribing.

The Liberty League also promoted its educational program by extensive use of the radio. Like so much of the free advertising that the organization received in the press, radio time was often given to the League "with the compliments of the radio companies." [5]

VIII

It was Shouse's original intention to organize the Liberty League into economic divisions as well as state divisions. In his initial statement to the press he listed seven economic classifications: homeowners, farmers, labor, savings depositors, life insurance policyholders, bondholders, and stockholders; and other economic divisions would be created "from time to time as may be found necessary." None of those which Shouse had listed ever materialized; but eventually the League did have two special groups, college students and lawyers.

Promoting the cause of the Liberty League in the colleges and universities was Otis T. Wingo, Jr., son of the Arkansas congressman, who began the work of organizing the National Intercollegiate Committee in January 1935. Within a year there were chapters in 210 colleges in 46 states, with 5192 members. Students, reported Wingo, were joining "at the rate of about 100 per day." By April 1936 there were 345 chapters with over 10,000 members, and at least one chapter in every state. Although the student organization included institutions both state and private, secular and denominational, the most successful chapters appeared to be at the state universities, especially Wisconsin, Virginia, North Carolina, Maryland, Illinois, Pennsylvania, and Nebraska.

The League not only caught on rapidly among college students but it also had considerable support from the other side of the desk. At least a dozen educators were prominently identified with its leadership. Edwin W. Kemmerer, Princeton University economist, monetary expert, and adviser to Herbert Hoover and a score of foreign governments, was a frequent spokesman and in 1935, at the annual meeting of the American Economic Association in New York, tried unsuccessfully to organize a committee of economists for the League. Dr. Samuel Harden Church, head of Carnegie Institute in Pittsburgh, was a member of the Advisory Council. Eight of the League pamphlets were based on the speeches of Walter E. Spahr, New York University economist, and Neil Carothers of the Lehigh University School of Business Administration. Albert G. Keller and

W. A. Wilson, both of Yale University, were active supporters. And the Yale political scientist Ray Bert Westerfield, G. W. Dyer, Vanderbilt University economist, the dean of the Columbia University Graduate School of Journalism, Carl W. Ackerman, and George Barton Cutten, a member of the Advisory Council and president of Colgate University, all lent the prestige of their names and positions to the cause of the Liberty League. One of the pamphlets, aptly entitled *Professors and the New Deal*, was devoted to the results of a survey of one hundred and fifty "leading educators." The not surprising conclusion was that the New Deal did not find acceptance with "the overwhelming majority of the academic profession." [6]

IX

The most ambitious program undertaken by the Liberty League on behalf of its student program was sponsorship of the ninth Annual Institute of Public Affairs at the University of Virginia in July 1935. Important New Dealers, including Raymond Moley, internal revenue commissioner Guy T. Helvering, several Cabinet officers, and "a score of Senators and Representatives" were invited to the week-long affair to defend the Administration in debate against a strong team of Liberty Leaguers on the topic "The Constitution and the New Deal." Representing the League were Nicholas Roosevelt, journalist of the New York *Herald Tribune*, Neil Carothers, J. Howard Pew, Walter E. Spahr, Raoul Desvernine, James W. Wadsworth, Captain William Stayton, and the journalist, Demarest Lloyd.

Moley and Helvering and possibly others had already accepted invitations when the Administration, fearing an ambush, passed the word through Charlie Michelson that they should back out. As a result, the ranks of the New Deal defenders were cut to Senators Rush Holt of West Virginia and Alben Barkley of Kentucky, Representative Fred J. Sisson of New York, Hugh Johnson, deposed head of the NRA whose New Deal fever had already cooled considerably, Mrs. Helen H. Miller of the AAA, and Dr. James Hart, Johns Hopkins University professor.

Despite the pro-New Deal sympathies of the audience, the Administration got the worst of it. The New Deal, argued Nicholas Roosevelt, had retarded recovery ("by meddling with business"); it was an alien philosophy, said Lloyd ("infected, if not permeated, by Fabian Socialism"); its fiscal policies were dangerous, warned Spahr ("money tinkerers" and "money meddlers"); the taxing power, complained Desvernine, was being used illegally ("a punitive weapon . . . an instrument of social control"); Pew scourged the Administration for interfering with free enterprise ("Government and business can't be mixed without harming both"); Carothers claimed the recovery program could not possibly work ("founded on economic error"); Stayton was frightened of Roosevelt's emergency powers ("history shows that men entrusted with power are likely to seek more of it"); and Wadsworth assailed the extension of federal power over industry and farming ("which rightfully came within the province of state control").

The country was much better off than it had been two years before, argued the defenders of the Administration. The Liberty League, they said, represented a fatal resistance to change in a changing world; it would perpetuate the past. The New Deal, said Professor Hart in summing up the arguments for the Administration, with its "orderly readaptation of the past," was the happy alternative to fascism.[7]

x

The success of the Voluntary Committee of Lawyers in the work of the United Repeal Council perhaps made it inevitable that the Liberty League would also enlist the help of the lawyers in the fight against the New Deal.

As early as September 1934 Raoul Desvernine offered to organize the lawyers; and on June 10, 1935, Shouse announced that a "Lawyers' Vigilance Committee" with Desvernine as chairman had volunteered its service to the League.

Like its counterpart in the United Repeal Council, the Lawyers' Committee had defense of the Constitution as its purpose. It offered to examine proposed legislation to see if it was "consonant with the American constitutional system and American traditions"; to "contribute its services" in test cases; to make its members "available for speaking" on behalf of the League; and to organize a general lawyers' committee to which all would be invited to join and to "volunteer their services in defense of the Constitution."

Desvernine had little trouble recruiting members. Large firms, many of whose important clients were already associated with the League, quickly fell into line and the smaller fry went along. In less than a year more than two thousand had joined the general lawyers' committee.

The parent organization, the Lawyers' Vigilance Committee or National Lawyers' Committee, numbered between fifty and sixty of the most talented lawyers in the United States: Raoul Desvernine, national chairman; John W. Davis; George W. Wickersham, whose report to President Hoover had aroused such bitter attack by the United Repeal Council lawyers' committee; Harold J. Gallagher and Frederic R. Coudert, Jr., of New York; Joseph Proskauer, friend and confidant of Al Smith; former Senator David Reed of Pennsylvania; James M. Beck; Joseph B. Ely, former governor of Massachusetts; Frank J. Hogan of Washington, D.C.; Merritt Lane, Robert McCarter, and Josiah Stryker of New Jersey; D. J. Kenefick of Buffalo, New York; George Roberts, a law partner of Henry L. Stimson; Forney Johnston, Birmingham, Alabama; J. Van Dyke Norman of Louisville; William H. Rogers, president of the Florida State

Bar Association; Ethan A. H. Shepley, state chairman of the Missouri division of the Liberty League; Ralph M. Shaw, chairman of the Illinois Liberty League; and twenty or thirty more of equal prestige.

This committee was broken down into a series of subcommittees, each subcommittee to concentrate on one piece of legislation and report back to the national committee. In August 1935 Desvernine announced that a group was at work on the National Labor Relations Act, and that work would soon begin on TVA, AAA, FCC, the Guffey-Snyder Coal Act, the 1933 Securities Act, and the Public Utility Holding Company Act.

The Lawyers' Committee was presumably volunteering its services without pay, and its only connection with the Liberty League was said to be that the League would handle the printing and distribution of its reports. However, at least a dozen members of the committee held some important post in the League: Desvernine, John W. Davis, Frederic R. Coudert, James Beck, Joseph Proskauer, David Reed, Joseph Ely, Ethan Shepley, Ralph Shaw, and others. Moreover, Shouse was instructed to give Desvernine $25,000, to be used "for such purpose as the Chairman of the Lawyers' National Committee shall authorize and approve." [8]

XI

At a news conference on September 19, 1935, the Lawyers' Committee released its first report.

"When a lawyer tells a client that a law is unconstitutional," explained Earl F. Reed, "it is then a nullity and he need no longer obey that law." Reed, chief counsel for Weirton Steel Company, was chairman of the subcommittee that drafted the report and the law that he was saying a client "need no longer obey" was the National Labor Relations Act. Both the subcommittee and the Lawyers' Committee agreed unanimously that the Act was unconstitutional on at least two counts: first, because it was an improper use of the interstate commerce clause; second, because it violated due process by intruding upon the right of contract.

The unfavorable opinion of the committee was not unexpected; it could hardly have been different. But the report nonetheless touched off a storm of protest that did not diminish for months. The *Nation* ran an article entitled "A Conspiracy by Lawyers" in which it pointed out that the report reflected only the opinion of corporation lawyers; no law professors or labor lawyers were consulted for their views. But more serious was the demoralizing implication of the report. "If lawyers turn themselves into an organized body dedicated to inciting the public to disobey the law," warned the *Nation*, "that is conspiracy." The *New Republic* belittled the lawyers, saying they "should not be taken too seriously"; that the report was simply a device for spreading propaganda on behalf of their clients, which was "not far above the level of criminal lawyers who try their cases in the newspapers."

The Administration maintained a discreet silence, all save the Secretary of the Interior. Harold Ickes, referring to the committee as "Chief Justice Shouse and his fifty-seven varieties of associate justices," said sarcastically, "one thing about it, Mr. Shouse beats the Chief Justice of the Supreme Court on salary; but then, he is a greater constitutional authority." If the League would double Shouse's salary, Ickes continued, he would "probably take on the work of the executive and legislative branches of the government as well."

On a more serious note Ickes charged that issuing the report before the court had an opportunity to rule on the National Labor Relations Act was "evidence per se of disrespect of the court." Shouse dismissed Ickes' scathing attack as the rantings of a "persistent denouncer."

The controversy over the propriety of a body of eminent lawyers declaring a law unconstitutional before the Supreme Court had a chance to review it and of encouraging clients to disobey the law was continued in the dignified pages of the *United States Law Review*. Editorially, the *Review* was most critical of what the committee had done. It was "just a little incredulous" that so distinguished a body of lawyers would declare legislation properly enacted by the Congress and approved by the President to be unconstitutional "before it has found its way into the courts or received judicial interpretation." The purpose of the report, the *Review* continued, could only be one of two things — to influence the courts or to arouse public opinion so that "confidence in the courts will be impaired should the legislation be held constitutional," and "neither purpose has anything to commend it." The editors expressed the hope that "wiser counsels and better judgment" would cause the lawyers to discontinue this phase of their activities.

The position taken by the *Review* did not go unchallenged. A member of the Lawyers' Committee, Charles A. Beardsley of Oakland, California, argued that they had done nothing more than express an opinion, that lawyers had always done this, that the law journals were full of articles questioning the constitutionality of legislation. In answer to Beardsley the editors repeated their earlier view, saying: ". . . there seems to us to be a wide difference between an expression of opinion in an article written by a lawyer for a law magazine, or an editorial note published in a law magazine, and a statement of an opinion which purports to have been formulated by a group of distinguished lawyers organized for the purpose of expressing that opinion, followed by its wide dissemination in the public press for the purpose of influencing public opinion. If not for this purpose, for what purpose the general publicity?"

Sveinbjorn Johnson, professor of law at the University of Illinois, took a more compromising position. Putting aside all other consideration, wrote Johnson in the *Review,* the lawyers had probably done more harm than good to their cause because the report made it "more embarrassing for the Court to concur in than to repudiate their views."

While the controversy raged, Shouse announced that the 40,000 copies of the report were gone and that a second printing had been ordered.[9]

XII

On November 17, 1935, the committee on professional ethics and grievances of the American Bar Association met in Columbus, Ohio, to consider possible disciplinary action growing out of the activities of the Lawyers' Committee. The grievance committee admitted that it was meeting to consider complaints that the lawyers' report was unethical and that it violated American Bar Association rules, but it would not divulge the source of the complaints.

One rumor had it that the complaints had originated outside the legal profession. The statements by important labor leaders, including William Green of the American Federation of Labor and Francis J. Gorman, vice-president of the United Textile Workers, that the lawyers involved should be disbarred gave foundation to the rumor. Another rumor alleged that the complaints originated with a group of lawyers working with government agencies.

Joseph L. Kaplan, general counsel for the National Support Roosevelt League, claimed that his organization was responsible for the inquiry on the grounds that the Lawyers' Committee was guilty of "maintenance" — the encouragement of litigation by offering free legal advice and assistance.

Whether it was "maintenance" or not, the Lawyers' Committee had offered free legal assistance. The same day that Reed released the report on the NLRA, Shouse announced that the Liberty League was setting up a free lawyer service for individuals and companies unable to pay the costs of litigation that would presumably follow from disobeying the Act. In a radio address a month later, James M. Beck renewed the offer of free legal aid with this warning: "We must defeat the sappers and miners of the New Deal who are insidiously undermining the very foundations of the constitution." (The next day, to the amusement of some and the irritation of others, the Hod Carriers' and Common Laborers' Union, Local 536, York, Pennsylvania, appealed to the Lawyers' Committee for free legal aid.)

It was eventually learned that the original complaint came from a member of the American Bar Association, an Atlanta attorney, Carl N. Davie, who branded the Lawyers' Committee "a vast free lawyer service for firms and individuals 'bucking' New Deal laws on constitutional grounds."

With justification, the grievance committee might have taken disciplinary action. Although Canon Twenty of the American Bar Association's *Canons of Ethics* read, "Newspaper publications by a lawyer as to pending or anticipated litigation may interfere with a fair trial in the courts and otherwise prejudice the due administration of justice. Generally they are to be condemned," the Lawyers' Committee was given a clean bill of health. ("The Committee is unable to see anything unethical or improper in such a course.") Liberty Leaguers were elated; but others saw it as another part of the legal conspiracy against the Administration.

Here was an early example of a difficulty that plagued the Liberty League throughout its life. To an extent hard to understand on the part of intelligent men filling important posts in American society, the officials of the League laid themselves, and thus the Liberty League, open to accusation, suspicion, and finally ridicule and political incapacity. Without indulging in what has come to be called the imputation of "guilt by association," it was easy for the opponents of the League, by exposing practices either suspicious, corrupt, or inept on the part of prominent members, to leave the impression that the League itself was involved or at least tarred with its members' brush. For Desvernine to have allowed himself and the Lawyers' Committee to be put in this position, is today very hard to understand.[10]

XIII

With the danger of censure by their colleagues removed the Lawyers' Committee resumed the offensive against New Deal legislation. The Liberty League is apparently unwilling to use the "orderly method" of contesting laws, said Chairman Hosford of the Bituminous Coal Commission, when the committee branded the Guffey-Snyder Bituminous Coal Conservation Act invalid "on four counts" (December 9, 1935); another report said the Potato Control Act was "flagrantly unconstitutional" (December 30, 1935); and when the Supreme Court ruled the Agricultural Adjustment Act unconstitutional the committee distributed a fifty-page pamphlet criticizing the minority opinion of Stone, Brandeis, and Cardozo (January 6, 1936).

None of these later reports created the heat that had been generated by the first one on the NLRA. This was due at least in part to the effective Administration counterattack.

No prominent New Deal spokesman except Ickes had openly criticized the Lawyers' Committee. But subtly (and sometimes covertly) Charlie Michelson began a campaign to neutralize the lawyers by ridicule and innuendo. An exhaustive report on the business connections of the lawyers was circulated within the higher echelons of the Administration to suggest that the committee was motivated by clients rather than by conscience.

In his "Dispelling the Fog" letter of October 20, Michelson ridiculed "The Little Supreme Court's ponderous assumption of infallibility in construing the Constitution" by printing a box score of cases won and lost by prominent members of the committee before the Supreme Court: John W. Davis (won 17, lost 15); James M. Beck (won 2, lost 8); George W. Wickersham (won 3, lost 3); Frederic R. Coudert (won 1, lost 2); Hal H. Smith (won 0, lost 1); Frank J. Hogan (lost two notable cases involving Albert Fall oil leases and the destruction of air mail contract records by former Assistant Secretary of Commerce, William P. McCracken); and so on.

The clever publicity director of the Democratic National Committee also planted the idea that the Liberty League had tried to do more than just influence the courts through the reports of the Lawyers' Committee. He cited the case of Justice John F. Carew of the New York State Supreme Court. Carew was a Roosevelt appointee when Roosevelt was governor of the state. It was well known that Carew had been approached on behalf of the Liberty League, an approach to which the judge had taken exception by stating publicly: "I regard this as impudence and I do not desire to receive this or any other communication of the kind."

Several distinguished jurists, among them William H. Ellis of the Florida Supreme Court, U.S. District Judge Merrill E. Otis, John H. Hatcher of the West Virginia Court of Appeals, Louisville's federal judge, Charles I. Dawson, and Pennsylvania Supreme Court Justice George W. Maxey, were known to be associated with the League in one way or another. The attempt to enlist jurists in the cause of the Liberty League, wrote Michelson, "makes me wonder if they have ever thought of approaching the members of the national tribunal of last resort."

Michelson knew better than that. But he also knew that with many unthinking people suggestion and fact were one and the same.[11]

XIV

During the late summer and early fall of 1934, the American Liberty League remained comparatively quiet. Shouse made several speeches, five in all, before the new year; but little was heard from the other big names of the League, Smith, Davis, Wadsworth and company. The main reason was that the organization was not yet completed and Shouse was reluctant to get the League involved in a congressional election until it was capable of functioning at full strength.

"Now that the elections are over," wrote Arthur Krock, "something will soon be heard of the American Liberty League." Krock never wrote truer words. Early in 1935 the Liberty League would launch a concerted and sustained attack upon the Administration of Franklin Roosevelt such as the country had not seen since the days of Andrew Johnson and Reconstruction. But in the late fall of 1934, the League suddenly encountered an adversary from a strange quarter, an adversary that wore two stars.[12]

4

SEMPER FIDELIS

No military officer of the United States since the late tempestuous George Custer has succeeded in publicly floundering
in so much hot water as Smedley Darlington Butler . . .

Time

Evidence was obtained showing that certain persons had
made an attempt to establish a fascist organization in this
country.

McCormack-Dickstein Committee

IN AUGUST 1948 newspapers across the country headlined the
dramatic story of Mrs. Oksana Kasenkina, a schoolteacher who
leaped from a third-floor window of the Russian consulate in
New York to avoid being returned to Russia. Mrs. Kasenkina's
jump to freedom followed the refusal of the Russian authorities
to honor a court release order issued by Judge Samuel Dickstein.

Judge Dickstein was well acquainted with oppression. Prominent in New York Democratic politics, a city alderman and
state representative, Dickstein was thirty-seven years old in 1922
when he was elected to the House of Representatives, where he
served until his resignation in 1945 to accept a judgeship on the
New York State Supreme Court. Born near Vilna in Russia,
the mild, bespectacled, scholarly son of Jewish immigrant par-

ents, Dickstein devoted his entire public career as legislator and jurist to fighting the battles of the underdog, the minority, the alien, the underprivileged. The Kasenkina affair was typical rather than unusual, and was reminiscent of the battles he had waged in Congress on behalf of other outsiders, first as a member and then as the chairman of the House Committee on Immigration and Naturalization.[1]

II

Smedley Darlington Butler was a fighter of a different type. By the time of his retirement in 1931, a major general with over thirty-three years' service, Butler was a Marine Corps legend. When the Spanish-American War erupted, young Butler astonished his Quaker parents (his father, Thomas S. Butler, was a lawyer and member of Congress for thirty years) by quitting Haverford School and accepting a provisional second lieutenant's commission in the Marine Corps. His gallantry at the age of seventeen — he had lied about his age — elicited from Theodore Roosevelt the opinion that Butler was "the finest fighting man in the armed forces."

Butler was in the Philippines for the insurrection there, then went on to China, where he was twice wounded in the Boxer Rebellion, and afterward, to Panama and Nicaragua. By 1914 he was troop commander aboard the *Minnesota* heading for Mexico because of the Tampico Incident. Posing as an eccentric entomologist, Butler checked the strength and disposition of Mexican troops all the way to Mexico City, a daring bit of madness which won him the first of two Congressional Medals of Honor. He won the second the next year in Haiti.

The great disappointment of his career was his failure to get into action with his command, the 13th Marines, in World War I. Chafing over his peacetime assignments, Butler took a leave of absence from the service in 1924 to become director of public safety in Philadelphia, a job that meant cleaning up the graft and corruption in the police and fire departments and the enforcement of prohibition. Two years later he was back with the Marine Corps and stayed on until his retirement in 1931. In 1932, running as a dry with the backing of Governor Pinchot, he opposed James J. Davis for the Republican senatorial nomination, but lost.

Butler was a colorful character even in a service noted for colorful characters. A stern disciplinarian (Old Gimlet Eye, the troops called him), with courage matched by his salty language, Butler was outspokenly contemptuous of brass hat military methods, a trait which endeared him to his troops, but probably cost him the post as Commandant of the Corps. He kept himself in hot water with his superiors: he once embarrassed the government with his tactless description of conditions in Nicaragua; he left his job with the city of Philadelphia after a noisy and public dispute with the mayor; and his remark about Mussolini (Butler called him "a hit-and-run driver") created an international incident marked by Italian protests, apologies from Secretary Stimson and from Butler, and an order from Navy Secretary Charles Francis Adams to have Butler court-martialed, an order later rescinded after tempers cooled.[2]

III

The careers of these two unusual men, Dickstein and Butler, crossed briefly but dramatically in the fall of 1934. Dickstein was disturbed by developments in Europe in the early 1930's. The spectacular rise of Mussolini and Hitler and the inroads of fascistic movements everywhere on the Continent, spawned in the backwash of war and the corrosive effects of depression, filled him with disgust and loathing. Wherever fascism triumphed his co-religionists suffered, were persecuted, were made the scapegoats. Dickstein was determined that this awful thing would not happen in America.

But it was happening here, or so it seemed. The 1930's were a time of severe testing for democracy in the United States. Using depression, want, and privation as the mask for their ideological treachery, messiahs and demagogues of every stripe, from fascists and racists on the extreme Right to Communists on the extreme Left, peddled their wares, sometimes boldly and blatantly, at other times secretly, deceitfully, and with cunning stealth, but always with the freedom befitting a democracy. If America sold its soul it would do so in the daylight, in the open marketplace of political ideas.

Despite the insidiousness of communism it was the thunder on the right that appeared the more dangerous, that created the greater sense of fear and urgency in the Depression Decade. In the forefront were such powerful figures as Huey P. Long and the Reverend Charles E. Coughlin. Behind them was a dismaying array of would-be Caesars, each strutting, posing, and tirading against that hour when he could come forth as savior and Führer.

There was the religious mystic and amateur economist William Dudley Pelley, who began his campaign to save America after a singular event in 1928. One night in his California cottage (alone, of course), Pelley died but was restored to life after spending seven minutes in eternity. The rest is history. Moving to Asheville, North Carolina, Pelley established the Foundation for Christian Ethics, Galahad College, and began publishing *Liberation*, a violently anti-Semitic paper. Roosevelt was really a Jew of Dutch ancestry, Pelley insisted, who had been foisted on an unsuspecting electorate by the Elders of Zion. Pelley's cure for the economic woes of the country seemed to involve forming the United States into one giant corporation with only native-born citizens as stockholders.

More ominous was his quasi-military force, the Christian Militia, clad in Silver Shirts and, wrote Pelley, dedicated to the mission of saving America, "as Mussolini and his Black Shirts saved Italy and Hitler and his Brown Shirts saved Germany." For a time a camp was established near Oklahoma City, the Officers Training School in Home Defense Tactics, to teach street-fighting and strong-arm tactics.

Pelley's Silver Shirt movement was the inspiration for a whole rainbow of colored-shirt organizations. There were: the National Blue Shirt Minute Men; the Sons of Loyalty, the brain-child of Richard S. Kaplan, a Gary, Indiana, attorney, who also affected blue shirts; the Khaki Shirts, a movement led by Art J. Smith that emerged from the Bonus Army's march on Washington; the Gray Shirts, more properly known as the Pioneer American Home Protective Association, which operated in New York and was dedicated to saving the home from "idealistic or Communistic college professors"; the Black Shirts, organized in 1930 by Holt Gewinner and the onetime candidate for governor of Georgia, Joseph Wood, who were anti-Communist, anti-atheist, and on the more practical side, anti-Negro; the Friends of the New Germany, with their authentic brown shirts smuggled in from Germany, singing their beery choruses of the Horst Wessel Song and practicing their storm-trooper exercises in streetfighting; the White Shirts, the disciplined force of the Crusaders for Economic Liberty, organized by George W. Christians of Chattanooga, Tennessee ("As soon as you are fully prepared and equipped to go to Washington," Christians instructed his local commanders, "report to the Commander-in-Chief of the White Shirts at Chattanooga, Tennessee, stating the number of men, how equipped and the time required to reach Washington . . ."); and an indefinite number of similar groups.

Besides the more or less well-organized groups, were those individuals with more or less nebulous followings acquired through the printed page or the lecture platform. Gerald L. K.

Smith, who converted Huey Long's organization into the Committee of One Million after Long's assassination; the Reverend Gerald B. Winrod, of Wichita, Kansas, sometimes described as "the Jayhawk Nazi" who had learned his anti-Semitism and anti-Catholicism firsthand from trips to Germany in 1934 and 1935; Lawrence Dennis, the ex-foreign service man who was the acknowledged intellectual leader of Right Wing extremist groups in the United States; James True of Washington, D.C., publisher of *Industrial Control Reports;* Charles Hudson of Omaha, publisher of *America in Danger!;* Major General Van Horn Moseley; Robert Caldwell Patton, notorious anti-Semite of New York; John Cecil of the American Immigration Conference; Captain James E. Campbell, associate of Moseley; George Deatherage of St. Albans, West Virginia; Dudley Pierrepont Gilbert; John Snow of the League for Constitutional Government; Allen Zoll of American Patriots, Incorporated; Mrs. Leslie Fry, head of the Militant Christian Patriots and the American League of Christian Women. The list could be extended almost endlessly.

It was the activities of these people and others like them that caused Dickstein such grave concern in the winter of 1933. Late in March 1934, his one-man crusade in Congress bore fruit when the House passed a resolution creating the Special Committee to Investigate Nazi Activities in the United States, better known as the McCormack-Dickstein Committee, the forerunner of the House Un-American Activities Committee.[3]

IV

Tuesday, November 20, 1934. The committee met in executive session in the supper room of the Association of the Bar, 42 West 44th Street, New York City, to hear the testimony of Major General Butler.

Butler had a bizarre tale to tell the committee. About the first of July 1933, he related, two men, William Doyle and Gerald MacGuire, called on him at his home in Newtown Square, Pennsylvania. Doyle was department commander of the American Legion in Massachusetts; MacGuire, a wounded veteran, was active in Legion affairs in the department of Connecticut. Doyle and MacGuire were more than a little vague about what they wanted from the general. They talked of being dissatisfied with the leadership of the Legion and of wanting to take steps to turn out its current administration (". . . help us in our fight to dislodge the royal family"). In any case, they were quite insistent that Butler should attend the Legion convention in Chicago. When Butler demurred, saying that he had not been invited, MacGuire said that it could easily be arranged for him to attend as a delegate from Hawaii or as a special guest since he, MacGuire, was chairman of the distinguished guest committee.

A few days later, testified Butler, Doyle and MacGuire called again. This time they proposed that Butler round up some two or three hundred veteran friends and take them to Chicago on a special train. They were to be planted in the galleries and when Butler appeared were to begin a demonstration demanding that Butler be allowed to speak to the convention. The speech, which MacGuire already had prepared, was one urging the Legion to adopt a resolution in favor of restoring the gold standard. From where, Butler wanted to know, was the money to come to pay for the trip of two or three hundred Legionnaires to Chicago? MacGuire said they expected to pay the entire expenses of the trip, and produced bank books showing some $42,000 on deposit in MacGuire's name.

On a subsequent visit, said Butler, MacGuire came alone. Doyle by this time had faded from the picture. Butler insisted on knowing where MacGuire had got all the money that he seemed so willing to spend on the convention project. He explained that it came from nine men who had contributed to a fund in amounts from $2500 to $9000. The object of the project was "to take care of the rank and file of the soldiers, to get them their bonus and get them properly cared for." One of the contributors, claimed MacGuire, was Grayson M.-P. Murphy. "What has Murphy got to do with this?" Butler asked. "I work for him. I am in his office," replied MacGuire. Murphy, a New York broker and treasurer of the American Liberty League, was a director of Guaranty Trust, and a number of other business concerns including Anaconda Copper, Goodyear, and Bethlehem Steel. Murphy, explained MacGuire, was one of the men who underwrote the formation of the American Legion (for $125,000) in Paris in 1919. "He is on our side, though," said MacGuire. "He wants to see the soldiers cared for."

The next time that Butler claimed to have seen MacGuire was about the first of September in Newark at the convention of the Twenty-ninth Division. MacGuire, according to the General, came to Butler's hotel room and offered him $18,000 in one-thousand-dollar bills to cover expenses of the Chicago trip. "MacGuire," said Butler, "you are being used by somebody, and I want to know the fellows who are using you. I am not going to talk to you any more. You are only an agent. I want some of the principals." MacGuire took the money and left, promising to send Robert Sterling Clark to see him.

Robert Sterling Clark was well known in Wall Street, an heir to the Singer Sewing Machine fortune whom Butler had known more than thirty years earlier as the "millionaire lieutenant" in the Boxer Rebellion. According to the testimony, a week later Clark came from New York to visit Butler at his home. Clark explained that the object of the Chicago trip and the speech about the gold standard was that Clark and his group did "not want the soldier to have rubber money or paper money. We want the gold. That is the reason for this speech."

When Butler replied that he did not think they were particularly interested in helping the soldier, that it looked "as if it were a big-business speech," Clark allegedly gave it to him straight. "You understand just how we are fixed," said Clark. "I have got $30,000,000. I do not want to lose it. I am willing to spend half of the $30,000,000, to save the other half. If you go out and make this speech in Chicago, I am certain that they will adopt the resolution and that will be one step toward the return to gold, to have the soldiers stand up for it."

Butler refused to have anything to do with Clark's plan, whereupon Clark called MacGuire in Chicago and told him he would have to put over the gold-standard resolution by flooding the convention with telegrams supporting it without any help from Butler. "The convention came off," Butler told the committee, "and the gold standard was endorsed by the convention. I read about it with a great deal of interest. There was some talk about a flood of telegrams that came in and influenced them and I was so much amused, because it all happened right in my room."

When next Butler encountered MacGuire he observed that the convention did not endorse the soldiers' bonus. "Well, we have got to get sound currency," said MacGuire, "before it is worthwhile to endorse the bonus." [4]

v

In November 1933, when Butler was about to depart on an extended tour to recruit membership for the Veterans of Foreign Wars, the General continued, MacGuire approached him again. "I want to go around with you, around the country," MacGuire told him. "I want to go around and talk to the soldiers in the background and see if we cannot get them to join in a great big super-organization to maintain the democracy." Butler indicated that he did not want MacGuire tagging along, but "I cannot keep you off the train."

MacGuire did not make the trip with Butler. Instead, he went to Europe and stayed until late in May. Butler had occasional notes from him, from Nice, the Riviera, from Berlin. Then late in August the General had an unexpected call from MacGuire asking to see him in Philadelphia at the Bellevue Hotel.

Butler met MacGuire late in the afternoon in a remote corner of the lobby. There MacGuire presumably laid all the cards on the table. He had been in Europe, he told Butler, "to study the part that the veteran plays in the various setups of the governments that they have abroad." He studied the situation in Italy, Belgium, Holland, and Germany, but was not impressed because "the use of the soldiers over there would never appeal to our men." In France, MacGuire had found what he was looking for. "I found just exactly the organization we are going to have," he exclaimed. "It is an organization of super-soldiers." He then proceeded to explain enthusiastically to Butler the organization of the Croix de Feu (Cross of Fire), a fascist-minded clique of French veterans. "Now," said MacGuire, "that is our idea here in America — to get up an organization of that kind." "What do you want to do with it when you get it up?" asked Butler.

At this point Butler's story became even more extravagant. The purpose of the organization as MacGuire explained it, he said, was to support the Presidency and defend the government. Roosevelt would approve it and go along with it because he was about at the end of his rope for money. "Now, did it ever occur to you that the President is overworked?" asked MacGuire. It would be a very simple thing to appoint a sort of super-secretary to take some of the burdens off the President. If Roosevelt would not accept this arrangement he could be forced to resign on the pretext of bad health; Garner, who was not the strongman type anyway, would also step aside, and the super-secretary (having in the meantime been appointed Secretary of State) would become President. Said MacGuire: "You know, the American people will swallow that. We have got the newspapers. We will start a campaign that the President's health is failing. Everybody can tell that by looking at him, and the dumb American people will fall for it in a second." Money, MacGuire allegedly told Butler, was no problem: ". . . we have got $3,000,000 to start with, on the line, and we can get $300,000,000 if we need it . . . you heard Clark tell you he was willing to put up $15,000,000 to save the other $15,000,-000."

"Now, there is one point that I have forgotten which I think is the most important of all," Butler told the committee. He had asked MacGuire what he was going to call the new organization:

> He said, "Well, I do not know."
> I said, "Is there anything stirring about it yet?"
> "Yes," he says; "you watch; in 2 or 3 weeks you will see it come out in the paper. There will be big fellows in it. This is to be the background of it. These are to be the villagers in the opera. The papers will come out with it." He did not give me the name of it, but he said that it would all be made public; a society to maintain the Constitution; and so forth. They had a lot of talk this time about maintaining the Constitution.

MacGuire, according to Butler, now came right to the point:

> When I was in Paris, my headquarters were Morgan & Hodges [sic]. We had a meeting over there. I might as well tell you that our group is for you, for the head of this organization. Morgan & Hodges are against you. The Morgan interests say that you cannot be trusted, that you will be too radical, and so forth, that you are too much on the side of the little fellow; you cannot be trusted. They do not want you. But our group tells them that you are the only fellow in America who can get the soldiers together.

In Butler's words, he was uncertain what to do about Mac-Guire's proposition. Eventually he went to Paul Comly French with the story. French, a Quaker, was a newsman, a reporter for the Philadelphia *Record* and the New York *Evening Post*, and in later years head of the Committee for American Relief in Europe, better known as CARE.

Butler poured out his story to French in September 1934, and French immediately began checking. Under oath, he told the committee of going to New York and of visiting MacGuire in his office on the twelfth floor of 52 Broadway.

French's interview with the bond salesman confirmed Butler's story in the essential details. He testified that MacGuire insisted that a fascist government was needed in the United States to save the country from the Communists and to save the capitalist system. The only people sufficiently patriotic to carry it off were the soldiers, and Butler was the ideal leader. ("He could organize a million men over night.") If Butler would accept, "we might go along with Roosevelt and then do with him what Mussolini did with the King of Italy." MacGuire estimated that at least half the American Legion and Veterans of Foreign Wars would follow Butler if he would accept leadership of the movement, if he would be the "man on the white horse." Several times, said French, MacGuire "brought in the names of various former national commanders of the American Legion, to give me the impression that, whether justly or unjustly, a group in the American Legion were actively interested in this proposition." [5]

VI

It was now late afternoon and time for the committee to hear MacGuire's rebuttal.

MacGuire's first session with the committee was a series of

emphatic denials. He denied having tried to get Butler to attend the Chicago convention or to speak for a gold-standard resolution. He had left no speech with Butler, nor had he suggested rigging the convention with two or three hundred legionnaires demanding that Butler be heard. He had neither shown Butler bank books nor offered him expense money. He denied that Clark had ever called him from Butler's home or that he had anything to do with sending telegrams to the delegates. He had never discussed with Butler the role of European veterans' groups or any sort of super-organization of veterans in the United States. According to MacGuire, his interest and that of Robert Sterling Clark in Butler was: (1) to recruit the talents and support of the General in the Committee for a Sound Dollar and Sound Currency, Incorporated, a group organized and chartered in Delaware and almost exclusively financed from Clark's own pockets; and, (2) to see if Butler would consider running for National Commander of the Legion. The sound-dollar committee, MacGuire explained, was intended to support President Roosevelt and "to educate the public"; "we were against the inflationists and the people who were trying to bring about inflation in the country."

That such a committee did exist there was no argument; MacGuire brought along and entered as evidence the anti-inflation literature of the organization and the audits of its funds.

MacGuire denied having discussed with French the plans for any sort of fascist coup. On the contrary, French had told him of various organizations that had been seeking the support of General Butler, and MacGuire had warned French that Butler should avoid becoming mixed up with these groups because they were either rackets or fascist-oriented or both. ("Why, I don't think the General ought to get mixed up with any of those affairs in this country.")

MacGuire was not entirely a satisfactory witness; he was "hanging himself by contradictions and admissions," according to Dickstein. His memory failed him at certain crucial points, particularly on matters relating to what was done with the nearly $154,000 received from Clark (or Albert G. Christmas, Clark's attorney) and turned over to him or to the Committee for a Sound Dollar and Sound Currency. It was later shown from bank statements that approximately $56,000 was returned to Clark's accounts. Of the remaining $97,000, $30,000 had been given to the sound-dollar committee, leaving about $67,000 unaccounted for. The only explanation of what became of this sum was from Christmas who told the committee that Mac-Guire had spent it for traveling and entertainment in the period from June to December 1933, fighting inflation and supporting sound currency. ("I think I began to discuss inflation with him early in 1933. We had many discussions about it. He thought he could spare some time to do some traveling so my thought was it would be a good idea for him to discuss this question with prominent people in various parts of the country. When I say 'prominent' I mean substantial citizens in different localities. And see if we could work up any sentiment for sound currency, and against inflation. I told him when he traveled that I expected him to travel in a way which would enable him to meet these substantial people and that he was to entertain lavishly.")[6]

VII

So far as the printed portions of the committee hearings were concerned, this was all there was to the Butler story. Butler had claimed that MacGuire and his associates were engaged in some sort of activities of a secretive nature to restore the gold standard, and about this there appeared little doubt. Those activities seemed only remotely connected with the American Liberty League: no more than that MacGuire worked for Grayson Murphy, the treasurer of the League; and that Murphy was said to have contributed funds to finance what Butler described as a super-veterans' organization.

But this was not all of the story. When the McCormack-Dickstein Committee finally published its findings in the Butler story they contained this important statement: "In making public the foregoing evidence, which was taken in executive session in New York City from November 20 to 24, inclusive, the committee has ordered stricken therefrom certain immaterial and incompetent evidence, or evidence which was not pertinent to the inquiry, and which would not have been received during a public hearing." It was not what the hearings included but what they supposedly omitted that caused the public furor and embarrassment to the Liberty League.

Butler charged, for example, that whereas included in the committee report was his testimony concerning the plans for a super-veterans' organization, and MacGuire's claim that a new organization would be announced in two or three weeks — "the villagers in the opera," MacGuire had called it, according to Butler — the committee omitted Butler's statement that "in about two weeks the American Liberty League appeared, which was just about what he [MacGuire] described . . . to me." Also suppressed, according to Butler and French, was French's testimony that MacGuire had said that he could get financing for a fascist coup through John W. Davis, a director of the Liberty League, and W. R. Perkins of National City Bank, an erstwhile member of the Liberty League's Advisory Council; that the guns would be obtained from Remington Arms through the du Ponts who had a controlling interest in the famous munitions company. Likewise deleted, claimed Butler, was his concluding testimony in which he urged the committee to question a number of notables on what he called the "Legion plot," including Grayson M.-P. Murphy, former governor Joseph Ely of Massachusetts, William Doyle, former department commander of the American Legion in Massachusetts, Frank N. Belgrano, Jr., national commander of the American Legion, John W. Davis, Alfred E. Smith, General Hugh Johnson, administrator of the NRA, Thomas W. Lamont, a partner of J. P. Morgan, General Douglas MacArthur, General Hanford MacNider, former national commander of the American Legion, and others. Johnson, MacArthur, and MacNider, according to Butler, had been mentioned by MacGuire as possible alternatives in the event Butler was unwilling to accept leadership of the plot. The supposed role of the others, among whom were some of the most prominent leaders of the Liberty League (Smith, Ely, Davis, Murphy), the General did not make clear. Despite the omission of this testimony from the committee's report, the names of these men were dragged into the affair through a bold breach of ethics on Butler's part when he permitted the New York *Evening Post* to publish a copyrighted statement some three days before he appeared before the committee.

The intent of the committee in omitting those parts of Butler and French's statements was quite clear and commendable: to protect the reputations of innocent parties. Early in the spring of 1935 Dickstein made a radio network speech defending the action of the committee:

> The testimony given by General Butler was kept confidential until such time as the names of the persons who were mentioned in his testimony could be checked upon and verified. The Committee did not want to hear General Butler's allegations without giving itself the opportunity to verify the assertions made by him. It did not feel like dragging into the mud of publicity names of persons who were mentioned by General Butler unless his statements could be verified, since untold damage might be caused to a person's reputation by public discussion of testimony which could not be substantiated. This accounts for the fact that when the results of the hearing were finally made public, references to Alfred E. Smith and others were omitted. They were wholly without consequence and

public mention might be misinterpreted by the public. . . . The Committee takes full responsibility for not paying any attention to this type of testimony. It should not be permitted to go out to the public. It would only result in needless subjection of prominent men to offensive criticism.

The desire of the committee to protect innocent persons was understandable, but it was probably a mistake to omit portions from the printed record. The names of these men were already involved; the fat was already in the fire; with those who looked no further than the headlines the damage was already done. To destroy the context by eliminating all references to them, however flimsy the evidence, however unjust, was calculated to create suspicion rather than to dispel it.[7]

VIII

This story of "a plot" was promptly denied by all of those named: "It's a joke — a publicity stunt. I know nothing about it. The matter is made out of whole cloth. I deny the story completely" (Gerald C. MacGuire). "I am completely bewildered. I will send my lawyer to represent me if the whole affair isn't relegated to the funny papers by Sunday" (Robert Sterling Clark). "A fantasy! I can't imagine how anyone could produce it or any sane person believe it. It is absolutely false so far as it relates to me and my firm, and I don't believe there is a word of truth in it with respect to Mr. MacGuire" (Grayson M.-P. Murphy). "A most serious libel has been committed" (Albert G. Christmas). "The American Legion is not involved in the slightest degree in any march on Washington" (Frank N. Belgrano). "Perfect moonshine! Too unutterably ridiculous to comment upon" (Thomas W. Lamont). "He [Butler] had better be pretty damn careful. Nobody said a word to me about anything of this kind, and if they did I'd throw them out of the window. I know nothing about it" (Hugh Johnson). Other American Legion officials branded the Butler story "horsefeathers" and General MacArthur said he was "amazed and amused."

The press, except for the more radical publications, handled the Butler affair with its tongue in its journalistic cheek. The unemotional *New York Times* was fairly typical: "What can we believe? Apparently anything, to judge by the number of people who lend a credulous ear to the story of General Butler's 500,000 Fascists in buckram marching on Washington to seize the Government. Details are lacking to lend verisimilitude to an otherwise bald and unconvincing narrative. . . . The whole story sounds like a gigantic hoax. . . . It does not merit serious discussion. . . ." *Time* Magazine, which said "there did not seem to be any plotters," discounted the whole affair: "No military officer of the United States since the late tempestuous George Custer has succeeded in publicly floundering in so much hot water as Smedley Darlington Butler." In later years George Seldes, who believed the Butler story, devoted considerable space in his *One Thousand Americans* angrily reviewing what seemed to him the whimsical and cavalier attitude with which the press ridiculed the Butler story off the stage.[8]

IX

Certainly the climate of the times was one congenial to the growth of fascist sentiments in the United States. That fascist groups did exist, did carry on their activities on a wide front, and were led by men numbering some who sincerely believed that they were destined to take control of the government is a well-established fact.

But the kind of affair that Butler was describing, a plan conceived, financed, and executed not by hot-eyed demagogues but by presumably sound, clearheaded businessmen was something else. By themselves, although the self-appointed fascist saviors of America may have been disconcerting and disgusting, they were not particularly dangerous. But if such extremists were enlisting the cooperation of outraged and frustrated businessmen and industrialists with the fascist buffoon, as was happening in Germany in the 1930's, the problem became one that could not be easily laughed off.

It is common knowledge that some business and industrial leaders, in their determination to defend their definition of democracy, did listen to the Lorelei voice of fascism, did lend support to some extremists, and in turn were used by extremists. The unfortunate fact was that some were so opposed to Roosevelt that they did not ask for credentials, they accepted without investigation any ally in the fight against the New Deal. This danger, helped along by indiscreet or worse actions by some business leaders, put ready ammunition into the hands of those who opposed the Liberty League. Let the League once be identified with radical rightists or with unwise leaders of industry whose fear of, or passion against, the New Deal led them to associate with such radicals, and the political power of the League would rapidly fade. It was a prime failure of the Liberty League and its leaders not to guard effectively against such associations.

The tolerance of extreme theories by some embittered members of the business community at the nadir of the economic crisis was noted by numerous discerning observers. In September 1932, Frederic A. Ogg, editor of the *American Political Science Review*, reported in *Current History:*

For a good while certain powerful elements have been toying with the idea that the way out of our troubles lies through the establishment of some form of economic and political dictatorship, and meetings of important personages are known to have been held in New York and Chicago, at which sentiment was tested out and possibilities discussed. It does not appear that anything more startling came out of these conferences than a more or less general consensus in favor of a coalition super-cabinet of bankers and industrialists. But in other quarters there has been less moderation.

Early the next year, Demarest Lloyd, who subsequently became one of the leading supporters of the Liberty League, could entitle an editorial in his magazine *Affairs* "Let Congress Abdicate":

> Popular government is a perilous extravagance in time of emergency. The present situation is more destructive than war and much more difficult for a popular government to handle. Large numbers of "the enemy" are within — demagogues, unscrupulous politicians, gangsters, voters who resist payment of taxes, blocs of voters, socialists, pacifists, communists. The enemies within enjoy all personal liberties; the right of free speech and ballot. . . . It is absurd to expect any democratic government to cope with them. We do not nominate the President-elect [Roosevelt] for the role of king or dictator. He is still too much of an unknown quantity. It is quite apparent that unless confusion is to become chaos, Congress, like a long line of unfit rulers in the past, should abdicate.
>
> It should delegate its powers and functions to a small group, not over a hundred of the most well-informed, intelligent and patriotic men in the country.

In May 1932, when Senator David A. Reed of Pennsylvania, who was later a prominent member of the Liberty League Lawyers' Committee, said, on the floor of the Senate, "I do not often envy other countries their governments, but I say that if this country ever needed a Mussolini it needs one now," he was merely saying what many were apparently already thinking. And there were others in government who were leaning precariously in this direction.

Butler's charge that big businessmen were incubating some sort of fascist move was the first but it was not the last. In 1937 Charles W. Ferguson, later a senior editor of *Reader's Digest,* in his *Fifty Million Brothers* reported that "following the re-election of Roosevelt in 1936 secret conferences were held in New York (at the Warwick Hotel and the Cornell Club) between gamin fascist leaders and die-hard businessmen who had worked for Roosevelt's defeat." These men were not named, but "it is said that they reached an agreement with certain miniature Mussolinis on the regional organization of the country for fascist action." Harold Lavine, the former editorial director of the Institute for Propaganda Analysis and a close student of subversion in the United States, related how in December 1938 some two hundred and fifty of New York's leading businessmen and industrialists assembled in the Empire Room of the Waldorf-Astoria for the annual meeting of the New York Board of Trade. Major General George Van Horn Moseley was speaker:

> Where does the defensive weakness of the nation lie, you ask? My answer is, primarily right in Washington, as our administration gives aid and comfort to our enemies who are operating within our very gates. . . . Our domestic enemies should be warned . . . not to excite the wrath of patriotic America, for once these patriots go into battle they will cure the disease definitely and make those massacres now recorded in history look like peaceful church parades.

Moseley ended his harangue with the warning that perhaps Washington and New York would have to be burned to rid them of the enemy ("It might be one way of reducing the bureaucracy"). Observed Lavine, "The industrialists cheered."

Over the years the rumors and allegations of "plots" and "conspiracies" of one kind or another engineered by businessmen against Roosevelt and the New Deal have continued to persist. The latest is that contained in the autobiography of

Cornelius Vanderbilt, published in 1959. In it Vanderbilt relates such "facts" as he was able to pick up by bits and snatches of a businessmen's plot to kidnap Roosevelt (after his election to an unprecedented third term in 1940) and to force a change in government on the eve of World War II.

None of this has any direct bearing on the Butler story except to suggest that the climate of the times was one in which it was possible to believe in a plot for a fascist coup executed by the country's businessmen. Certainly the press did not take Butler seriously, nor did the country at large appear unduly alarmed. But in the McCormack-Dickstein Committee's final report in February 1935 there appeared this brief appraisal of the Butler incident: "Evidence was obtained showing that certain persons had made an attempt to establish a fascist organization in this country. There is no question but that these attempts were discussed, were planned, and might have been placed in execution when and if the financial backers deemed it expedient."

So far as the American Liberty League was concerned, however, the committee's conclusion that there was some substance to Butler's story did not mean that the League was involved. On the contrary, the committee's refusal to call prominent League members named by Butler to testify and its refusal to print irresponsible testimony (testimony "wholly without consequences," Dickstein had called it), involving such men as John W. Davis, Alfred E. Smith, and others could only mean that the committee was giving the Liberty League a clean bill of health. After momentary embarrassment by Butler's wild charges, the Liberty League seemed to emerge from the affair unscathed. But such were the times that some people were easily spooked; and with the unthinking ones allegations, no matter how incredulous, were accepted as facts. From the Butler yarn there remained a residue of suspicion. The League was now more vulnerable to future attacks, attacks of perhaps not so serious a nature but no less unworthy, attacks against which there was no adequate defense.[9]

5

THAT MAN IN THE WHITE HOUSE

Disregard for the Constitution requires that the New Deal stop itself or it must be stopped.

Jouett Shouse

The fact is, though it is called the New Deal, it is not a new deal. It is the same weapon of despotism which monarchs and dictators have used since history began. There is no escape from its malignity. . . . In short, unless annihilated, it will annihilate the Republic.

Ralph M. Shaw

FOLLOWING THE November elections and the temporary embarrassment of the Butler episode, the American Liberty League launched the most intense and concentrated campaign to propagate conservative political and economic thought that the United States had ever witnessed. To a philosophy that was at once a combination of Social Darwinism, laissez-faire economics, Old Testament apocalypse, and Constitution and ancestor worship, the Liberty Leaguers now often added a savage hatred of the man who had come to symbolize their torment and frustration.

II

Not a few — men like Al Smith, Jouett Shouse, and others — had reason to dislike Roosevelt because of some personal unpleasantness with the President. The Shouse-Raskob feud with Roosevelt, for example, began in the early spring of 1932. Shouse was the hand-picked choice of the auto magnate for permanent chairman of the 1932 convention at the Chicago Stadium. When the arrangements committee met in April, it was apparent that Shouse had quietly rallied to himself considerable support for convention keynoter, the spot for which Roosevelt had Senator Alben Barkley of Kentucky in mind. Shouse pressed his candidacy; but the Roosevelt people stalled until Governor Byrd of Virginia proposed a compromise: Barkley for keynoter and Shouse for permanent chairman. This was what Shouse and Raskob had wanted in the first place; however, Shouse refused to accept the compromise until the New York governor pledged his acceptance of the arrangement. By telephone, Roosevelt said he had no objection to the committee's "commending" Shouse for the post of permanent chairman.

Two months later Farley informed the press that the Roosevelt forces would seek the election of Senator Thomas J. Walsh of Montana as permanent chairman. The aroused opposition now accused Roosevelt of breaking a solemn pledge.

There may have been bad faith on both sides. As a member of the National Committee, Shouse had possibly violated his neutrality by urging that uninstructed delegations be sent to Chicago, something that could only have done harm to the Roosevelt cause. Farley was correct in arguing that the arrangements committee had no authority to pick the permanent chairman, that there was a difference between "recommending" and "commending" Shouse for chairman. But in accepting the minimum obligation implied in the "battle of semantics" Roosevelt was violating the spirit of the agreement if not the content.

John W. Davis carried the fight to the convention floor, but Walsh was elected over Shouse by a vote of 626 to 528.[1]

III

The career of Smith and his break with Roosevelt was one of the tragic stories of modern politics. From a humble beginning on New York's Lower East Side, Smith fashioned a warm concern for the underdog, the support of the Tammany organization, and a natural talent for politics into a career that carried him from borough alderman, county sheriff, and state senator to four terms as governor of the Empire State. By 1924 he was a leading Democratic aspirant for the Presidency.

Although his stand on prohibition and his religion made him suspect in the eyes of rural America, particularly the South, Smith was the idol of the eastern industrial states. These issues, wet versus dry, industrialism versus agrarianism, Catholic versus Protestant, provoked a disastrous deadlock between Smith and William Gibbs McAdoo at Madison Square Garden in 1924 which gave the nomination to John W. Davis. At Houston four years later Smith could not be denied. With dissident Southerners temporarily pacified on the prohibition question and the delegates charmed by Franklin Roosevelt, the man who had electrified the convention four years earlier with his "Happy Warrior" speech, the Smith success story — from Oliver Street to Pennsylvania Avenue — moved another step nearer reality.

Hoover's overwhelming victory was a crushing, disillusioning experience. Frustrated because the White House had eluded him and galled by the vision of what might have been, Smith laid the blame for his defeat in the wrong place. Liquor and religion, no doubt, played an important part in the election; but the decisive factor was the complacency of prosperity, the universal desire to continue the leadership and policies which were credited with that prosperity and promised even better times ahead.

Smith never understood this. Defeat, he believed, had come

because the American people would not accept that which was Catholic or big-city as being quite respectable or American. "I was probably the outstanding victim of the last half century of a whispering campaign" was the way he summed up his rejection by the electorate, a cruel half-truth that he found increasingly hard to live with.

The break between Smith and Roosevelt antedated 1932. Smith thought Roosevelt was too superficial and conceited, too opportunistic. "An ineffectual young man," he had called him. Nevertheless, the name was magic, and Smith had urged Roosevelt to run for governor in 1928 to strengthen the national ticket in New York.

It was embarrassing that Roosevelt won by a narrow majority and Smith failed to carry the state. Later, he was offended because Roosevelt failed to consult him or seek his advice on matters of state, and was annoyed that Roosevelt could find no place in the Administration for Smith's favorites, particularly Belle Moskowitz. Although Smith made the nominating speech when Roosevelt again ran for governor in 1930, he was infuriated by the way he thought Roosevelt had neglected his duties as governor while exploiting the office to enhance his chances for the presidential nomination in 1932.

By the time the faithful assembled at Chicago the two men were more than rivals for leadership of the party. Smith, realist enough to know the party could not risk nominating him again but tormented by the knowledge that whoever was nominated was almost certain to win, thought that a Roosevelt victory would be a calamity. Determined to stall the Roosevelt bandwagon at all costs, the "Stop Roosevelt" forces rallied around Smith.

Except for the fight to preserve the two-thirds rule, the Smith-Raskob-Shouse team was outmaneuvered at every turn. Although he knew it was inevitable, Smith was hurt that his party did not offer him a second chance. He campaigned indifferently in the East, against Hoover rather than for Roosevelt, and soon after the election became editor of the *New Outlook*, a position from which he became increasingly critical of the Administration.

During 1933 and early 1934, Smith made little effort to temper his contempt for the New Deal or the apparent ineptness of New Deal administrators. He brooded over Roosevelt's failure to invite him to fill a conspicuous spot in the new Administration to which, as the elder statesman of the party, he thought he was entitled. "The Administration should call upon the ablest, the soundest, and the most experienced men we have. But that is not being done," he told his daughter, Emily Smith Warner. "What about yourself?" she asked. "Would you accept an appointment?" "What else could I do?" was Smith's melancholy reply. "Under conditions as serious as they are now it would be any person's duty to serve if he were called upon."

But Smith was never called. As he became genuinely alarmed by the steady drift of government to the Left, it was not surprising to find him identifying himself with his old friends among the powerful conservatives of the Liberty League.[2]

IV

For each one who knew Roosevelt, who had suffered some hurt, real or imaginary, at his hands, there were countless others who did not know him at all but who had grown to hate him nonetheless with an unrelenting and unappeasable hatred. The Roosevelt Haters (the term was probably coined by Marquis Childs) were first in evidence as early as 1934; by 1936 they were a well-defined cult, exhorting one another with a theology of hate, often garnishing their sermons with scandalous stories, and some raising anthems of obscene parody and doggerel.

Whatever form the expressions of hate adopted, the Roosevelt

Haters included a large group with a common social origin. That origin was the American economic aristocracy. "Regardless of party and regardless of region, today, with few exceptions," said *Time* in April 1936, "members of the so-called Upper Class frankly hate Franklin Roosevelt." In a piece for *Harper's* in May, Marquis Childs wrote that most of the upper economic echelon was beginning to share "a consuming personal hatred" for the President.

Much of the anti-Roosevelt sentiment certainly resulted from adverse legislation, policies inimical to this group's interests, or the heavy hand of bureaucracy ("government by busybodies," the League called it), sometimes capricious, often arbitrary, always omnipresent. But the hatred of Roosevelt the man was something quite different from an honest difference of opinion or divergence of convictions. Businessmen had taken credit for prosperity, now they were receiving the blame for poverty; and hatred was a way of shifting that blame. Overnight, men who were the heroes of prosperity became the villains of depression, and hatred was a retreat wherein many could seek to recapture some measure of their self-esteem. Hatred was a compensation; it kept them from hating themselves for their fall from the sun.

In their thesaurus of hate, Roosevelt was a "renegade Democrat," an "extravagant," "destructive," "vacillating," "unprincipled charlatan." A "cripple," an "invalid" lacking physical stamina, a captive, psychologically, who was morally "weak," intellectually "shallow," unbelievably "gullible," a "dupe" (surrounded by "radicals," "crackpots," "quarterbacks," and "foreign-thinking brain-trusters, some of whom were better known in Russia than in the United States"). Nor was this the worst of it. From Newport to Miami, from Wall Street to Park Avenue, in country club locker rooms, the cathedral-like hush of bank offices, in board rooms and carpeted law offices, in hotel suites and cabin cruisers the broad stories passed: Roosevelt was an inveterate liar, immoral (hadn't you heard about his affair with Frances Perkins?), a syphilitic, a tool of Negroes and Jews, a madman given to unprovoked gales of immoderate laughter, an alcoholic, a megalomaniac dreaming his dreams of dictatorship.

How Roosevelt could be a mental and physical weakling and a dictator simultaneously was never quite clear. But this was hardly a matter of concern to those with ears to hear and eyes to see. Roosevelt was a dictator. Anyone with a grain of sense knew it. The Liberty League knew it, and in its publications said so: e.g., "The President Wants More Power," "Will It Be Ave Caesar?" "New Labels for Old Poisons," "The Way Dictatorships Start." A speech from the floor of the House by Pennsylvania Representative Clare Fenerty, reprinted as a Liberty League leaflet, described Roosevelt and the New Deal as "the only willfully subversive Government in our history." On the eve of the 1936 Democratic convention, Shouse returned to his oft repeated charge that the New Deal was an attempt "to set up a totalitarian government." In a speech before the Kansas City Lawyers' Association, reprinted as a Liberty League pamphlet ("Shall We Have Constitutional Liberty or Dictatorship?"), James A. Reed said bluntly: "Cannot you now understand that Roosevelt desires to pass laws utterly destructive of liberty . . . ? Louis XIV never went so far. Neither Mussolini nor Hitler, nor Stalin of Russia, have gone so far."

That Roosevelt was a dictator there was no doubt; but Liberty Leaguers were not quite sure what kind. Some thought he was a fascist, others believed him a socialist or Communist, while others, to be absolutely sure, said he was both. To the first group belonged men like William H. Rogers, president of the Florida State Bar Association (". . . brought us to the verge of fascism"). League publications played frequently on the fascist charge ("The principle underlying the New Deal . . . was similar to the . . . policies of Fascist Italy." "The New Deal

. . . and Fascism have three chief characteristics . . . " ". . .
the acts of the administration . . . have veered from the ex-
tremes of fascism . . ." "The President's power can be compared to that of Mussolini without danger of exaggeration."
". . . toward a Fascist control not only of agriculture but of
a major section of the manufacturing and distributing industries").

The claim that Roosevelt was a socialist or Communist and
the New Deal was a Marxist conspiracy occurred more frequently and persistently than the fascist charge. Senator Hastings branded the New Deal a "morass of socialism." James
M. Beck called it "wild, socialistic schemes." "We have now in
fact, although not in form," said Beck, "a totalitarian socialistic
state . . ." Forney Johnston of the National Lawyers' Committee referred to Roosevelt as "a Democrat dealing from the bottom of the Socialist pack." Walter E. Spahr of New York
University charged that the New Deal was moving "toward a
thorough socialization of our major economic institutions."
President Roosevelt, said Demarest Lloyd at the University of
Virginia Institute of Public Affairs, had "surrounded himself
with Reds and Pinks" and, instead of carrying out the Democratic platform of 1932, had "covertly and blandly put over
the 1932 Socialist Party Platform . . ." The New Deal,
warned J. Howard Pew, had "already traveled a long sector of
the road toward socialization." Judge Charles I. Dawson of
Louisville, a member of the National Lawyers' Committee,
castigated Roosevelt and the "motley crew of socialists, parlor
pinks and silly sentimentalists with whom he had surrounded
himself." James A. Reed, in a speech before the Farmers Grain
Dealers Association of Illinois early in 1936, charged that in the
hands of Franklin Roosevelt the Democratic flag of Jefferson,
Jackson, and Cleveland had been replaced by one of "varying
shades of Bolshevism, Socialism, and Communism . . . with red
predominating."

The most serious charge of communism came from the League's star performer, Alfred E. Smith. Late in January 1936, at a dinner sponsored by the Liberty League in Washington, Smith drew the battle line along which the League would fight the New Deal in the election year. ("There can be only the clear, pure, fresh air of free America, or the foul breath of communistic Russia.")

By 1936 the League had apparently made up its mind that the New Deal was more communistic than fascistic; but there were still some who were not sure. Among these was Raoul Desvernine, chairman of the National Lawyers' Committee, who wrote a book in 1936, *Democratic Despotism*, in which he likened the New Deal to both communism and fascism. Ralph Shaw, chairman of the Illinois division of the Liberty League, was another who was uncertain about classifying the New Deal. In a speech to the Georgia Bar Association, Shaw said that the "heterogeneous laws" of the New Deal were "so full of unsound, absurd, uneconomic, irreconcilable and contradictory policies" as to defy classification; but they "were and are deliberately designed to Sovietize or Nazi-ize the Republic . . ." As late as December 1935 the League issued a pamphlet (*Alternatives to the American Form of Government*) in which it analyzed three European dictatorships (Russian, Italian, German) "whose underlying theories bear upon present attempts to regiment industry and agriculture in the United States." [3]

v

If the Liberty League was not always certain what Roosevelt and the New Deal were ideologically, it was certain that the New Deal meant destruction of the Constitution.

For the Liberty League, protection of the Constitution was its *raison d'être*, its moral issue. "If the League has taken issue with the New Deal it is only because the New Deal has taken issue with the Constitution.") Preserving the integrity of this document was a worthy enterprise that any American citizen could and should espouse, and there is no doubt that many Liberty Leaguers espoused it in all sincerity. But beyond this, defending the Constitution was noble, it was patriotic and no one could find fault with it. Accordingly, for the League to appear as the knight errant of the Constitution was to imply that the President and his Administration were its enemies, seeking to ignore it, to pervert and destroy it. Defending the Constitution served another practical purpose, that of giving to the specific objectives of the League a measure of righteous immunity. The motives of those who cherish the Constitution are as much beyond question as those of ministers and grandmothers.

The pose of the Liberty League as the handmaiden of the Constitution may well have been sincere; but it was also conscious, deliberate, and calculated. When the former members of the AAPA were being alerted to the formation of the League, Captain Stayton wrote them pointing out that no matter how strong or efficient the new organization might be it would have trouble achieving its objectives "unless it has a moral or an emotional purpose" and thereby created "a moral or an emotional issue." "Nor do I believe," continued Stayton, "that many issues could command more support or evoke more enthusiasm among our people than the simple issue of the 'Constitution.' " The aged secretary of the Liberty League wrote further:

> The public ignorance concerning it is dense and inexcusable, but, nevertheless, there is a mighty — though vague — affection for it. The people, I believe, need merely to be led and instructed, and this affection will become almost worship and can be converted into an irresistible movement. . . . I think our first appeal should be to the effect that the Constitution is per-

fect; we do not seek to change it, or to add or to subtract from it; we seek to rescue it from those who misunderstand it, misuse and mistreat it. . . .

And we should remember that he who takes the "Constitution" for his battle-cry, has as his allies the Fathers of old. It will be of inestimable aid to quote Washington, Franklin, Hamilton, Adams, Jefferson, Madison, Monroe and other mighty men of the past, and to recall the Supreme Court's stirring opinions handed down by Marshall and his fellow justices.

From Shouse's initial press conference until the League passed into history six years later, the League regarded itself as the champion of the Constitution. ("The necessity for this association . . . has become apparent in the continual gnawing at the vitals of the Constitution.") There were no other enemies abroad in the land seeking to undermine the Constitution save Roosevelt, to hear them tell it. James A. Reed, in a Constitution Day speech at the Chicago World's Fair, charged Roosevelt with "wrecking the Constitution." Ogden Mills, in a speech called "Constitutional Liberty," warned that the New Deal meant "the death of democratic institutions." On Constitution Day 1935, Liberty League speakers, including James M. Beck, Albert C. Ritchie, Bainbridge Colby, and Jouett Shouse, built their speeches around the general theme that the New Deal was a program deliberately conceived and executed in defiance of the Constitution. According to League publications, virtually every major piece of New Deal legislation was unconstitutional, and in the administration of those laws New Dealers "in high places" had "eaten away vital portions of the Constitution by direct attack and by subtle usurpation." The League expressed the hope that if this did not disturb their digestion it might at least "disturb their consciences."

Of the 135 Liberty League pamphlets, 21 had the word "Constitution" or an adjectival form of it in the title, and all of these came during the first nine months of 1936, when the League sought to make the constitutional question a major issue of the campaign. ("The issue is not whether the Constitution shall be amended, but whether it shall be destroyed.") There were as many more under other titles in which the Constitution was the principal theme (e.g., "Where Are We Going?" "Government by Experiment," "The Supreme Court and the New Deal," "New Deal Laws in Federal Courts," "The President Has Made the Issue").

To bolster its constitutional attack on the New Deal, the League leaned heavily on the theme that Roosevelt was personally responsible (". . . the President has done more than any previous President, in fact alone among the Presidents of the United States, has spoken and acted to impair popular respect for . . . a written Constitution"). Liberty Leaguers consistently charged that the New Dealers, knowing full well that their measures were unconstitutional, sought to delay as long as possible a judicial determination of those laws, a charge for which there appeared to be ample justification. They continually cited the case of the NRA and Roosevelt's "intemperate, bitter denunciation" of the Supreme Court, a reference to his "horse-and-buggy" outburst over the Schechter decision. But the *pièce de résistance* the League offered as proof that Roosevelt was the arch-enemy of the Constitution was his note to Representative Samuel B. Hill regarding the Guffey-Snyder Bituminous Coal Conservation Act. "I hope," wrote the President, "your committee will not permit doubts as to the constitutionality, however reasonable, to block the suggested legislation." [4]

VI

Preoccupation with the Constitution carried with it the obligation to defend the Supreme Court, at least so long as the high tribunal interpreted the supreme law of the land to the satisfaction of the League. The five pamphlets, devoted exclusively to

the Supreme Court ("The Supreme Court and the New Deal,"
"New Deal Laws in Federal Courts," "The Constitution and
the Supreme Court," "A Layman Looks at the Supreme Court,"
"Shall We Plow under the Supreme Court?"), portrayed it as
the last bulwark of the Constitution and individual liberties
against a rapacious executive who had already succeeded in reducing the legislative branch to a rubber stamp. Thus the Supreme Court was "the guardian of the people against office
holders and politicians" (William H. Stayton); "forthright defender of the Constitution"; "the free and untrammeled agency
. . . to uphold American institutions" (Albert C. Ritchie);
"has always thrown the powerful circle of the Constitution as
a defense around the humblest as well as the greatest of American citizens" (Borden Burr); "the one last thin line that has
stood between the American people and the destruction of the
form of government in which they believe" (Jouett Shouse).

For an organization, however, so directly descended from the
Association Against the Prohibition Amendment — many of
whose members violated as well as opposed that article of the
Constitution — for this organization now to champion the Constitution so righteously opened it to cynical doubts. It was one
of their own leaders who strongly pointed out this hypocriti-
cal aspect of the League's Constitution-worship. In a speech
before the New York Chapter of the American Institute of
Banking, George Barton Cutten, a member of the League's National Advisory Council, said he admired Roosevelt's consist-
ency in that, when the Eighteenth Amendment was part of the
law of the land, he showed little regard for the Constitution and
he "has shown little since." Softly ironical, sweetly sarcastic,
the president of Colgate University continued:

> . . . Some others who are now expressing their unbounded
> love and concern for the Constitution were not so expressive
> five years ago either in precept or practice. I have no doubt but

that some present here thought it a great lark to flout the Constitution then, who are expressing overflowing adoration for it
now. Well, you are reaping what you sowed — it was you who
taught law makers to make a football out of the Constitution,
and you cannot blame them for refusing to listen to your
avowals of tender solicitude now.

At one point the Liberty League was prophetically correct.
In 1936 Secretary of Agriculture Henry Wallace wrote in a
foreword to Irving Brant's book, *Storm over the Constitution*,
"The important thing . . . is to elect Presidents who will
nominate the right men to the Supreme Court." The League
took violent exception to Wallace's callousness and to the theme
of his later book, *Whose Constitution?*, and devoted an entire
pamphlet to it, "A Reply to Secretary Wallace's Question —
Whose Constitution? The Dominant Issue of the Campaign," an
answer prepared by Raoul Desvernine. In it the chairman of
the Lawyers' Committee decried the methods that New Dealers
had used in trying to get judicial blessing for their program: the
resort to the defense of crisis and emergency, to pleading on the
basis of sympathy and humanitarianism, to appealing to public
opinion, to flooding the courts with test cases in the hope that
they would waver and capitulate under the weight of litigation ("judicial attrition," the League called it) while delaying
and procrastinating to prevent test cases of other New Deal
measures. Failing in these, said Desvernine, the Administration
would try in one way or another to influence and control future
decisions of the Supreme Court. Judge Dawson put the issue
quite bluntly:

> Does any man or woman within the sound of my voice doubt
> that the President hopes, if re-elected, he will have the oppor-
> tunity within the next four years to place upon the Supreme
> Court enough judges holding his own constitutional views to
> change the whole current of constitutional construction in this

country? Do any of you doubt that if such an opportunity is presented, that is exactly what he will do?

The League thus correctly anticipated the court reorganization plan of 1937.[5]

VII

New Deal irreverence for the Constitution and the judiciary the League regarded as part of a general conspiracy to destroy the federal system. Already, as the League saw it, the Administration had succeeded in making a mockery of checks and balances and the separation of powers by debauching the legislative branch. By 1936 Roosevelt, they felt, had usurped the legislative function and was ruling the land through more than fifty new agencies and by means of 1500 executive orders having the force of law. The impotence of the Congress was a recurring theme with the League: "Congress has abdicated"; ". . . has surrendered all of its power to the executive branch"; "a nonentity"; "little more than a rubber stamp to approve Executive direction"; "has exercised little volition"; "in despair because of its own incompetence"; "crawl like spaniels to the heel of the Executive." A debilitated, demoralized legislature an accomplished fact, the judiciary under heavy attack, the President was well on the way toward creating an all-powerful, centralized government. The "obliteration of the constitutional dividing lines between coordinate branches," warned the League, "lays the foundation for a potential dictatorship."

Destruction of checks and balances and the traditional separation of powers was, it was argued, only part of "a three-fold movement" under the New Deal toward centralized government. The other two phases involved encroachment upon the rights of the states and upon the liberties guaranteed to the people in the Bill of Rights.

For ballast against the growing power of the central government the League became intently interested in the welfare of the states. Again and again the League railed against Henry Wallace's proposal in his book *Whose Constitution?* that perhaps the time had come to substitute a cooperative commonwealth for the system of states, since they "mark no economic boundaries that make sense." Roosevelt was charged with "persistently attempting" to destroy local government and to substitute for it "all-powerful federal authority similar to the current dictatorships in several European countries." Albert Ritchie was expressing the sentiment of the League when he told the Ohio Bar Association in Toledo that unless New Deal measures were abandoned they would destroy the dual system of government and the integrity of the states. The transfer of power from the states to the federal government could end only in making the national government "master of our souls," Joseph B. Ely warned the Chicago Union League Club. "It is the complete reversal of the Jeffersonian theory of government," said the former Massachusetts governor. Those attending a United States Chamber of Commerce banquet in Washington applauded when Fitzgerald Hall told them that it "was not Ulysses S. Grant who effected the near-destruction of 'States' Rights,' but rather the man who invented 'Federal Aid.'" Hall, president of the Nashville, Chattanooga and St. Louis Railway and member of the Liberty League Advisory Council, meant that it was largely through federal aid that the central government was gradually and insidiously invading those areas properly reserved to the states.

The League revolted against the National Resources Committee's proposal that the field activities of the federal government be regrouped into ten or twelve regional centers, criticizing the plan as a deliberate attempt to by-pass the states, to set up "satrapies." And it added that Washington was "rapidly becoming inadequate for the horde of playboy experimenters who have taken up their abode on the banks of the Potomac."

The sapping of the states' powers by the New Deal, claimed the League, was rivaled only by the loss of individual freedoms. During dark depression days people had tolerated, had even encouraged the government to take their liberties in exchange for food, warmth, and safety. In language reminiscent of Benjamin Franklin the League warned that those willing to exchange liberty for temporary safety were deserving of neither; in fact, they held, under Roosevelt the people had neither. The New Deal, "by congressional usurpation and administrative fiat," had undertaken to "regulate the most intimate details in the lives and businesses" of the people; the people had realized too late that they were no longer safe or free, but now "must toil or play at the dictate of their overlords in Washington." [6]

VIII

A common criticism of Liberty Leaguers was that they took themselves too seriously. They often, in truth, laid themselves open to the charge that theirs was a pompous, righteous, pharisaical approach; an attitude that reminded some of the blue-nosed characters prominently featured in the anti-prohibition cartoons of the AAPA. They could not laugh at themselves; they lacked a sense of humor. Stuart Chase of the *Nation* summed it up: "Their whole attack has been tight-lipped, long-nosed, fanatically ungenerous and intolerant . . ." The League might retaliate by saying that with the Constitution and the survival of the federal system at stake there was nothing funny, nothing to laugh about.

But others could laugh at the League, and frequently did. The dinner of the Gridiron Club in December 1935 was such an occasion. The setting for one of the skits was the Acropolis in Athens. Onstage marched nine Delphic oracles dressed in armor (the first two ceremoniously bearing a golden box), who turned out to be Liberty Leaguers Jouett Shouse, John W. Davis, James M. Beck, David A. Reed, Bainbridge Colby, Frank J. Hogan, Thomas N. McCarter, George Wickersham, and Frederic R. Coudert.

The oracles launched into a gay tune:

> "Oh it's time to take your places,
> You'll hear the verdict soon;
> It's better than the races,
> On a Monday afternoon.
>
> "You'll hear what folks were thinking,
> Back in eighteen hundred ten,
> And Latin words a-linking
> What happens now with THEN."

"But what is in that box?" an Athenian citizen wanted to know. "The sacred foundation of our being. It tells us what to do and when to do it," came the reply. "Could I see it?" "Of course not," was the answer. "When anyone examines it, it changes color like a chameleon." Refusing to be put off, the citizen asked, "How can one tell what it means?" "Once a week, revelation is given when wise persons announce what it means — that week." "Permit me," said a retainer stepping toward the golden container, "to exhibit the historic charter on which our freedom rests. The Contribution List of the Liberty League." "It is your duty," said Chief Justice Shouse of the Oracles, "to protect this sacred document with your life and uphold it with your cash." [7]

IX

The Liberty League's charge that Roosevelt was doing violence to the Constitution and the federal system was fairly predict-

able; in defending the document, the Supreme Court, the separation of powers, checks and balances, and the duality of state and
national government, the League was on firm footing.

While one could hardly disagree with what the League was
defending, there was substantial area for disagreement with
how it went about it. After all, asked critics, was the picture
as grim as the League was painting it? Had nothing comparable
ever happened before? To pretend that our history had been
placid, a slow, even, uninterrupted growth of the Republic, with
no trouble, no disturbances, no chaos, no challenging of the established system, was to suppose a colossal ignorance of American history on the part of the League or of the public, or both.
Franklin Roosevelt was hardly the first to flaunt the system or
upset the status quo. More serious was the implication that all of
this was cunningly deliberate and calculated, that Roosevelt was
purposefully intent on wrecking the Republic and superimpos-
ing upon its ruins a totalitarian state with himself as dictator.

Here was a new dimension in the League's criticism. It was
more than a matter of criticizing the Administration in terms
of its wisdom, its efficacy, the short and long range results of its
policies. The new dimension was morality. The League stood
for that which was traditional, that which was "natural," hence,
that which was virtuous and good, morally good. The New
Deal was not bad in the sense that it was imprudent or unwise;
it was morally bad. The New Deal was immoral. As Ralph
Shaw put it: "Can crimes be turned into virtues by a mere
change of terminology?" One proof of New Deal immorality
was Roosevelt's apparent determination to raise issues that
would set class against class, a purpose designed to perpetuate
the New Deal in office. He was setting up "a straw man"
merely for the purpose of knocking him down, the League
maintained, "with the incidental hope of diverting attention
from the ghastly waste, the mad extravagance and the unjustified experiments of his own administration."

As evidence, the League cited Roosevelt's radio address from the White House in September 1934, when he had said: "I am not for a return to that definition of Liberty under which for many years a free people were being gradually regimented into the service of the privileged few." They made much of his speech in Atlanta a year later: "I can realize that gentlemen in well-warmed and well-stocked clubs will discourse on the expenses of government and the suffering that they are going through because the government is spending money for work relief." They recalled his State of the Union message in January 1936, when he denounced "entrenched greed" and "unscrupulous money changers," accusing them of stealing "the livery of great national constitutional ideals to serve discredited special interests." They pointed to his Jackson Day speech of 1936, when he had said, "Our enemies are the forces of privilege and greed within our borders"; and his acceptance speech in Philadelphia when he had referred to them as "privileged princes" and "economic royalists."

To suggest that classes existed in America and that their interests might be in conflict, argued the League, "was both socially wicked and economically wrong." It was "government by denunciation." Shouse stated his organization's position: "The League is opposed to any attempt to divide this country into classes and blocs." "The present Administration," said Forney Johnston of the Lawyers' Committee, "has, under the high tension of depression, done more to create class, occupational and regional prejudice than any Administration in history . . ." "Insofar as I am aware," said Jouett Shouse, "no other President of the United States ever resorted to such methods in the attempt to further his political fortunes." William R. Perkins of the Lawyers' Committee put it more strongly. Addressing the Sphex Club of Lynchburg, Virginia, on the eve of the 1936 election, Perkins (without mentioning names) denounced "the demagogue who, with pious phrases, but for his own personal

glory, does that most despicable and devastating of all things —
incites class against class, plunders the rich to purchase the poor
— and thus under the guise of love for mankind kindles fires of
hate that bring high and low into a common ruin of dissension,
bankruptcy and revolution."

What made the class struggle so tragically dangerous in the
Liberty Leaguers' minds was that there were no facts which
proved such class differences existed. "The Constitution recog-
nizes no class distinctions," a Liberty League *Bulletin* read.
"Mr. Roosevelt seeks to establish them." Creation of these arti-
ficial class differences, Ernest T. Weir told the Union League
Club in Chicago with bitter sarcasm, had brought the nation to
the ironic position where they, the successful businessmen,
were ". . . the selfish obstructionists in the way of the multitu-
dinous, altruistic, and celestial plans which, if unimpeded,
would make everything right with the country."

The League maintained that its views had nothing to do with
the fact that many of its members were men of wealth; they
believed as they did because they were thoughtful, patriotic
Americans. Or, as Demarest Lloyd put it: "It so happens that in
its inception there were some wealthy persons among the organizers of the American Liberty League." Throughout its
struggle with the Administration, the League took Roosevelt
to task for publicly stating the obvious, while insisting that the
uniform wealth of its leaders was purely accidental and incidental, that their economic status had nothing to do with their political affiliations.

This position was not so ingenuous as it might sound. On the
contrary, it was quite consistent with the philosophy of nine-
teenth-century conservatism. Theirs was the philosophy of
Social Darwinism, of Fiske and Youmans and Spencer, a philosophy that they might have learned at the feet of William Graham Sumner; in fact, some of them had.

Life, they believed, was a struggle, a competition, "a root,
hog, or die" existence, Sumner had called it. Life was like a

race in which the runners start equal, but the prize is to the swift, "he who shows the most conscientious training, the greatest ability, and the greatest character." The only obligation of government in this competitive endeavor was to "provide the training of the runners" through education and to serve as "the umpire of fairness" in the race. This meant, of course, that there were those who succeeded and those who failed; it meant that there was an elite of the swift and strong: this was "natural" and did not justify setting class against class.

To the Social Darwinists, the success of the swift and the able could be measured in financial terms. They could still hear Sumner asserting confidently and unashamedly that millionaires were the finest blooms in the garden of America's competitive civilization. Business, then, deserved respect; businessmen, that class that had made America great, were deserving of admiration and emulation; industry deserved a position of power in the American system; "the business of America," said Coolidge, "is business."

Conversely, poverty resulted from the innate inferiority of the poor, the slow of foot; in short, most economic and social problems were the result of individual incompetence. (Thus the difference between rich and poor was the result of natural, inherent, innate qualities, not the result of economic conditions or degree of opportunity.) This too, after all, was "natural"; it did not mean that there was anything wrong with the system.

Many Liberty Leaguers accepted this philosophy of the elite sincerely, without question, accepted it as self-evident. In a speech to the Michigan Association of Congregational Churches, S. Wells Utley, president of the Detroit Steel Casting Company and member of the League Advisory Council, could say in all sincerity: ·

> They contend that there is a tremendous disparity in the distribution of the "good things of life," due to greed, corruption, and crookedness in the economic system; I contend that

the maladjustment is not nearly so great as they claim; that the distribution of wealth under our system is infinitely more wide-spread than ever attained by any other; that what maladjustment there is, is due largely to the difference in human capacity and human capability; that the amassing of wealth honestly made is but a badge of service performed to the community, and that the remedy of the defects of the present system lies not in the destruction but in the improvement of the character of the race, through Christian education. They claim that the present depression is quite different from those of the past, and was brought about by the criminal errors of a few of the bankers and business men; I claim that it is world-wide, brought about by the errors of the race, of yourself and myself as much as anyone else; that it is not essentially different from other depressions; that after all these periodic slumps are only nature's brakes to keep us from dashing to our own destruction.

The whole theory of the New Deal, said Ralph Shaw, could be summed up in a few sentences:

The New Deal is nothing more or less than an effort spon-sored by inexperienced sentimentalists and demagogues to take away from the thrifty what the thrifty or their ancestors have accumulated, or may accumulate, and to give it to others who have not earned it, or whose ancestors haven't earned it for them, and who never would have earned it and never will earn it, and thus indirectly to destroy the incentive for all future accumulation. Such a purpose is in defiance of everything that history teaches and of the tenets upon which our civilization has been founded.

The New Deal, with its social legislation, was striking at the "natural" order of things according to President George B. Cutten of Colgate University:

Nothing could threaten the race as seriously as this [New Deal measures]. It is begging the unfit to be more unfit. Even such a measure as old-age insurance, which I am sure must touch the sympathies of every one, especially if he has the intelligence to think the thing through, removes one of the points of pressure which has kept many persons up to the strife and struggle of life.

William R. Perkins of the Lawyers' Committee put it even more succinctly. Speaking of the successful businessmen, he asked: "Who but they developed and established this great country of ours commercially?" [8]

x

If there were a natural order of things which inevitably made some men superior to others, so were there immutable, eternal, natural laws governing the economic environment in which men must function. The League accepted this premise unreservedly. Economic conditions were mysteriously but nonetheless naturally cyclic. Depression, any depression, was natural; it was, as one League spokesman put it, a sort of cathartic, a physic to purge the economic system of harmful poisons; it is "the process of eliminating these poisons" (Neil Carothers). This was what Utley meant when he asserted that "after all, these periodic slumps are only nature's brakes to keep us from dashing to our own destruction."

If depressions were natural, even desirable in a sense, then recovery from depression would inevitably follow if nature was allowed to run its course. The idea of a natural recovery was not a hypothesis or a matter of wishful thinking with the Liberty League: it was a tenet of the faith.

At this point, the Leaguers faced an embarrassing discrepancy that their opponents were quick to point out. If depression, recovery, and prosperity were natural processes, how could businessmen claim credit for the one without assuming responsibility for the other? Or, put the other way around, if prosperity could be created by conscious effort, why could not depression be avoided by conscious effort? Why should permanent prosperity be unattainable and those who worked for it denounced as utopian dreamers?

The government and a large segment of the population discarded the idea of natural recovery at about the same time. In the worst of the depression good men came face to face with a stark, dreadful truth: thrift, honesty, willingness, skill, and need were not the answers to "No Help Wanted" signs; the slogans and clichés of free enterprise offered little hope to a stricken people. On the contrary, men turned to government as their last hope; hungry and without work, they were in no mood to sympathize or temporize with the conservative's fear of economic experimentation and unorthodoxy.

In his acceptance speech at Chicago, Roosevelt made it clear that he rejected the natural recovery thesis. We were told, he said, that "economic laws — sacred, inviolable, unchangeable — cause panics which no one could prevent. We must lay hold of the fact that economic laws are not made by nature. They are made by human beings." The events of nearly a decade did not shake that conviction. In 1940 the President repeated his faith in the idea that men could control their economic fate:

> There were some in those days who chanted that nature had to run its course of misery, that deflation could not be stopped, and that the depression was only the working of natural economic laws in a system of free enterprise.
>
> The American Government . . . decided to reject that philosophy of inaction and irresponsibility and indifference to the destitution of its citizens.

The League's answer to this was that the depression "was not essentially different from other depressions," the worst was al-

ready over before Roosevelt took office. Had he just let
things alone, the country would have rebounded quickly,
stronger and more prosperous than before its malaise. But in
those days, businessmen likewise had lost their nerve and turned
to government for help. This they were loath to admit. When
the worst had passed and they recovered their composure, they
insisted that the New Deal was interfering with recovery, sug-
gesting darkly that perhaps the Administration was deliberately
retarding prosperity for political reasons.

In the spring of 1935, Neil Carothers assured a nationwide
radio audience that the United States was emerging from the
depression; but "these two years of experimentation have retarded the progress of recovery . . . from six months to one
year." What the country now needed was rest from "experiments and economic sleight-of-hand," an assurance of relief
from "further interference." A few weeks later, Carothers
was telling his audience at the University of Virginia Institute
of Public Affairs that recovery "comes automatically, of itself.
It develops when the inevitable processes of deflation and liquid-
ation are complete." This process, he contended, was completed
by 1932; by the summer of 1933 recovery was on the way.
Then the New Deal appeared on the scene and "for two years
past, recovery has been at the door, begging admittance."

Not only had New Deal measures failed to bring recovery,
insisted the League, but in most instances they had been a definite handicap, a detriment to recovery. By 1935 the Liberty
League was openly questioning motives as well as methods. At
the outset, New Deal tinkering could be dismissed as misguided
but well intentioned. Eventually suspicions were aroused that
the Administration was deliberately retarding recovery, pro-
longing the depression, magnifying the crisis in order to perpetuate themselves in power and as a screen behind which to re-
design the Republic. Suspicion became suggestion; suggestion
became assertion. More and more the League came to read new

meaning into Roosevelt's remark that he would either be America's greatest President or he would be its last. Many shared the conviction of New York University Professor Walter E. Spahr, who doubted that the "Administration intends that recovery shall come." [9]

XI

At this point the League imagined that it saw the New Deal for what it really was: Roosevelt's interference in a natural recovery had as its ultimate goal a planned economy for the United States; a planned economy could mean only one thing, dictatorship. According to one Liberty League leaflet, the Administration was bent on substituting a planned economy "for the economy of nature and the plan of Nature's God." In another place it insisted that stretching the commerce, general welfare, and "necessary and proper" clauses of the Constitution, unreasonable delegation of legislative powers to the executive, pyramiding of the bureaucracy, unrestrained use of executive orders for lawmaking, and all the other attempts to extend federal power were intended "to facilitate economic planning and to accomplish social ends."

For Liberty Leaguers, whose habits of thought presumed that economic matters were, *per se*, outside the competence of government, economic planning was deplorable. Not only was it unnatural, but, in order to accomplish it, government "must be able to dictate . . . the activities of citizens"; such planning "calls for a modification of the dual form of government"; "is in conflict with the system of free enterprise"; "is abhorrent to American constitutional principles"; "is out of place in a democracy." What economic planners never understood, wrote J. Howard Pew, was that government and business could not be mixed without harming both any more than "you can mix pure

water with contaminated water and get anything but contaminated water." When government interfered with business
it was interfering "with natural processes that Government
doesn't understand," Pew contended; but worse, planned
economy was "necessarily dictated economy." All planned
economies (from the Egyptian pharaohs to Stalin), explained
Pew, came out at the same place—"lower living standards, national decay and the sacrifice of liberty." This conclusion was
inevitable "whether the dictator is a usurper by force or is
elected under the forms of popular government." Democracy,
said another League pamphlet, could not live side by side with
economic planning, because planning and regulation were always "a part of Mercantilism and Fascism." [10]

XII

Another of the principal charges leveled by the Liberty League
against Roosevelt was that of "broken promises," a charge so
politically attractive that the Republicans adopted it as their
own in the 1936 campaign. In general, this referred to the
Democratic platform of 1932 and Roosevelt's failure to carry
out all its pledges in good faith. Specifically, it applied to the
President's failure to cut government spending.

Although the League had applauded the Economy Act and
publicly congratulated Roosevelt for his veto of the Bonus
Act, economizing was short-lived. When New Deal programs
began involving unprecedented expenditures the League was
more than annoyed; it was frightened. And it reacted in such
terms that its opponents could convincingly reply, "Of course
they are scared, because large spending can mean for them only
one thing — higher taxes."

Fear of taxation, while it was unlikely to arouse much sympathy, was not to be despised. Back in August 1934, when the

League was in its formative stage, Captain Stayton had circulated a series of memoranda among the former members of the AAPA, one of which read in part:

> It is true that to a limited extent the power of federal officials (for this term I include the Congress) was legally broadened by the Income Tax Amendment.
>
> But, again, it is by sheer usurpation that the Income Tax Amendment has been given its present administration. I shall refer to this matter later in these letters, but for the present let me state that if the Income Tax Amendment had been fairly and honestly interpreted to mean what the people understood it to mean when it was passed — if it had not been honey-combed by usurpations — that Amendment would only very slightly have expanded the powers of federal officials, and would have been an almost unobjectionable piece of constitutional legislation; — whereas, as now used in practice, it is the source of nearly all our calamaties [*sic*] and woes and is being made as an instrument to re-distribute wealth, to communize the nation, and to confiscate the property of one man and dole it out to others.

Stayton believed the most important work the new organization being formed could undertake would be "a constitutional resistance to illegal forms of taxation and squandering." Elaborating on this theme, Stayton believed it would be a mistake if the League openly advocated repeal of the Sixteenth Amendment for at least two reasons: "If men connected with the world of finance advocate such a repeal, they will be misunderstood . . ."; "A campaign for the repeal of the Income Tax Amendment would carry no emotional appeal to the mass of the people and would be devoid of the necessary 'moral issue.'" His recommended course was for the League to work toward a reinterpretation of the Sixteenth Amendment and the income tax laws. By basing its appeal solely on constitutional principles and in the name of economy, he believed the League could force a cut in federal expenditures from twelve billion dollars to perhaps three or four billions annually. This, he said, was a "bearable" sum because taxes could likewise be lowered.

When the League went to work on New Deal spending it played up the idea that economy in government was a virtue just as thrift was a virtue for the individual. Government expenditures were a "spending debauch," a "saturnalia," "unreasoning prodigality," "spendthrift policies," "bookkeeping sleight-of-hand," a "riot of extravagance." In a radio speech, Jouett Shouse went to great length explaining how the federal budget was like a household budget. What happened if a family spent more than it earned? What about "nest eggs" and the "sudden necessity for hospitals and doctors"? "Isn't it the same with Government?" he asked rhetorically.

The approach to spending as related to taxation was what the salesman calls identification. Liberty Leaguers naturally avoided too much overt complaining about their own taxes being too high. The approach was: "*You* have got to pay more taxes"; "*Your* government has got to reduce its expenditures"; "What are *you* going to do about it?" In the long run, warned the League, taxes and spending would harm everyone because it was "*your* public debt," and in four years that debt had increased "$576 per family"; "You Owe Thirty-one Billion Dollars" was the title of a Shouse speech. New Deal tax policies were dangerous because they deprived business of adequate surpluses against possible future depressions; they were checking the development of new industries; they were particularly burdensome to small and struggling businesses; they demoralized business by "blindly penalizing bigness"; they were part of the Administration's discredited plan to redistribute wealth; they reflected Roosevelt's perverse refusal to reduce expenditures. In short, New Deal tax measures were bag and baggage of the planned economy schemes that were retarding recovery.

One of the government's largest expenditures was for direct

relief, a matter that gave the Liberty League unusual trouble. Although it was privately thought that too much was being expended on relief measures, CCC, NYA, WPA, and the like, Liberty Leaguers were wise enough not to say so publicly. For them to claim that the Administration was extravagant with relief would be to imply that those receiving it should not have government beneficence and, that if given the opportunity, the Leaguers would reduce those expenditures. Neither of these possible implications had anything to commend it from a political standpoint.

Acknowledgment of the necessity of federal relief and recognition of the political impossibility of opposing it combined to make the League confine itself to criticism of relief administration and ridicule of waste and boondoggling. Jouett Shouse made it clear that the League was not opposed to relief (". . . we must care for those who are in distress"). But it was opposed to shifting responsibility and policy from the legislature to the executive, in handing over huge sums to the President with virtually no strings attached. The abdication by Congress of "its proper responsibilities" was inviting "a very material change in our government." As Shouse explained it to the Philadelphia County League of Women Voters, the proposed 1935 work-relief budget ($4,880,000,000) was the "most revolutionary, the most unjustified and the most unwise attempt at absolute delegation of legislative authority to the Executive that we have ever witnessed in this country."

The danger was twofold according to Shouse: first, the relief program invited an even larger bureaucracy; and second, it could be used as a political weapon. If relief were abused, Shouse told the Beacon Society of Boston, it could be used to build a political machine just as was commonly the case at the local level: "Distribution of largess from the public treasury is one of the most ancient devices by which bureaucracies and other undemocratic governments have sought to maintain themselves in power."

Shouse suggested that funds for direct relief should be provided by the federal government but administered by the Red Cross; administration of work relief should be delegated to the states and supported by mutual contributions of states and federal government.

The waste and boondoggling that certainly existed, although it was perhaps an unavoidable part of the relief program — as big as it was and as hastily organized — was the target of frequent barbs by the League. A regular feature of the League *Bulletin* cited examples of waste or exotic work projects: street dancing, teaching pinochle, building a boardwalk that was under water during high tide, and so on. A pamphlet entitled *Dangerous Experimentation* was caustically critical of New Deal relief measures, calling them dangerous and based on "half-baked theories." Here, once more, however, the League sometimes laid itself open to devastating attack. League criticism of a shoe-repairing project in Mineola, New York, as boondoggling, brought an angry, sarcastic reply from Senator Robinson of Arkansas, who told his Senate colleagues: "I think you people read the accounts of the severe winter through which we have just passed. As the Liberty League implies, think how demoralizing it must have been, with the thermometer 10 degrees below zero, to have Uncle Sam supplying funds to repair the damaged shoes of children who were forced to trudge back and forth to school. The du Pont brothers must have been shocked when Shouse showed them that classic example of undermining the moral fiber of children on relief." [11]

XIII

It went without saying that New Deal spending for relief and all the rest would involve government regulation and a consequent loss of some freedom, besides requiring an infinitely larger budget and higher taxes to meet the increased cost of government activities. But did it have to be attended by a ruinous inflation, an impairment of the national credit, and a wrecking of traditional banking practices? The Liberty League did not think so.

When businessmen argued the cause of deflation, balanced budgets, a sound currency, and what seemed to them, at least, a sound banking system, they were open to the charge that consciously or unconsciously they were pleading the cause of their own security. Behind the talk about freedom, initiative, enterprise, risk, and all the other terms businessmen like to use that suggest their rugged individualism, there is the need for security, for calculability, for certitude. In short, the cornerstone of business is contract. To business, money is a form of contract; in this case a contract between government and the owners of money. If businessmen are to sleep well and know peace of mind, contracts must be honored. If business is going to grow, then money must be predictable, not only for the moment but for the indefinite future.

The New Deal was making predictability increasingly difficult for business. For example, the League bitterly opposed Roosevelt's Banking Act of 1935. The argument was that it would give the President too much power over the banks and open the way for political influence. Whenever management rather than supervision became the policy of government toward banking, financial ruin seemed near at hand because "the fiscal requirements of Treasuries rather than of industry and agriculture tend to become the prime consideration . . ." Countries where banks were subject to political control had produced "the outstanding examples of disastrous inflation." With such control as the New Deal banking program contemplated, and with the power it would give to the party in office, "the freedom of the people can disappear overnight," warned Walter Spahr. Speaking for the League, Neil Carothers just

about said it all when he told his audience at the University of
Virginia:

> Our monetary system has become an indescribable and un-
> nameable mixture of debased gold coin, debased silver coin, and
> paper, and every day a useless and dangerous mass of dead silver
> is pumped into the vaults, further diluting and adulterating the
> mixture behind the irredeemable paper that we use. . . . The
> materials for a disastrous inflation of currency and credit have
> been built up, and no one knows when these inflammable ma-
> terials will set ablaze. Our currency measures have disorganized
> foreign trade, cruelly embarrassed the gold standard countries
> of Europe, deepened the misery of China, and retarded recovery
> the world over.
> . . . And the excuse for these disastrous errors has been
> emergency. It was obvious from the beginning that there never
> was an emergency which justified abrogation of contract and
> confiscation of property and violation of the Constitution.

Thus business, Shouse told his radio audience, "has been beset
not only with every kind of regulatory legislation but with
the fiscal uncertainties that have resulted from going off the
gold standard, devaluing the dollar, increasing deficits as a result of unprecedented extravagance and waste, and an unbalanced budget."

The League's theme was consistently what these policies
would do to the little fellow. New Dealers called it a play
upon his fears and usual ignorance of economic matters. So
Ray Bert Westerfield could title his radio speech "How Inflation Affects the Average Family"; Walter Spahr could call his
speech "The People's Money" and warn that New Deal inflation could only "involve serious losses for a people and im-
poverishment of the people"; Edwin W. Kemmerer called
inflation "a sad irony" because it was a subtle way for government to finance itself out of "the endowments of public welfare institutions, our schools, colleges and hospitals, out of the

life insurance of millions of our people and out of the savings of the poor, the foresighted and the thrifty"; inflation, said Neil Carothers, is the "primrose path to destruction" which hurts everybody, rich and poor, "but it falls most heavily on the wage-earner, on the little fellow." [12]

XIV

It is not fair simply to write off the Liberty League as composed of uncompromising conservatives and diehard reactionaries who took it out on the Administration for spite and for whatever satisfaction obstructionism would give them, or frustrated soreheads and persistent denouncers who opposed everything. Some of its members may have been all of these things. Certainly it contained some of the most antiquated political minds in the land. It had within its ranks many who had personal reasons for seeking revenge, men who were too emotionally involved in their views to see that they just might be wrong, but it had, both among its leaders and its rank and file members, sincere conservatives who distrusted and feared the trend of the times and of the New Deal. From whatever variety of motivations, the fact is that the League did oppose nearly everything that the Administration tried to do. Of all the Roosevelt policies, the League approved only the Economy Act, the veto of the Bonus Act, the President's opposition to the thirty-hour-week proposal of Senator Black. It gave a reasonable, qualified approval to the Wagner-Doughton bill (the Social Security Act), although it thought the law should be worked out more carefully and its several parts should be passed as separate laws.

Otherwise, it found little in the New Deal to sanction. "We are neither for nor against the administration," Shouse had said. "We shall support it when we can. We shall not hesitate to

oppose it when that course seems necessary." As events turned
out, the League found itself to be mostly in opposition: the
Bankhead farmers' home bill ("would produce a government-
sustained peasantry"); the Public Utility Holding Company
Act ("a calamitous blow"); the Agricultural Adjustment Act
("economic and political quackery," "this legislative monstros-
ity"); the Potato Control Act ("another step toward Socialism"); and on and on.

But the League was a great deal more than reaction, ridicule,
and revenge. It was the most articulate spokesman of American
conservative political thought in the decade of the 1930's; and
in this role its importance was not inconsiderable. Its conservatism was easily predictable. Its membership, or at least its leaders, often thought of themselves as an elite minority who had
risen to positions of wealth, power, and prestige through their
own efforts, talents, and merit. A system that permitted the
maximum of individual self-reliance was not only desirable but
essential if the man of ability was to have a chance at satisfy-
ing his desires, his ambitions, his self-expression, and self-fulfill-
ment. Any number of prominent Liberty Leaguers had traveled the road from rags to riches, and a system that made this
possible must be desirable. What they had done others could do
if they had the necessary qualities; what had been so good for
them must be good for others. The fact that a man could go as
far as he was able was proof that no class system existed, and
the League resented Roosevelt's attempt to create one. The
League would not admit what his supporters claimed — that
Roosevelt was not stirring up class consciousness but, rather,
capitalizing on that which already existed.

The League, refusing to fight the New Deal on the basis of
an economic class alignment, sought to identify its views with
the national interest, to capitalize on the sentimental and sacred
symbols of our national heritage, to couch its objections in
moral terms. Thus the motive of the League, to save the Con-

stitution and the Republic, was morally good; the New Deal program was immoral because it threatened the Constitution, which was sacred; New Deal spending was immoral because thrift is virtuous; enhancing the power of the national government was immoral because it could only be at the expense of states' rights, which were sacrosanct; collective action was immoral because individualism was morally right, the one was democratic, the other socialistic; government regulation was an invasion of privacy; relief always was suspect because it tended to undermine self-reliance; excessive taxation was little better than theft; debt was prodigality.

From the theory of the élite followed the concept of the limited role of government in a democracy. The League extolled the Jeffersonian view about the best government being that which governed least. It was equally lavish in its praise of Hamilton; but this presented no problem to anyone but the historical purist; the New Deal itself frequently praised Jefferson and followed Hamilton. It was important only that with the average citizen Jefferson and Hamilton were familiar names out of our past, national heroes, and their pictures were on money and stamps. Government's proper role seemed to the League that of the fair and impartial judge and umpire, seeing that all its sons had an equal start, equal opportunity, and that no one took unfair advantage of his fellow. Particularly must government refrain from violating private property. "If one thing," said Shouse, "more than another has been proved by historical experience it is that the denial of property rights has always been the prelude to a denial of human rights."

The gravest danger, according to the League, was from government unbridled. So frequently was this stressed that opponents could claim, and did, that for the League depression was no threat; foreign powers with their alien ideologies were no threat; business was no threat; business could combine, form trade associations, cooperate, whereas labor unions were de-

plored since a free labor market being proper, unions or anything else that interfered with the labor market were improper.
Monopolistic business was proper because somehow it was a
natural outgrowth of natural tendencies. Thus ran the Administration's description of the League's philosophy, and whether
or not it was a fair picture, it was an effective one politically,
and one to which the League all too often laid itself open.

Imbued with a Social Darwinist philosophy, the League was
critical of nearly everything the Administration undertook to
do. Its criticisms included these principal points: (1) New Deal
measures endangered the Constitution; (2) centralization of
power tended toward tyranny and dictatorship; (3) the New
Deal was predicated upon coercion rather than voluntary cooperation; (4) all the various manifestations of New Deal economic planning were dangerous and deceitful; (5) government
regulation of business was based on false economic theories; (6)
New Deal measures in the name of reform had retarded a natural recovery; (7) regimentation of agriculture was a cure
worse than the disease; (8) most New Deal measures were socialistic or fascistic, or both; (9) New Deal tax policies were
damaging to private enterprise; (10) New Deal spending and
unbalanced budgets were threatening a disastrous inflation;
(11) banking policies were designed to subject the banking
community to political control; (12) monetary policy impaired
the credit of the United States and endangered the national
currency.[13]

xv

The American Liberty League represented something that was
new and unique on the political stage in America. Here was a
group who had long been on the side protested against; now
they were in the unaccustomed role of protester.

But the role of the League was not negative all of the time, nor even a greater part of the time. As Shouse observed at the Bankers Club in New York: "It [the American Liberty League] has frequently been referred to as a representative of conservative thought of the country. I maintain that a better definition . . . is the assertion that it represents the constructive thought of the country."

What did it have to offer the country as an alternative to the New Deal? On the eve of the election year the League published a pamphlet, "A Program for Congress," in which it offered a series of recommendations which, if effected, would "put the nation's house in order." These, in part, stated that: (1) Treasury deficits should be brought to an abrupt end by reducing expenditures to the level of receipts; (2) for direct relief, moderate appropriations should be continued for a limited time; thereafter relief should be handled by the states with loans from the federal government if necessary; (3) expenditures for work relief should be halted immediately; public works on a reduced scale should be continued but only on projects that could not be undertaken by private enterprise; (4) inequities in taxation should be eliminated and taxes on business and the individual should be eased rather than increased; (5) Congress should reject inflationary currency proposals and politically oriented banking measures and plan for a revision of monetary laws along sound lines, meaning, probably, a return to the gold standard; (6) all legislation that was a part of the New Deal program of economic planning should be defeated, and such legislation as might be necessary to withdraw the government from competition with private business should be enacted; (7) the "death sentence" provision of the Public Utility Holding Company Act should be repealed and the socialistic activities of the TVA should be curbed; (8) further study of the Social Security Act should be undertaken with a view to transferring its operation to the states; (9) all restrictions on agriculture based on the false theory of scarcity should be repealed; (10) the Canadian trade agreement should be nullified, and hereafter the Senate should guard more jealously its power to veto treaties; (11) governmental bureaucracy should be overhauled and the New Deal agencies should be thoroughly investigated and perhaps abolished; (12) the Congress must reassert its responsibility for preserving the Constitution and the traditional form of government.[14]

XVI

Critics of the Liberty League were quick to point out that this "positive" program was hardly constructive in the sense that it offered anything new. To follow the recommendations laid down meant restoring the status quo ante-New Deal. This, Roosevelt had said many times, he would not do.

So the lines were drawn for the election year. As Ogden Mills put it, the choice of 1936 would be between the New Deal and the system of the Founding Fathers as interpreted by the Liberty League: ". . . after one hundred and fifty years of unparalleled progress to abandon the American scheme of life?" The League knew where it stood. The New Deal must "stop itself or it must be stopped," Shouse told a group of reporters as he embarked for Europe late in the summer of 1935. "There is no escape from its malignity," Ralph Shaw told the Georgia Bar Association. "In short, unless annihilated, it will annihilate the Republic."

As 1935 turned into 1936 the League led off the election year with its strongest political card. Its trump was Alfred E. Smith.[15]

6

ALFRED IN WONDERLAND

It is no exaggeration to say that the League has been the most discussed and in some high quarters the most "cussed" organization in the recent history of America. When before has a President of the United States, pretending to address the Congress on the State of the Union, devoted a large part of his speech to an organization such as this?

Jouett Shouse

Unmaking a President is sometimes nearly as sweet as being one yourself.

Arthur Krock

. . . considered as a political effort, it was one of the major tactical blunders of modern politics.

James A. Farley

A DINNER at the Mayflower Hotel in Washington late in January launched the League's anti-Administration campaign of the election year. The dinner was a magnificent affair. Harold Ickes confided to his diary that he had been told it was to be "the biggest banquet ever held at the Mayflower" and tables would have to be placed in the main corridor to handle the overflow crowd of two thousand guests. Jouett Shouse announced he had turned down four thousand requests for tickets, yet they continued to pour into National Press Building headquarters at the rate of seven hundred a day. Those who could not get tickets for what some irreverently called "dinner with the du Ponts" could hear the proceedings on the radio; and Indiana Republicans dutifully advanced the hour of their banquet in Indianapolis so they could follow the broadcast on the Columbia network.

What gave the banquet such significance was the announcement that Al Smith would be the principal speaker. For days Washington was astir with excitement in anticipation of the speech scheduled for January 25. Almost daily there appeared columns in the press by political analysts discoursing knowingly on Smith's probable strategy. Contemplating an attack upon the New Deal, friends of the League went about with looks of smug self-satisfaction, and Administration officials, already wary of the growing power of the League, became increasingly irritable and short-tempered.[1]

II

As tension mounted it was the League that injected the welcome comic relief.

Shortly after Christmas the *New York Times* printed the story that the First Lady had invited Smith to be an overnight guest at the White House while in Washington for his speech, an offer which Smith had declined, explaining that he would be accompanied by such a large party "as to tax the hospitality of the White House." This, the story continued, was not the first time; at least once each year since Roosevelt's election Smith had been tendered an invitation to the White House and each time had spurned it.

The story brought immediate denials from Smith. He insisted there had been only one previous invitation. Back in November 1933, accompanied by John J. Raskob and his personal physician, Dr. Raymond P. Sullivan, Smith had had tea with the Roosevelts. New Yorkers, celebrating New Year's Eve, had something to chuckle about when the *Times* admitted that the White House had confirmed Smith's version of the affair.

Unscrambling the matter of earlier invitations did nothing to alter the interesting aspects of the most recent one. Defenders of the President blandly argued that it had been made in good faith to an old friend of the family. The opposition, noting Roosevelt's reputation for treachery and intrigue, insisted that the whole incident had been staged to embarrass their champion, to force him to reveal his intentions in advance of the Liberty League dinner. In either case, Smith had been put in a difficult position. If he was not going to attack Roosevelt there was really little excuse for declining an invitation to stay at the White House. If he was going to attack the President he could hardly belabor his host and accept his bed and board all in the same evening.[2]

III

Smith's dilemma was amusing to some but not to John Raskob and Pierre du Pont, who were beset by troubles of their own. With the Smith speech only two weeks away the details of their tax case became front-page news.

Following the disastrous market crash in 1929, Raskob and du Pont had sold each other large holdings of stock well below the original purchase price. After the first of the year these transactions were reversed. It appeared that they had exchanged Baltimore and Ohio and Warner Brothers stock in almost equal amounts. To complete the deal, du Pont had thrown in General Motors and Kennecott Copper for Raskob's National Cash Register and Anaconda Copper stock. In this brief exchange of certificates the two had emerged only $46.86 apart on cross

sales totaling just under thirty million dollars. For income tax
purposes these sales involved deductible losses.

The investigation of the transaction dragged out for years
amid charges and countercharges, the Treasury Department
muttering darkly about "identical certificates," "matched
checks" and "postdated letters," du Pont and Raskob complaining of "hounding and harassing tactics." On January 10, 1936,
Guy Helvering, Commissioner of Internal Revenue, claimed
that, "in line with the close relationship between du Pont and
Raskob, they concocted a scheme to take losses," thus reducing
their taxes by nearly two million dollars. The Revenue Bureau
disallowed the transaction; the Board of Tax Appeals upheld
the disallowance; a circuit court in turn upheld the tax appeals
decision; and eventually the Supreme Court dismissed a cer-
tiorari application.

Disposition of the case was anticlimactic; it was the timing of
the charge on the eve of the Smith speech that rankled. Raskob
and du Pont complained of "the tyranny which a government
bureau can inflict on a citizen." "This attack . . . is quite well
timed with respect to the dinner of the American Liberty
League to be given in Washington next week," said Raskob,
and was proof of the need for an organization like the League if
the country were to avoid "losing our constitutional form of
government" to one of "innumerable alphabetical bureaus"
which could "dictate the conduct of the daily lives of each and
every one of us." Raskob did not mention that the Bureau had
voiced its first objections to the transaction as far back as December 1932, before the Roosevelt Administration took office.[3]

IV

If the timing of the Revenue Bureau's decision was a deliberate
attempt to embarrass the League on the eve of the Smith speech,

it was only part of a campaign that had begun with Roosevelt's State of the Union message on January 3.

The State of the Union speech in 1936 was another example of Roosevelt's unerring instinct for the theatrical effect — for the first time in history a President would deliver the speech at night. Upon hearing of the decision to have a nocturnal session, Republican National Chairman Henry P. Fletcher charged Roosevelt with "undisguised politics," "the first speech of the campaign," and demanded (unsuccessfully) equal radio time.

Fletcher's charges were correct. It was shortly after eight o'clock when the President braced himself before the microphones in the House chamber and launched into such a sharp attack upon New Deal critics that to one Democratic observer it made the session "seem like a party rally."

The basis of the New Deal, said Roosevelt, was the shift of government away from private and selfish interests and toward the concept of the public interest ("We have returned the control of the Federal Government to the city of Washington"). Accomplishing this had not been easy ("We have earned the hatred of entrenched greed"). The "unscrupulous money changers" had resisted any alteration in the status quo ("They offer to lead us back round the same old corner into the same old dreary street"). To justify that resistance the opposition had sought to brand the New Deal as a dangerous alien philosophy ("They steal the livery of great national constitutional ideals to serve discredited special interests"). If the critics of the New Deal were sincere, invited the President, let them demand of Congress a repeal of all New Deal legislation ("In other words, let action be positive and not negative").

But, said an aroused President, their motives were not sincere. Their efforts were directed toward the ignoble purpose of restoring the status quo ("They realize that in thirty-four months we have built up new instruments of public power. In the hands of a people's government this power is wholesome and proper. But in the hands of political puppets of an economic autocracy such power would provide shackles for the liberties of the people. Give them their way and they will take the course of every autocracy of the past — power for themselves, enslavement for the public"). And their technique is the use of fear (". . . they engage in vast propaganda to spread fear and discord among the people. . . . But such fear as they instill today is not natural fear, a normal fear; it is synthetic, manufactured, poisonous fear that is being spread subtly, expensively and cleverly by the same people who cried in those other days — 'Save us, save us, else we perish' ").[4]

V

The President's harsh words and the Liberty League's rebuttal set the political tone of the election year. Roosevelt's budget message two days earlier Jouett Shouse branded "deceitful" because the budget could be balanced; instead, it was a "riot of extravagance" providing for "the greatest orgy of peacetime spending by any nation in the history of the world." The State of the Union message, said Shouse, was "the most dangerous speech that ever came from a President of the United States"; to which Senator Robinson of Arkansas replied: "Had Mr. Roosevelt recited the Ten Commandments they would first have accused him of plagiarism, and second, found some ulterior motive for his quoting the Decalogue." The sole motive of the Liberty League, said James Farley, was to undermine and shake the confidence of the people in the Administration's program for the purpose of restoring the government to the "same crowd that wrecked it before." Echoing the words of the President, Farley challenged the League to have Congress repeal New Deal legislation if it dared.

Later in the week Farley returned to the attack. On January 9, at a meeting of the Democratic National Committee in Washington to complete plans for the Philadelphia convention, Farley charged that the campaign would not be on issues but would be "a campaign of defamation" ("Our opponents will make this the bitterest and certainly the dirtiest political struggle that any of us here can remember"). The objective, he asserted, would be to restore the status quo ("The assault will be financed with the largest slush fund on record, contributed for the most part by those who have neither public conscience nor private scruple, who are only interested in getting back inordinate privileges"). The motive would be hate and fear ("In the ranks of our foes you will find not only the financial gangsters whose extortions were so largely responsible for bringing on the Hoover panic, but others, who, for one reason or another, hate Franklin D. Roosevelt, or who are accessories of the exploiters").[5]

VI

In the midst of these verbal skirmishes the annual Jackson Day dinner in Washington gave Roosevelt the second opportunity within a week to attack the Liberty League in a major speech.

An enthusiastic crowd of nearly two thousand assembled at the Mayflower Hotel for the annual occasion. On the wall above the dais that set apart the long speakers' table, hung the flag-draped painting of Andrew Jackson, borrowed for the occasion (and insured for $25,000) from the Corcoran Gallery of Art. Everyone who was anyone in the Administration was present, some willingly and some not so willingly, judging by the Liberty League charge that Farley had dunned government employees for tickets. Mrs. Roosevelt appeared briefly and acknowledged the applause before departing to have dinner with the Young Democrats of Washington and to hear her husband's speech by radio.

It was nearly eight o'clock when the spotlights flared on, the draperies beneath the picture of Jackson parted, and the President made his way the four short steps to his brocaded chair as the strains of "Hail to the Chief" were heard.

Roosevelt used the occasion for attacking the League by analogy. A century earlier entrenched wealth had opposed Jackson just as it was opposing Roosevelt: "An overwhelming proportion of the material power of the country was arrayed against him." Then as now the press was antagonistic: "The great media for the dissemination of information and the molding of public opinion fought him." Then as now the forces of conservatism and reaction were contemptuous: "Haughty and sterile intellectualism opposed him. Musty reaction disapproved him. Hollow and outworn traditionalism shook a trembling finger at him." As it had been in Jackson's time so it was now: "It seemed that sometimes all were against him — all but the people of the United States." [6]

VII

So the suspense mounted, the headlines expressing the air of expectancy: "Coming Smith Speech Stirs Party Leaders," "Many Guesses as to Smith's Speech Policy," "Capital Awaits Smith Attack on the New Deal," "Ex-Governor Leaves for Washington to Address Liberty League."

It was an unusual audience in an improbable setting that greeted the former governor to the familiar music of "The Sidewalks of New York." Present, besides two former presidential candidates (Al Smith, John W. Davis), were former governors (Joseph B. Ely, Albert Ritchie), ex-senators and congressmen (Hiram Bingham, David Reed, James A. Reed, James Beck), and a handful of sitting Republican representatives (Bacon, Crowther, Wadsworth, New York; Knutson, Minnesota; Michener, Michigan; Robison, Kentucky; Rogers, Massachusetts; Taylor, Tennessee). No top-rank members of the Administration appeared; but among those in attendance who had recently fallen from grace and been expelled from the New Deal heaven were Silliman Evans, veteran newsman and Assistant Postmaster General, Treasury adviser James P. Warburg, Dean Acheson, Undersecretary of the Treasury, and former Director of the Budget Lewis Douglas.

From the ranks of business, finance, management, and law were assembled many of the most prominent names in America: Winthrop W. Aldrich, Robert V. Fleming, Ernest T. Weir, John J. Raskob, J. Howard Pew, Alice Roosevelt Longworth, Eugene Meyer, Rufus Choate, Jay Cooke, Philip H. Gadsden, A. P. Haake, George Houston, Robert L. Lund, Colby Chester, Raymond Pitcairn, Joseph Proskauer, Frederic Coudert, Raoul Desvernine, Robert M. Guggenheim, J. B. Lippincott, Grayson Murphy, Mrs. Charles Sabin, Robert L. O'Brien, "an even dozen du Ponts," and two thousand more of equal prominence representing a substantial portion of the corporate wealth of the United States, or, as one reporter put it, the "greatest collection of millionaires ever assembled under the same roof."

A *New York Times* reporter described the scene like this: "Jammed elbow to elbow, tailcoat to tailcoat, fluttery bouffant dress to sleek black velvet dress, the tables set so closely together in the main ballroom that the ushers in the Confederate grey mess coats and black pants scarcely could wiggle between the anti-New Dealers, Democrats and Republicans alike gathered to hear the magic, rasping voice of Alfred E. Smith belabor the present administration." [7]

VIII

Dinner over, it was time for speechmaking. According to the *New York Times,* Smith listened "with obvious impatience" to the preliminary speeches of Charles I. Dawson, Louisville's federal judge who had ruled against the Administration in an early test case of the NIRA ("The issue in the coming election, therefore, is clear. That issue is not whether the Constitution shall be amended but whether it shall be destroyed"); and Dr. Neil Carothers of the Lehigh University College of Business Administration, who described himself as "a good Mississippi Democrat who went to Lehigh to teach economics to Northern Yankees" ("They [the American people] will not long support a government, whatever its objectives, when its only program is experiment, its only policy is expediency, and its only philosophy is opportunism"). Five blocks away on the second floor of the White House, Franklin Roosevelt, entertaining a group of intimates at a stag dinner, tuned in in time to hear Borden Burr, Birmingham attorney, introduce the featured speaker simply as "Al Smith of America."

The applause was deafening. At sixty-two with deeply silvered hair, his once full, ruddy face already growing hollow with age, Smith, attired in white tie and tails, was still a commanding figure as he stepped to the microphones. Eschewing any mention of the New Deal or Franklin Roosevelt by name, Smith treated his audience to a speech with the stinging sarcasm and biting wit that had become his trademark.

He began quietly, sadly, with an avowal of love for the Democratic party . . . ("It is not easy, it hurts me to criticize a Democratic administration"). But there were dangers . . . class against class ("You can't soak capital without soaking labor at the same time") . . . government by bureaucracy ("instead of what we have been taught to look to: government by law") . . . draining the resources of the people ("to pool and redistribute them, not by any process of law but by the whim of the bureaucratic autocracy") . . . the platform of 1932 ("Why wasn't it carried out? . . . there is only one man in the United States of America that can answer that question")

. . . socialism replacing representative democracy ("The young brain-trusters caught the Socialists in swimming and they ran away with their clothes. . . . There can be only one capital, Washington or Moscow. There can be only the clear, pure, fresh air of free America, or the foul breath of communistic Russia. There can be only one flag, the Stars and Stripes, or the flag of the godless Union of the Soviets. There can be only one national anthem, The Star-Spangled Banner or the Internationale").

Pinning the Communist label to the New Deal was the essence of the Smith speech. But the biggest ovation of the night came when he leaned toward the microphones, "twisted his mouth in a snarling expression," and warned that at the next Democratic convention he and his friends could "either take on the mantle of hypocrisy or we can take a walk, and we will probably do the latter." (Shouse repeatedly pleaded for silence; radio time was passing swiftly.)[8]

IX

It had been a busy weekend for the leaders of the Liberty League. The night before the Smith speech John W. Davis was the featured banquet speaker of the American Bar Association at the Waldorf-Astoria in New York. Speaking very slowly, emphasizing each point with utmost solemnity of manner and delivery, the handsome, courtly lawyer accused Roosevelt of violating his oath of office, of transgressing the Constitution — "surely the mortal sin," Davis called it.

But it was the Smith speech that created the storm (a storm Smith avoided by departing with his wife for Palm Beach). Whereas Republicans were encouraged by the incipient split in the Democratic party and Liberty Leaguers were delighted ("It was perfect," Pierre du Pont; "He gave a splendid definition of democracy," John Raskob), Democratic reaction was mostly one of anger tinged with sadness. "It was the speech of a great man gone wrong," said Senator O'Mahoney of Wyoming, who had helped organize the West for Smith in 1928. "There was no doubt that it was Mr. Smith who was speaking," said the South Carolinian James F. Byrnes. "I recognized the voice. It was the voice of Oliver Street, but the thought of Wall Street." "Before Mr. Smith begins to speak for Democratic voters," said Eugene P. Connolly, president of the Association of Knicker-bocker Democrats, "we suggest that he come down from the eighty-sixth floor of the Empire State Building to the side-walks of New York, particularly those leading to the home relief office." With Smith's record of progressive labor legisla-tion while governor of New York, Alexander F. Whitney, president of the Brotherhood of Railroad Trainmen, could not understand his attack upon an Administration that had finally "given labor a fair break." Gazing down into the street from his room in the Commodore Hotel, Whitney could only con-clude that Smith had "sold his birth-right for a mess of pot-tage" and had alienated labor which was "100% behind FDR."

What happened in the House of Representatives on Monday after the speech may have been a case of laughing because it hurt so much. During the debate on the Department of In-terior appropriation bill, Clifton A. Woodrum, an ardent New Dealer from Roanoke, Virginia, seized the opportunity to an-swer Smith. The American Liberty League dinner reminded him of a county fair where two locomotives were run together because an American "will go anywhere to see somebody bust hell out of something." Smith, he said, had "already walked" and "moved up town." How well do we remember, remem-bered Woodrum, the Chicago convention of 1932 when Smith and "little Johnny Raskob, and little Jouett Shouse, and those other spoiled little boys who can't take it . . . gathered up their blocks and paper dolls and slid out of sight!" When

Woodrum finished his satire the Democrats rose and cheered; and Representative Gassaway of Oklahoma apologized to his colleagues for the one hundred and four speeches he had made for Smith in 1928.

Across the aisle Republicans could not bear to hear Democrats abusing a Democrat. Knutson of Minnesota (who had attended the Liberty League dinner) paid Smith the highest compliment within the power of a Republican to bestow by somehow likening him to the martyred Abraham Lincoln. While Democrats heckled, New York congressman Hamilton Fish, Jr., vigorously defended Smith. At one point, Knutson, tie askew and face flushed with rage, demanded that Speaker Joseph W. Byrns defend Fish against "these political fleas." Fish shrugged off the hazing, remarking that "where the feathers fly is where the shot hit." After one particularly pungent observation by Fish the irrepressible Knutson leaned across and shouted to his Democratic tormentors: "Laugh that off, damn you!"

Later in the week, during discussion of the Indian schools appropriation bill, Scott (California), Young (Ohio), and the aptly named Maury Maverick (Texas) engaged in some prearranged horseplay at the expense of the Liberty League. Scott proposed an amendment that money should not be used "hereafter" to pay salaries of instructors "teaching or advocating" American Liberty League ideas. Maverick agreed with the amendment but thought that it should be amended further to include Communists. Amid gales of laughter, Young urgently insisted that Scott include Communists in his amendment, observing: "Does not the gentleman agree with me that the only difference between the American Liberty League and the Communists is that the Communists seek to divide all and the League seeks to take all?" Scott then offered a substitute amendment when the veteran chairman of the Ways and Means Committee, Robert Doughton, went along with the gag, ruling that "hereafter" implied permanent legislation which was against House practice in appropriation bills.

At this point, Edward Taylor of Colorado, who was in charge of the bill and failed to understand that it was all a hoax, raised a point of order, but explained at some length (and much to the merriment of the House) that it was not out of any love for the Liberty League. Temporary Speaker Doughton ended the farce by upholding Taylor's point of order and the House got on with the serious business of educating the aborigines.[9]

X

Among Administration leaders who were uneasy about the Smith speech none regarded it more gravely than the Secretary of the Interior. Ickes favored putting Smith and the League on the defensive with "a savage attack" prior to the speech and had said so to everyone who would listen. With the speech less than a week away, Ickes complained to his diary that "we have done absolutely nothing to discount this speech or to counteract it."

Ickes' complaint was not quite true. The public statements of both Roosevelt and Farley had presaged what was to come. The League would be discredited, not by any logical refutation of its philosophy, but by making it synonymous with greed and hereditary wealth, by parading its well-heeled members as the defenders of a system as obsolete as the spinning wheel and muzzle-loader.

The remarks of Lewis Schwellenbach in the Senate two days before the Smith speech became typical of the kind of things the Administration supporters would say about the Liberty League before 1936 was over. Swept into office in the Democratic tide of 1934, the free-wheeling, swashbuckling, extroverted Washington senator had quickly become a dependable

Administration hatchetman. He brought up the Raskob and du Pont tax case, violently attacking these men's motives and charging Raskob with passing a "rubber check" for more than four million dollars, a check readily honored by Bankers Trust Company, which "recently contributed $20,000 to the American Liberty League." The "contribution" in fact was a perfectly proper loan secured by the required collateral and later repaid.

Turning to Smith he reminded him that Roosevelt had nominated him for President on three separate occasions (1920, 1924, 1928), and in 1928 had endangered his precarious health and risked his life for Smith in running for the governorship of New York to strengthen the national ticket. Smith, said Schwellenbach, had been duped by "all the . . . leeches, rascals, crooks, and bloodsucking lawyers who control the American Liberty League."

Except for Schwellenbach's attack, what Ickes mistook for inactivity was actually a matter of strategy. Since it was not certain what form Smith's attack on the Administration would take, the wisest course was to let Smith lead and then counterpunch. There had been private exploratory talks involving Roosevelt, Farley, Steve Early, and Charlie Michelson in which names had been bandied about of likely candidates to answer Smith. The President apparently leaned toward Indiana's governor, Paul V. McNutt; but Early did not think that McNutt had sufficient national prestige to take on Smith. Early's choice was Joe Robinson of Arkansas, who had been Smith's running mate in 1928, a suggestion Roosevelt and Farley readily accepted. Michelson favored a general counterattack rather than a specific rebuttal. A formal reply to the Liberty League speech, thought Michelson, "would be dignifying Smith unduly."

Michelson's position aroused the suspicions of both Ickes and Early. Michelson and Early had been cut from the same herd. A Virginian in his late forties, a product of the liquor, black

coffee, and sandwiches school of journalism, Early had emerged
a profane, rough-and-tumble reporter and recognized ace of
the Associated Press. He had first joined the Roosevelt team in
the 1920 vice-presidential campaign. But his attachment to
Roosevelt was personal rather than ideological. Politically he
was as uncommitted as Michelson.

Early doubted Michelson's loyalty to Roosevelt and com-
municated those doubts to Ickes. Ickes, suspicious of everyone
who had not confessed his political convictions in the dogmatic,
unknown tongue of the Progressives, believed the worst. At
Chicago, in 1932, Michelson had shifted allegiances from Raskob and Shouse to Roosevelt without batting an eye; but according to Early, he was "opposed to Roosevelt," "did not like
him," and was "really with Shouse and Al Smith and that
crowd." Occasionally, said the President's press secretary,
Shouse and Michelson had lunch together in some remote corner of the Mayflower Hotel dining room "with their heads
almost touching" as they chatted. Only Ickes could have believed that a traitor with a foot in both camps would have
broken bread with the enemy in the glaringly public Mayflower Hotel.[10]

XI

Despite his own mental reservations, the Democratic publicity
director completed arrangements with the Columbia Broadcast-
ing System and the morning after the Smith speech Farley announced that Robinson would answer Smith in a half-hour
speech three nights later.

Quite by accident, Ickes beat the Administration to the
punch. On Monday night following the League dinner Ickes
was scheduled to address the Washington Town Hall at the
Shoreham Hotel. He was dressing when he received a call
from Mike Straus, a veteran hand of the Universal News Service

and director of information for the Public Works Administration. Straus had come upon the remarks made by Smith in the 1928 campaign to Hoover's charge at Madison Square Garden that he was advocating a socialistic state. A few evenings later in Boston, Smith answered the charge, saying that "the cry of socialism had always been raised by powerful interests that desired to put a damper upon progressive legislation." It was a charge, said Smith, which had been raised by Republican reactionaries and which he had been fighting "for twenty-five years."

At the Shoreham, Ickes arranged for Senator Barkley, a member of the panel, to ask a loaded question so that Ickes could quote both from Smith's reply to Hoover and from his "shelve the Constitution" speech. Smith had been the speaker at a dinner of the Catholic Conference on Industrial Problems at the Hotel Astor in February 1933. On that occasion he had said that a depression was the same as a state of war. The Great Depression had already done more damage to the American people than World War I. The only thing to do was "to lay aside the red tape and the regulatory statutes" and "do what a democracy must do when it fights." And what, Smith asked rhetorically, does a democracy do in a war? "It becomes a tyrant, a despot, a real monarch. In the World War we took our Constitution, wrapped it up and laid it on the shelf and left it there until it was over."

The Town Hall meeting went off just as Ickes and Barkley planned it. The quotes from Smith's earlier speeches "brought down the house," and the next day President Roosevelt called Ickes "to give [Ickes] a pat on the back." [11]

XII

Robinson chose an Old Testament passage, Genesis 27:22, as a text for his reply to Smith: "The voice is Jacob's voice, but the hands are the hands of Esau." The complaints he hurled at the Administration Robinson compared with past statements by Smith; point by point the Senate majority leader tried to show that New Deal legislation embodied the social-justice measures Smith had been advocating for nearly a quarter of a century.

In 1928, said Robinson, when Smith had fought for causes of social justice and democratic principles, when he had campaigned on behalf of the common men and women, he was opposed by "stock-ticker patriots" who regarded him as "a potential enemy of his country." The voice of Jacob pleading the cause of justice and charity was drowned out "by greed and privilege hiding behind a murky and malodorous smoke screen." But now it was 1936 and a new campaign, and to the amazement of all, here was Smith "enthroned in the camp of the enemy, warring like one of the Janizaries of old against his own people and against the men and women with whom he fought shoulder to shoulder in the past."

It was the voice of Jacob but the hands of Esau when Smith charged the New Deal with being socialism: "When I advocated workmen's compensation, child welfare, a factory code, low income housing, state-owned water power," he had once said, "I was referred to many times by my political opponents as a Socialist" (speech before Alumni Association of Harvard University, June 22, 1933). As for Smith's charge that the New Deal farm-relief program was unconstitutional; he had once vigorously supported the McNary-Haugen bill, a bill far more drastic in its use of the taxing power than the AAA: "I would sooner have a short shake hands with the fellow that knows how to do it than listen for a week to the fellow who knows how to tell you what the trouble is," Smith had then proclaimed (Jefferson Day speech, April 13, 1932). Did the New Yorker now claim that the NIRA was an octopus smothering business big and small? Not long since, he had insisted that "the slightest reflection on these facts should dispose of the claim, from whatever source it came, that the National Industrial Recovery Act shakes the firm foundations of our Constitution, or marks revolution in our government and in the conduct of our everyday life" (speech, August 22, 1933). Had the New Deal broken faith by failing to reduce expenditures? Again, Robinson answered with Smith's own words: "Now if it is all right to put the credit of the government behind business, let the credit of the government be used to keep the wolf of hunger away from the doormat of millions of people" (Jackson Day speech, January 8, 1932).

And now Robinson was talking directly to his old running mate in coolly formal and reprimanding tone: "It was strange to see you in such company, Governor Smith. Within a few feet of the table at which you sat were members of the power trust, some of whom you denounced by name in 1928. The policies of the Liberty League have become the platform of the Un-happy Warrior." In a word, said Robinson, the famous brown derby had been exchanged for "the high hat."

Smith was not satisfied. The country was entitled to an answer from the President; "Poor Joe merely beclouded the issue." But Roosevelt maintained a discreet silence. "I am keep-ing very quiet in regard to Al Smith," he wrote to his friend, George Foster Peabody, in Warm Springs, "and I think few if any others will make reply." [12]

XIII

Sunday, the next day following the Smith speech, was an un-usually busy one for the Western Union office in Washington. More than a thousand telegrams were delivered to the National Press Building headquarters of the Liberty League, about "95% commendatory." In the week that followed, Shouse re-ceived more than nine thousand requests for copies of the speech. Another two thousand letters were sent directly to Smith, letters containing contributions for the League totaling more than $2300, mostly in amounts of $1 to $10.

John Raskob was so elated by the response that he sent out several thousand letters at his own expense with a poignant appeal for others to join the League. He explained at length how from a youth of modest circumstances he had achieved great financial success, a success that had come "from accomplishments made possible under our form of government, accomplishments impossible under a socialistic, communistic or other form of government which fails to encourage initiative." Join the American Liberty League, Raskob importuned, and help us "root out the vicious radical element that threatens the destruction of our government." [13]

XIV

In the initial clash of the campaign between the Administration and its critics Smith and the Liberty League had drawn first blood. In January the League was a sensation. With the charge that the New Deal was communistic, an alien "ism" subverting the Constitution, poisoning the economy and destroying the foundations of the Republic, it had a cause that any patriotic American could espouse, a cause raised by one of the most genuinely beloved men ever to appear in American politics.

There were those, however, who saw the Smith speech in another light. "Historians of this political year," Arthur Krock speculated, "may unanimously conclude that its contribution was a rich one to the President." It was, many felt, ironic as well as sad to hear Smith make Roosevelt out a Stalin for the benefit of the Liberty League; if the speech gave the League its issue — communism, it gave the Administration one equally good — selfish Big Business. Farley recognized the vulnerability of the

League (". . . even a novice could see how incongruous it was for the man who had risen from the 'Sidewalks of New York' to be announcing his political stand before an audience of wealthy potentates"); rightly or wrongly, the financial angels of the League were identified in the public mind with economic and social privilege, and the dinner only served to highlight that fact. It was from this point of view that the politically wise James Farley called it "one of the major tactical blunders of modern politics." Jouett Shouse admitted years later that not having Smith speak in one of his old familiar haunts among the people who knew him best was probably the worst single mistake the Liberty League made in 1936.

Next to the Communist charge, the threat to "take a walk" created the greatest concern in Democratic ranks. There were those who were unduly alarmed over a possible split within the party. Yet dramatic as it was, Smith had left himself poor alternatives: if he did not bolt, no harm was done; if he did walk, where was he to walk to?

Despite the negative possibilities the first round went to the League, at least on points. Editorializing from Washington on the eve of the Smith speech, Arthur Krock predicted that he would "move far out on a limb . . . and, if he does not saw it off behind him, he will hold up the saw in glittering menace." As it turned out, Smith did saw off the limb; but he and the League gave the Administration some anxious moments before the limb hit the ground.[14]

7

RUN, DON'T WALK

If you fail, then patriotic voters of all parties will know unhesitatingly to what standard they must rally. . . .

Alfred E. Smith

Roosevelt's friends took the American Liberty League seriously. So did he.

Samuel I. Rosenman

IN THOSE EARLY MONTHS of 1936 prospects for Roosevelt's re-election did not look nearly so bright as the outcome might indicate. After the unprecedented victory in the midterm election of 1934 the President's popularity began to sag, hit bottom in the winter of 1935, and did not begin an upward climb until after the Liberty League dinner late in January 1936. Political pollsters, whose reputations for infallibility had not yet been tarnished by the *Literary Digest*'s embarrassment at predicting a Landon victory, were pointing out that between December 1934 and December 1935 Roosevelt's popularity had skidded precipitously from 66 per cent to 40 per cent. A secret poll taken in the spring of 1935 by the Democratic National Committee found Roosevelt less popular than at any other time since taking office.

There were a number of reasons for this. With at least a measure of prosperity returning, the old fears, the panic, the hysteria that marked the first years of the depression were beginning to subside. The normally conservative elements, the bankers, business leaders, the legal profession, and their middle-class allies, began to weigh the New Deal by conventional standards and found it wanting. It was this disenchantment of the Right which found expression in the formation of the Liberty League late in August 1934, and throughout 1935 the voice of conservative opposition mounted in volume and intensity like the chorus of a Greek tragedy.

The defection of the conservatives was serious but unavoidable. Roosevelt was convinced that nothing would placate business short of an abject apology, a hat-in-hand repentance, and a hasty retreat to pre-depression patterns when government performed, but always with a glance at the wings for a nod or a frown from its business mentors.

More ominous was the groundswell of discontent from the masses, the marginal farmer, the unskilled and semiskilled workers, those who were barely white-collared, the old and indigent, the unemployed, a discontent that was ripe for exploitation by the sincere extremist, the demagogue, the unprincipled, or the political lunatic. The Huey Longs, the Eugene Talmadges, the Upton Sinclairs, the Francis Townsends, the Charles E. Coughlins, and a score of other messiahs grew like bacteria in the fetid, politically diseased air of depression. This discontent from beneath eroded still further the President's popularity and threatened the unity of the Democratic party, especially in the South and Far West.

The wave of social legislation which characterized the New Deal in 1935, while it quieted some of the popular discontent, only incensed the Administration's conservative critics the more. The Works Progress Administration, authorized by the Emergency Relief Appropriation Act with a budget of nearly five billion dollars, was assailed as a scheme to buy the votes of the lazy and slothful (". . . partisan loyalty has remained an essential in obtaining employment in governmental emergency agencies"). The Resettlement Administration seemed to the opposition proof that the New Deal was bent on collectivization in the Soviet fashion and was called "Tugwell's Folly." The Federal Power Act, extending the rate-fixing powers of the Federal Power Commission, and the TVA amendments were interpreted as assaults upon private power ("a vast experiment in State Socialism"). Establishment of a National Youth Administration and a doubling of appropriations for the Civilian Conservation Corps were denounced as indoctrination programs, schemes to seduce the youth of the land, to mold them into the raw manpower for a colored-shirt fascist army of Roosevelt the Dictator ("Let us not forget that Federal control of education and recreation is one of the most important steps toward Fascism or Communism"). The Social Security Act was denounced as socialistic ("the people must support themselves and in addition support government"). The National Labor Relations Act (the Wagner Act) appeared to be needlessly anti-business ("its salient features are not consistent with the requirements of due process"). The Potato Control Act (". . . makes a travesty of constitutional liberties"), the Banking Act ("makes our monetary and banking structure subject to the whims of political influence"), the new AAA amendments ("new schemes for overcoming laws of nature"), the Public Utility Holding Company Act ("designed to bring about government ownership and operation of utilities"), and the Guffey-Snyder Bituminous Coal Conservation Act ("a program of government ownership") all seemed the irresponsible deeds of a vindictive executive lusting for power. The Revenue Act of 1935, which raised the surtax to the highest rates in history ("a gesture to satisfy radical agitation for a redistribution of wealth"), smacked of Huey Long's share-the-wealth plan in sophisticated disguise.

Commencing in January 1935 a series of court decisions, the Schechter poultry case and the Amazon Petroleum case, which paralyzed the NIRA, the Louisville joint stock land bank case which voided the Frazier-Lemke Farm Mortgage Act, the Alton Railroad Company case which struck down the Railroad Retirement Act, and the Humphrey case decision limiting the removal powers of the President, put the Administration on the defensive and added to its embarrassment.

With the criticism from above becoming daily more articulate and personal, with the persistent rumblings of discontent from below and irrational leaders to egg it on, badgered by an almost universally hostile and unsympathetic press, faced with an incipient party split, and with the Republicans, still badly disorganized and leaderless, showing signs of rejuvenation, Roosevelt eyed his political future in the election year with concern and apprehension; and no wonder.

Experienced political writers of the *New York Times* were reading the President's doubts and misgivings in 1935 with such statements as: ". . . however brave his words, Roosevelt finds his back to the wall"; ". . . his [Roosevelt's] present path is uphill"; "the Democrats have plenty of trouble"; "the outlook is for a close election." [1]

II

"Dear Breck," the letter began in the almost unreadable Roosevelt scrawl. "Dear Breck" was Breckinridge Long, able and distinguished diplomat whose lengthy career had carried him from St. Louis and its Indian mounds to the ancient hills of Rome. "We are facing a very formidable opposition," Roosevelt confided to his ambassador, "on the part of a very powerful group among the extremely wealthy and the centralized industries." This bit of understatement to his friend from the Wilson Administration was the President's way of saying that the election year was off to a bad start.

Just after New Year's the court struck down the Agricultural

Adjustment Act. In a decision reminiscent of the E. C. Knight case that had paralyzed the Sherman Antitrust Act for a decade back in McKinley's time, Justices Hughes, Roberts, and the "Four Horsemen" ruled that Congress could not use the taxing power to regulate agriculture. Not only did the decision impair the farm program, but it exposed the Treasury to a host of recapture suits for recovery of money paid in, a process that eventually upset the budget predictions by nearly a billion dollars and forced the President to ask for new taxes to offset the losses.

A week later the Administration received another blow to its prestige. Back in November 1933, because of disagreement over the Warren gold-purchase policy, Roosevelt had fired Dean Acheson, Undersecretary of the Treasury. Acheson's dismissal was followed in rapid succession by the resignations of Dr. Oliver M. W. Sprague of Harvard, James P. Warburg, and Assistant Secretary Thomas Hewes. The same day that he let Acheson go, Roosevelt brought in Henry Morgenthau, who soon replaced the ailing William Woodin as Secretary of the Treasury. Late the next summer the smoldering feud between Roosevelt and his budget director, Lewis Douglas, came to a head ending with the resignation of Douglas.

In Morgenthau, Roosevelt had a loyal, trusted Dutchess County neighbor and friend who had performed effectively in Albany and later in Washington at unrewarding chores with the Federal Farm Board and Farm Credit Administration. Although the President sometimes entertained private doubts, the presence of the intense and methodical Morgenthau at the Treasury helped the Administration weather the storm. But the frequent shakeup of key personnel reflected the mounting dismay, both in and out of the Administration, over financial policy.

On January 17, 1936, trouble erupted again in the Treasury. Undersecretary T. Jefferson Coolidge and Assistant Secretary L. W. "Chip" Robert, Jr., broke with Roosevelt over emergency spending and refunding policies. The presence of Coolidge, representing as he did two great citadels of Americanism — he was a Boston banker and lineal descendant of Thomas Jefferson — gave the business world reassurance that the New Deal could not be all bad. The break, despite the "Dear Jeff" letters, was an unpleasant one, accompanied by caustic comments of self-vindication that evoked from the President a reminder of the good sportsmanship with which a predecessor (Acheson) had taken his enforced "resignation."

The Liberty League Smith speech that followed a week later was at once a climax and a denouement. All that had happened in the preceding months was minor skirmishing compared to this priceless moment of Smith's frontal assault on the New Deal. Nothing that followed would recapture the excitement, the spine-tingling scent of victory, the warm satisfaction of a mission accomplished which the Smith speech inspired. Everything else was anticlimax; this was Gettysburg. Surveying the wreckage in November, Liberty League leaders would look back to that high adventure in January and realize that they had shot their bolt too soon.

A reaction favorable to the President set in almost immediately. The unfavorable verdict in the AAA case elicited no recriminations, no "horse-and-buggy" outbursts from Roosevelt. He accepted the decision with disarming aplomb and set about philosophically to repair the damage with the Soil Conservation Act, an Act that the League described as a "new AAA . . . risen from the ashes of the old, [which] offers even greater freedom of experiment than its predecessor to a group of theorists whose record has been one of tragic blunder." His request for only $1,500,000,000 for relief in the new fiscal year (as contrasted with $4,880,000,000 in 1935) was reassuring; and there was something courageous about his asking for new taxes in an election year to compensate for the losses caused by the AAA decision.

The Smith charges, after the initial shock wore off, likewise
redounded to the advantage of Roosevelt. The effect was to
create not fear and alarm but anger and resentment. The un-
lettered and unsophisticated, if not the Liberty Leaguers, sensed
that the New Deal program was hardly the raw material from
which totalitarian states were made; nor did dictators spring up
on small nibbles and bites of power. The totalitarian states of
the twentieth century had sprung full grown like Minerva from
the head of Jove where governments, paralyzed by fear and
depression, were doing too little, not where they were doing too
much. Dictators, the Hitlers, Mussolinis, and Stalins did not
evolve by gradual accretions of power. Theirs had been a grab
for power, a grab in which they had astounded the world by
their utter ruthlessness, colossal ego, and the vulgar enormity of
their nerve. By 1936, if Roosevelt had entertained ambitions to
become a dictator ("You know," said Garner, "in spite of all
this talk, the Boss could never be a dictator"), he was already
four years too late. To the public at large any attempt to make
him out a dictator in 1936 was an absurdity.[2]

III

Early in 1936 it was still too soon to tell how the rank and file
were going to react to the Liberty League challenge. Buoyed
by the initial impact of the Smith speech, Shouse could claim at
the annual dinner of the Bondmen's Club in Chicago in February that Roosevelt "faces almost certain defeat in November;
some two million Democrats will take a walk to vote Republican." The same week in Washington, John L. Lewis was telling
his United Mine Workers convention that they should give all
they could to the Democratic campaign fund. "Because," roared
Lewis, "in downtown New York, agents of the Liberty League
and the Wall Street financial interests are boasting that the

political opposition to President Roosevelt can raise enough money to elect a Chinaman to the office if they want him."

The formidable quality of the League could not but cause concern at Democratic headquarters. Farley fretted about the "financial war chest" with "no bottom" and Michelson wrote later that the volume of wealth represented by the League's membership "scared" them. "Roosevelt's friends," said Judge Rosenman, "took the American Liberty League seriously. So did he."

The opposition believed that Roosevelt could be beaten and leaders of the American Liberty League were convinced that they would wield the balance of power. They had support for this belief from a reliable source. At 8 to 5 on Roosevelt, those dispassionate students of the laws of probability, the professional bettors, had made the opening odds on Roosevelt the least favorable on a President seeking re-election since the Wilson-Hughes contest in 1916. But how to use that power most effectively?

Four courses seemed open to the League: (1) attempt to control the Democratic party; (2) undertake a third-party movement; (3) maintain a posture of neutrality; or (4) exert control over the Republican opposition.[3]

IV

At the 1932 convention the Smith-Raskob-Shouse forces had successfully blocked the Roosevelt maneuver to kill the rule that required a candidate to garner two thirds of the convention votes for nomination, a rule that had been haunting Democratic conventions since Andrew Jackson's assault on King Caucus. It was their only victory of the convention, and a hollow one at that after the Hearst-Garner-McAdoo delegation joined the Roosevelt camp ("the great betrayal," Shouse called it), giving the New York governor the necessary margin and preventing any stampede to Smith or Newton D. Baker.

A brooding, chastened opposition would try again what it failed to do before — block the nomination of Franklin Roosevelt. With the two-thirds rule still in effect, the League's strategy would be to try to control enough delegates to produce a deadlock and then swing the convention to a conservative compromise candidate. There was talk that in the event of a stalemate Governor Smith would put the name of Joseph B. Ely in nomination as a compromise choice, repaying a debt left over from the 1932 convention when the Massachusetts governor had nominated Smith.

Admittedly it was a long shot; but, superficially at least, the strategy made good sense. Led by men well-known to the public and prominently identified with the Democratic party for a great many years it could be reasoned that the influence of the Liberty League would run wide and deep through such Democratic figures as Smith, Raskob, Davis, Reed, Shouse, Ely, and others. As part of this plan the Liberty Leaguers were prepared to support any Democrat willing to oppose Roosevelt for the nomination, including Eugene Talmadge, Henry Breckinridge, and possibly even Huey Long, until his assassination in September 1935 removed his threat.

Roosevelt had feared the Louisiana senator. Long had vigorously supported the Roosevelt candidacy in 1932, and for some time had been a powerful and effective Administration spokesman in the Senate. Of the political lunatics that dotted the landscape in the early '30's Long was in a class alone. Wise in politics, a veteran campaigner, a proven vote-getter with a powerful state machine, Long was more than strut, bluff, and noise.

Considering how Long had tried "to steal the national spotlight" from Roosevelt in 1932, there was "no doubt on earth," Farley declared later, "that, in the back of his mind, he was already looking forward to the day when he would be a candidate for the Presidency." After the break with Roosevelt, Long had begun working openly to get the nomination in 1936.

The share-the-wealth movement gave him a running start. Begun as a palpable appeal to the fear or greed, or both, of voters in Louisiana, the idea had spread like a virus throughout the Deep South, swept northward across the Ohio River into the industrial East, and rolled like a tumbleweed into the Midwest and Far West, eventually claiming by 1935 some 6,000,000 to 7,000,000 members.

In preparation for the campaign of 1936, Farley and the Democratic National Committee had conducted a secret poll to get some estimate of Long's strength. "His probable support was not confined to Louisiana and nearby states," wrote Farley. The poll revealed that his strength was fairly evenly divided between North and South, with no appreciable difference between rural areas and industrial centers. Even rock-ribbed Republican Maine "was ready to contribute to Long's total vote in about the same percentage as other states. . . ."

Farley had concluded that Long, running on a third-party ticket, might be able to draw between 3,000,000 and 4,000,000 votes. In a close election this number could hold the balance. For example, it appeared that Long would command upward of 100,000 votes in New York, a critical state in any national election. A vote of that size, Farley warned, "could easily mean the difference between victory or defeat. . . ."

Roosevelt, anxious over the burgeoning strength of the Louisiana senator, had expressed to Raymond Moley the thought that he might have to move to woo away Long's support. We must "steal Long's thunder" was the way Roosevelt put it. Word leaked that time at several Cabinet meetings had been spent considering ways to break Huey.

Meanwhile, Long's attacks upon the Administration had become ever bolder. His leadership of the successful fight against the World Court embarrassed the Administration; his wild charges against Farley forced a Senate investigation into the letting of contracts for the New York City Post Office Annex;

and his personal attacks upon the President became scandalous ("Prince Franklin," "Knight of the Nourmahal," "faker," "liar").

The presidential boom for Long, if that is what it was, came to a sudden end on September 8, 1935. It had been a grueling session at the State House in Baton Rouge. At 9:30 P.M., Senator Long strode briskly from the House chamber and crossed the rotunda. As he neared the office of Governor Oscar Allen, a slight, bespectacled man in a white suit stepped hesitantly from behind a pillar, pressed an automatic pistol to Long's side, and fired one shot. A guard grappled the man to the floor. Other guards rushed up, guns drawn, and began pumping bullets into the assassin. Dr. Carl A. Weiss, aged twenty-nine, a Baton Rouge physician whose father and father-in-law were bitter foes of the senator, was shot sixty-one times.

Tuesday, September 10, Huey Long died.[4]

v

That Long expected someday to be President there can be no doubt. Late in 1935 there appeared posthumously his book *My First Days in the White House*, an extraordinary piece of irrational candor.

In it Long anticipated the creation of a coalition administration to implement his share-the-wealth program, a coalition in which he planned to include many of the ranking conservatives of the country. Among his first acts in the White House would be the dispatching of a brief note: "I hereby appoint Alfred E. Smith to be Director of the Budget." His Cabinet appointments included a number of surprises: William E. Borah, Secretary of State; Smedley Butler, Secretary of War; Herbert Hoover, Secretary of Commerce; Franklin D. Roosevelt, Secretary of the Navy; Edward Keating, Secretary of Labor; and Frank Murphy, Attorney General.

The dream continued. To the White House, a few days later, President Long called the country's financial leaders for a dinner conference. He inquired of Winthrop Aldrich whether he thought John D. Rockefeller, Jr., would head a committee of businessmen, bankers, and industrialists to draft plans for implementing the share-the-wealth program. "I believe so, Mr. President," Aldrich was made to reply, "but I should like to confirm that by telephone." "Call him now," Long ordered. Aldrich called New York, talked briefly to Rockefeller, then smiled and nodded to Long. The President beamed. "That's fine. His services will allay fear throughout the business world."

Having secured Rockefeller to head the committee, President Long appointed additional members to serve: Andrew W. Mellon ("his face lighted with real pleasure when I made the appointment"), Winthrop W. Aldrich, Pierre S. du Pont, Irénée du Pont, Owen D. Young, Charles M. Schwab, Bernard Baruch, and others. In Long's dream world it was a "friendly dinner" and a most successful conference, during which Pierre du Pont "rather startled his associates" by saying he was heartily in favor of the share-the-wealth program.

Could there ever have been any reality to the dream? Say that depression conditions had dragged on, perhaps even worsened, and in a moment of national aberration the electorate had made Long President. Would he dare think of turning to these men to carry out his plans? With the publication of the fantasy there were those who asked if there was any reason to suppose they would cooperate. Although it was categorically denied by Shouse and others, it was widely rumored, but never proved, that Long had been offered substantial backing by prominent Liberty Leaguers and Republican ultraconservatives ("all of these Republican elements are flirting with Huey Long and probably financing him," Roosevelt once said in a Cabinet meeting). For all his rantings, Long was on good terms with the financial interests in Louisiana, who had often found him an amiable ally. Such an alliance need not have been surprising. There may well have been at least some rich men who would sacrifice much in exchange for assurances of protection by a Louisiana yokel with a Macedonian complex. As noted before, no proof was ever forthcoming that Liberty Leaguers in any way backed Long, but there were those who believed the rumors, and they certainly did no good to the political strength of the League.[5]

VI

The Talmadge candidacy was quite another matter.

Talmadge was fifty-one years old in 1936. Stocky, deliberately ungrammatical, with a heroic shock of hair over his forehead that had become his trademark, Talmadge (city born and bred) had used his office as Commissioner of Agriculture to build an unbeatable machine in rural Georgia. The farm vote elected him governor; his promise, which he fulfilled, of a three-dollar automobile license for every car in the state made him a national figure.

Talmadge was a bitter foe of the New Deal, the relief and farm policies particularly, the cotton processing tax specifically. Throughout 1935 he kept in close touch with Huey Long amid rumors of a third-party movement or a concerted drive to deprive Roosevelt of renomination. With the death of Long, Talmadge decided to go it alone.

Late in January, a week after the Smith Liberty League speech, there met in Macon, Georgia, what backers described as the Grass Roots Convention to begin the Talmadge "boom." Self-styled Jeffersonian Democrats of seventeen southern and southwestern states were invited to consider ways of counteracting "the appearance in government of theories and actions which are alien, foreign, and inimical to America and Americanism."

The invitations went out over the signature of John Henry Kirby, Houston lumber and oilman and head of the Southern Committee to Uphold the Constitution, who personally favored his fellow Houstonian and director of the Reconstruction Finance Corporation, Jesse Jones, as a replacement for Roosevelt. Another sponsor was the handsome, flamboyant Gerald L. K. Smith, sometime Disciples of Christ preacher and self-appointed successor to Huey Long as head of the share-the-wealth movement. When Smith announced to the press (in Talmadge's presence) that he was joining forces with the governor to fight Roosevelt's renomination, Talmadge had said simply: "Just quote him."

With the 7000-seat auditorium less than half full for the two-day meeting and fewer than 150 attending from other states, the convention was something less than a success. But if the meetings lacked numbers they did not lack enthusiasm. While the band blared "Dixie" and "Put On Your Old Gray Bonnet," overalled cotton farmers and wives in faded calico stamped and clapped, shouted encouragement ("Take off your coat!" "Pour it on!" "Give it to 'em, Gene!"), and, between ear-splitting rebel yells, shouted their promise to help drive the "dadgummed foreigners" out of Washington.

Despite obvious appeals to racial and religious bigotry, there was much in the Macon meeting to appeal to the Liberty League. There was ridicule of the New Deal: "The way to bring back prosperity in this country is through scarcity — have less to eat and less to wear!" . . . "burned up wheat and oats" . . . "plowed under cotton" . . . "paid a premium to get to cut a good brood sow's throat" . . . "telling him what to plant on his land — and how little." In between were interspersed some of the basic views of the League's philosophy: "The federal government is working consistently to tear down states' rights" . . . "Pay up the national debt!" . . . "Cut down the expense of the Federal Government" . . . "Stop all competi-

Jouett Shouse, President of
the American Liberty League, 1934–1940.

Irénée du Pont.
Photograph by Karsh.
Courtesy of
E. I. du Pont de Nemours
& Company.

John W. Davis.
Photograph by
Pach Brothers.

Alfred E. Smith addressing the American Liberty League
dinner at the Mayflower Hotel, Washington,
on January 25, 1936. *Wide World Photos.*

Cartoon by Berryman in the *Washington Star* for August 25, 1934. *Courtesy of the Franklin D. Roosevelt Library, Hyde Park, New York.*

The Spirit of '35. Cartoon by Jerry Doyle in the *New York Post* for January 12, 1935. *Courtesy of the Franklin D. Roosevelt Library, Hyde Park, New York.*

Filling in for the Court. Cartoon by Duffy
in the Baltimore *Sun* for September 18, 1935.

The Reserve List. Cartoon by Rollin Kirby
in the *New York World-Telegram* for November 12, 1935.

Just Practicing! Cartoon by Berryman in the *Washington Star*
for September 9, 1934. *Courtesy of the Franklin D. Roosevelt
Library, Hyde Park, New York.*

Puzzle: What Is the Little Boy Waiting For? Cartoon by
Marcus in the *New York Times* for January 19, 1936. *Courtesy
of the Franklin D. Roosevelt Library, Hyde Park, New York.*

tion of the government with private industry!" . . . "Cut taxes!" . . . "Rewrite the platform of 1932!" . . . "The New Dealers have tried by billions of dollars to hold back a natural recovery due this country" . . . "Let's don't allow a bunch of Communists to have four more years."

At least no one could claim that the Liberty League was involved in the charges which an Atlanta grand jury investigated that WPA funds and workers had been used to wrap and mail copies of the *Georgia Woman's World*, an anti-Negro publication distributed to delegates at the Macon meeting and later mailed to select groups by Kirby's Southern Committee to Uphold the Constitution.

Its lead story began: "Notwithstanding the fact that he was elected by the Democratic Party President Roosevelt has . . . permitted Negroes to come to the White House Banquet Table and sleep in the White House beds. . . ." An editorial blasting Roosevelt's Jackson Day speech said: ". . . when Jackson got to be president he didn't put in Republicans, Socialists, Communists and Negroes to tell him how to run these good old United States." The publication also sought to slander Mrs. Roosevelt with what came to be called the "nigger pictures" — pictures that showed her flanked by two young ROTC officers on the occasion of a visit to Washington's Howard University to address the Women's Faculty Club.

The cheap and dangerous mixing of the Southern Committee to Uphold the Constitution in such racist fanaticism clearly shows that it was of such a nature as should have warned any responsible citizens from backing the committee. Yet the fact is that much of the financial backing for the Macon meeting came from Liberty Leaguers. John J. Raskob and Pierre du Pont each gave $5000 because they "believed in the principles" of those backing the Southern anti-Roosevelt movement. Other contributors included prominent members like Lammot du Pont, Henry B. du Pont, Irénée du Pont, Alfred P. Sloan, Alvan

Macauley of Packard Motor Company, S. H. Curlee, a clothing manufacturer, and E. W. Mudge and L. F. Mudge of Weirton Steel Company.

It is impossible to believe that any political passions were strong enough to lead men of such prominence and position to disregard the ugly operations of the committee. Yet in contributing without enough investigation to discover what sort of group they were supporting, they certainly failed in their responsibility to the nation and damaged their own cause almost beyond repair.[6]

VII

Although he was a bitter foe of the New Deal, Henry Breckinridge lacked the demagogic qualities of Long or Talmadge. A prosperous New York attorney and lifelong Democrat, Breckinridge was Assistant Secretary of War in the Wilson Administration. A conservative even among conservatives, he had seconded the nomination of Virginia's Harry Byrd at the Chicago convention in 1932.

The Breckinridge candidacy was the only serious attempt in the preconvention months to test the power of Roosevelt vote for vote. Never a serious contender, nevertheless the Colonel played to the hilt his role of stalking horse. He entered primaries in four critical states, New Jersey, Ohio, Pennsylvania, and Maryland "just to give Democrats a fair chance to vote against the New Deal."

Although in Maryland Breckinridge had the support of Howard Bruce, Democratic national committeeman, who, with the late Governor Albert Ritchie, was prominent in Liberty League affairs, most conservative Democrats were reluctant to support him openly and the Liberty League denied publicly that he was a member of that organization.

There were at least two reasons for this. First, they de-

murred at the idea of a showdown test of voting strength at
that stage of the campaign. Second, Colonel Breckinridge had
support from some questionable quarters, and perhaps those
who contributed at Macon were more careful in their investigations in this case. The chairman of his Maryland campaign
committee was Thomas F. Cadwalader, a director of the Southern Committee to Uphold the Constitution and also a leader in
the Association for the Defense of the Constitution, a local organization of about 10,000 members. Breckinridge had attended
the Macon convention, but not as a delegate. Breckinridge likewise had the support of another group of constitution defenders,
the Sentinels of the Republic, who favored repeal of the general welfare clause, and who professed "great admiration" for
Governor Talmadge's stand against federal income taxes.

As shall be seen later, these organizations were not always
what they appeared to be.[7]

VIII

Behind the scenes a bitter fight was being waged on another
front for control of delegates to the Democratic National Convention. According to Farley, the Liberty League was "openly
boastful" of its power to recruit convention votes in New
Hampshire, Connecticut, Rhode Island, Massachusetts, New
York, Pennsylvania, and Maryland, although Shouse, as we
shall see, denied this. It was assumed that Talmadge would
control the Georgia votes. To make certain, charged Farley, he
was "heavily financed by the identical wealthy gentlemen who
were sponsoring the Liberty League." It was supposed that the
vote of the Long machine in Louisiana would be lost to Roosevelt at Philadelphia. Rumors of other revolts within the Democratic ranks came from such widely scattered places as Florida,
Alabama, Minnesota, and California.

It was confidently believed that as many as two hundred delegates and maybe more could be mustered against Roosevelt's renomination. Reviewing the situation two years later in *Behind the Ballots*, Farley wrote: "If the opposition captured all the convention seats they set out to get, or even a substantial part of them, the result would have been a very serious situation indeed."

Opponents of the New Deal believed they could be more successful in recruiting convention votes if they worked for uninstructed state delegations rather than slates that were openly anti-Roosevelt. The revolt against an instructed delegation in New Hampshire was led by John S. Hurley, a self-made lawyer who had learned his politics the hard way in the Amoskeag Mills. Farley got his way by beating the Hurley faction back in line with a patronage club. The effect of the New Hampshire fight, the first state to choose delegates to the convention, was to take some of the edge off similar revolts in other states.

In Connecticut the Fitzgerald wing of the party, strong supporters of Al Smith, fought bitterly against Tom Spellacy and the New Deal wing for an uninstructed delegation. The effort very nearly succeeded. It required the personal intervention of Farley (who arranged a compromise whereby New Deal national committeeman Archibald McNeil resigned in favor of Dave Fitzgerald) to salvage a Roosevelt-instructed slate.

In Alabama the anti-New Deal state committee refused to certify the slate of delegates introduced by national committeeman Judge Leon C. McCord. It took legal action to get McCord's list of Roosevelt supporters on the ballot for the May preferential primary. On June 20, Representative Burdick of North Dakota charged Farley with buying the convention votes of the Louisiana delegation — the "Second Louisiana Purchase," according to one wag. This was an understandable way of describing it. The feud between the Administration and the Long organization, which had recently won an impressive victory in the Louisiana primaries, ended amicably with a meeting between

Farley and Governor Richard Leche in New York. For convention support the Administration appeared willing to restore patronage that had been curtailed during the vendetta with the late senator and to drop the pending income tax evasion charges against the important Longite, Seymour Weiss. Meanwhile, in North Carolina, C. L. Shuping, member of the Democratic National Committee and campaign manager for anti-New Deal Senator Josiah Bailey, was talking of a bolt from the Roosevelt camp.

Joseph B. Ely gave up his struggle with Governor James M. Curley for control of the state delegation from Massachusetts. Ely was having dinner in a Boston restaurant when the primary results in New Hampshire were announced. Complaining bitterly of "the greatest patronage organization this country has ever seen," the former governor surrendered, observing grimly: "One lone Democrat can't lick four billion dollars and he is foolish to try."

In the contest for convention votes the Democratic leadership countered the League's strategy by insisting on a safe slate of delegates pledged to the renomination of President Roosevelt in every state where the opposition threatened. In each case this insistence upon a showdown resulted in a Roosevelt victory and revealed a vital weakness of the League, its lack of important popular support. It also revealed the almost insuperable advantage of the Administration, which controlled the vast machinery of patronage.

By early spring the League had given up any hope, if it ever had any, of preventing the renomination of Roosevelt. Shouse insisted later that the League had not tried to stop Roosevelt because "a president always gets the nomination without opposition if he wants it. Such an effort would have been useless." In any case, the story was the same everywhere. The Talmadge movement was so thoroughly discredited that Talmadge withdrew from the June primary and the election was called off be-

cause Roosevelt was the only entry. In announcing his with-
drawal the governor said in Atlanta, "I will support whatever
candidates and platform are adopted in Philadelphia." But he
canceled his hotel reservations and refused to attend the convention.

Henry Breckinridge, who also refused to attend the convention, was overwhelmed in the New Jersey, Ohio, Maryland, and
Pennsylvania primaries. Al Smith, although he was acceptable
to all New York factions as a delegate because of his status in
the party, had no influence in choosing the rest of the delegates.
In the other states where only weeks before trouble had been
brewing, the revolts had all burned themselves out before the
faithful assembled in Philadelphia.

But before abandoning hope of influencing the convention the
Liberty Leaguers threw one more scare into Democratic ranks.[8]

IX

From his Liberty League speech down to the eve of the Democratic convention in late June, Al Smith maintained an ominous
silence. As a former presidential candidate, Smith was entitled
to a place in the New York delegation if he wanted it. With the
convention less than a week away, he still refused to say
whether he would serve.

Smith did not go to Philadelphia. He sulked at his summer
cottage at Hampton Bays, Long Island; but his presence could
hardly have been felt more in Convention Hall had he been
there in the flesh. On the Saturday before the convention, Farley received an open telegram to the delegates signed by Smith,
Bainbridge Colby, James A. Reed, Joseph B. Ely, and Daniel
F. Cohalan.

Prepared earlier that week in Smith's Empire State Building
offices at a meeting of the Liberty League's Executive Commit-

tee, and sent from John Raskob's summer home in Maryland, the message read:

> As men who believe in the principles . . . of the Democratic party, as . . . personified by Thomas Jefferson, Andrew Jackson and Grover Cleveland, we urge you . . . to emulate their examples. . . . We submit therefore that . . . you must first be Americans . . . you must take the heavy hand of government off of business . . . balance our budget . . . put an end to the series of deficits . . . not throw away . . . the domestic market of the United States of America. You must put an end to the orgy of spending. . . . You must preserve the constitution. . . . You must . . . keep our country free from entangling alliances. . . . You must . . . put an end to the campaign . . . to buy the Presidency by the misuse of funds. . . . These are hard tasks. . . . They would necessarily involve the putting aside of Franklin D. Roosevelt. . . . But if you do not act . . . you should put aside the name of the party. . . . We hope for the best. . . . If you fail, then patriotic voters of all parties will know unhesitatingly to what standard they must rally in order to preserve the America of the great leaders of the past.

The confusion that followed was fair indication that the telegram caught the Democratic leadership by surprise. Senators Alben Barkley, temporary convention chairman, and Joseph T. Robinson, permanent chairman, were in conference with Roosevelt at the White House on convention strategy when they learned of the telegram. "No comment" was the reaction of all three. Farley masked his surprise with the thought that "considering their connection with the American Liberty League their views were to be expected." Representative John O'Connor called it "an impertinence." McAdoo thought it would help rather than hurt Roosevelt; and Attorney General Cummings observed loftily that "this was a matter which delegates were competent to decide for themselves."

There was still the problem of what to do with the telegram. Should it be read to the convention? Should a reply be made? If so, by whom? If it were read it might ignite a demonstration; if it were not, the opposition could charge Farley with suppression.

Farley huddled with other party leaders. Senator Joseph Guffey and the Pennsylvania people favored reading the message the first night of the convention after the speech by Joe Robinson in the belief that the gallery would hoot it down. Farley was afraid to risk a noisy demonstration going out over the air, and the others agreed with him. The decision was not to read the telegram; and, if possible, to head off any parliamentary maneuvers to have it read from the floor. As for a reply, it was tentatively agreed that one would be forthcoming at the William Jennings Bryan Memorial Breakfast at the Penn Athletic Club, where Josephus Daniels, ambassador to Mexico, Secretary of Commerce Daniel Roper, and Senators Barkley, Sheppard, Murray, Wagner, McKellar, and Thomas were scheduled for brief speeches. At the last minute, however, it was decided that the speakers would refrain from mentioning it.

Although the Smith telegram provided the delegates with their liveliest topic of conversation in hotel lobbies, bars, and coffee shops, and charged Convention Hall with an atmosphere of excitement and expectancy, outwardly at least the convention came off with hardly a ripple. At the appointed time John E. Mack of Poughkeepsie, former justice of the New York Supreme Court who had nominated Roosevelt in 1932, again did the honors. Mack's nominating speech was the start of an incredible eight-hour eulogy of Roosevelt, replete with bands, roaring galleries, tumultuous demonstrations, and an unbelievable fifty-seven seconding speeches representing every state, territory, and the District of Columbia. The session ended with an exhausted convention renominating Roosevelt by acclamation.

The only incident traceable to the Smith telegram occurred on Thursday night. While a demonstration was in progress on the floor, three huge "Al Smith" banners were suddenly unfurled in a corner of the upper balcony and a group of about fifty began chanting, "We want Al Smith!" Joe Marinelli, deputy attorney general of Pennsylvania, grabbed at the nearest banner and was rewarded for his valor by being knocked backward over three rows of seats with a left hook to the jaw. State troopers and city police closed in, broke up the fight, and hustled the belligerents out of the hall and through a basement corridor amid shouts of "Throw them out!" "Lynch them!" from other gallery spectators. After the melee an entire block of seats in the gallery was vacant except for one lone man in shirtsleeves triumphantly waving an Al Smith banner upside down. It was learned later that the demonstration was a hoax: the "demonstrators" were young Republicans from Philadelphia's Second Ward.[9]

X

As a political maneuver the effectiveness of the Smith telegram was impaired by an obvious flaw. Except for former governor Ely, each of the signers had very personal reasons for wanting Roosevelt ditched. Roosevelt incurred the wrath of Senator James Reed of Missouri when he, like Smith, ran out of the money at the 1932 convention. For more than a year Reed had been predicting that if the Republicans nominated a good man Roosevelt would be beaten. Cohalan, a former New York Supreme Court judge, had been nursing a grudge that dated back to 1911. While leader of a group of Democratic young Turks in the New York State Senate, Roosevelt had fought Tammany Hall to a standstill over the election of former Lieutenant Governor William F. Sheehan to the United States Senate. In the compromise that broke the deadlock, Roosevelt accepted Judge James A. O'Gorman in preference to Cohalan, a choice for which Cohalan had never forgiven him. Only recently Cohalan had been urging a coalition of Democrats and Republicans against Roosevelt. Colby, Woodrow Wilson's onetime law partner and Secretary of State, represented the Hearst wing of the Democratic opposition. Hearst had supported Roosevelt in 1932, but more recently the strong man of San Simeon was claiming credit for having "discovered" Alf Landon. The bitter Smith-Roosevelt feud was common table talk even among the politically unsophisticated.

The day after the telegram story broke it was learned that a number of disenchanted Democrats, who might have opposed the New Deal on other than personal grounds, had refused to sign it; among them, John W. Davis, Lewis Douglas, and Bernard Baruch, who urged Smith not to send it.[10]

XI

Thus far in the convention no official notice was taken of the telegram incident and the President made no mention of it in his acceptance speech.

One hundred and five thousand people filled Franklin Field to witness the second act in the Roosevelt drama of accepting the nomination in person. In 1932 he had flown to Chicago. Tonight, Saturday night, June 27, 1936, he was arriving less dramatically by train. It drizzled all afternoon and in the early evening heavy showers set in. But as the presidential train pulled into the station at 9:28 (on time, according to the station master), the rains stopped and a big half-moon appeared in the sky to the south.

Lily Pons sang the national anthem. Senator Pat Harrison of Mississippi thanked the huge crowd for its patience and for brav-

ing the inclement weather. Vice-President Garner accepted his
nomination with dignified brevity. At ten o'clock Senator Robinson introduced the President.

Roosevelt's acceptance speech is perhaps best remembered for
two well-turned phrases: "rendezvous with destiny," coined by
Tom Corcoran, and "economic royalists," by Stanley High, a
preacher-turned-journalist, who, shortly after the election, was
dropped as a presidential speech writer and wound up in the
Willkie camp four years later.

The American people, said Roosevelt, triumphed over political tyranny in 1776; but the Industrial Revolution created a
new form of tyranny — economic.

> For out of this modern civilization economic royalists carved
> new dynasties. New kingdoms were built upon concentration
> of control over material things. . . . Through new uses of
> corporations, banks and securities, new machinery of industry
> and agriculture, of labor and capital — all undreamed of by the
> fathers — the whole structure of modern life was impressed into
> this royal service.
>
> It was natural and perhaps human that the privileged princes
> of those new economic dynasties, thirsting for power, reached
> out for control over government itself. They created a new
> despotism and wrapped it in the robes of legal sanction.
>
> The election of 1932 was the people's mandate to end it.
> Under that mandate, it is being ended. . . . The royalists of the
> economic order have conceded that political freedom was the
> business of the government, but they have maintained that eco-
> nomic slavery was nobody's business.
>
> The economic royalists complain that we seek to overthrow
> the institutions of America. What they really complain of is
> that we seek to take away their power. . . . In vain they seek
> to hide behind the flag and the Constitution.
>
> In the place of the palace of privilege we seek to build a
> temple out of faith and hope and charity. It is a sobering thing
> to be a servant of this great cause.

To some generations much is given. Of others much is expected. This generation of Americans has a rendezvous with destiny. I accept the commission you have tendered me.[11]

XII

Slowly the car circled the track, the President smiling and waving to the crowd amid a shower of confetti. It was 10:46, and it was over. As the presidential party disappeared under the concrete stands at the end of the field, an anonymous voice boomed over the public address system: "Let's have no accidents on the way home. Tonight is Saturday night and we have plenty of time to get home."

The record does not show whether the advice was heeded. One thing was certain, however. The American Liberty League, now christened by Roosevelt "economic royalists" who sought "to hide behind the flag and the Constitution," had caused no accidents at the convention. Smith's "walk" and all other efforts to influence the Democratic party had thus far failed.

But there was still the election, and it was more than four months away.

8

AS MAINE GOES, SO GOES VERMONT

. . . we arrived at the conclusion that a gaping hole existed in the battle-lines of the opposition. Wishing to take advantage of that, the Democratic National Committee's first "battle-order" was to ignore the Republican Party and to concentrate fire on the Liberty League.

James A. Farley

Never before in all history have these forces been so united against one candidate as they stand today. They are unanimous in their hatred for me — and I welcome their hatred.

Franklin D. Roosevelt

THE THIRD-PARTY IDEA figured only remotely in Liberty League strategy for 1936. In American history the record of third parties was not an impressive one, and the leaders of the League knew history even if they did not always understand it. They lacked the *sine qua non* of a political party — a popular program, an uncomplicated slogan, an appealing promise; their glorification of the Constitution might inspire reverence but not action. They had no great leader, no one who could weave a spell, bring a shout to the throat, or move to tears. Nor did they have, as Theodore Roosevelt once put it, any political "loaves and fishes."

There may have been more discussion of a third party after the election than before. Jouett Shouse from the beginning visualized the League as the intellectual nucleus for a reorientation and realignment of parties, an idea that was often discussed in executive committee and one on which there was complete agreement. After the election he explored the possibility with a number of responsible persons including Harry Byrd of Virginia, North Carolina's Max Gardiner and Senator Josiah Bailey, David Reed, former senator from Pennsylvania, and others. It was no secret that Alf Landon likewise favored creating a new party after his humiliation at the polls. Late in February 1937, Landon and Shouse were house guests of a mutual Republican friend at Howey-in-the-Hills in north-central Florida where they talked about third-party possibilities until dawn.

Republican National Chairman John Hamilton was approached after the election by Republicans and Democrats alike with the idea of a coalition constitutional party. It was Alfred P. Sloan who called him to New York. Arguing that the Republican party was beyond saving, Sloan insisted that Hamilton undertake the organization of a new party. Sloan said he spoke ("carried the word," according to Hamilton) for the du Ponts, General Motors people, and others "whose names were legion," warning that if a new party were not undertaken before the next election they might withdraw their financial support from the Republicans. Hamilton, in his tour of the states, found no sympathy for the idea at the local level. In a lengthy report to the Republican National Committee he argued that the idea was neither desirable nor feasible. The committee agreed and the idea was discarded.

Such discussion as there was of a new party during the election year stemmed from the pledged support of Joseph B. Ely to Al Smith if he chose to run as an independent. In January, when the Liberty League was still confident that the election was going to be close, some members reasoned that if the League were to launch a "Constitutional Democratic Party" and put forward Smith as the candidate (an idea that William Randolph Hearst openly supported), perhaps it would split the vote in New York and Massachusetts and turn the election against Roosevelt. This possibility did not get beyond the talking stage because Smith balked and refused to consider the idea.[1]

II

An opportunity for voters to oppose Roosevelt through a third party came unexpectedly from a source far removed from the League.

For a number of years the Reverend Charles E. Coughlin, pastor of the Shrine of the Little Flower in Royal Oak, Michigan, had been attracting a local following with his sermon broadcasts. As the depression deepened and the mood of the country changed, the radio priest changed with it. People, it seemed, were more interested in their bellies than their souls, so Coughlin's sermons became less religious and more economic. Diatribes against Wall Street bankers and the ineptness of Republican leadership gave way to far-reaching demands for the socialization of industry and banking.

Coughlin at first supported the New Deal; but his monetary views were as capricious as Roosevelt's, and by 1935 he had turned the full fury of his National Union for Social Justice movement against the President. A hypnotic speaker with a touch of hysteria, one who perspired easily and flushed dramatically, Coughlin dispensed a mixture of economic mumbo jumbo, moralistic clichés, and the mystery of the clerical collar into a mass movement of several million followers (nine million according to his exaggerated figures). By 1936 he had turned the warmth of his smile upon a hard-working but obscure Dakota congressman.

The Coughlin choice for President was William Lemke. A son of frugal German immigrants, Lemke had spent a lonely and cheerless childhood breaking the Dakota prairie and absorbing the strict Lutheran fundamentalism of his parents. Venturing East long enough to get a law degree from Yale, he returned to North Dakota and dedicated his career to the work of the Nonpartisan League.

Organized in 1915 among wheat growers of North Dakota, the Nonpartisan League promoted a remarkable — and for that day, radical — program of state ownership and operation of grain elevators, warehouses, and credit facilities, minimum wages, and strict control of banks, railroads, and assorted private business enterprises. Gaining control of the state government of North Dakota in 1916, the League moved on into some six neighboring states during the war years.

It was in this school of political unorthodoxy that Lemke learned his trade. From 1917 to 1921, he was both a member of the Nonpartisan League executive committee and chairman of the state Republican committee. After a variety of political posts and a term as attorney general of North Dakota, he moved on to Congress in 1932 as a Nonpartisan Republican. In Washington, Lemke attacked his job with the cold, fierce intensity of a Dakota winter, and on June 20, 1936, the austere (he neither drank nor smoked) and undistinguished-looking representative with gray, thinning hair announced himself as the self-appointed candidate of the Union party with Thomas C. O'Brien, Boston attorney, as his running mate.

The frightful odds deterred him not at all — he had spent a lifetime fighting for unpopular and lost causes. Besides, he was not alone. The same day, Father Coughlin endorsed his candidacy; and additional succor was on the way. Dr. Townsend and Gerald L. K. Smith also rallied to the Lemke banner.

Townsend, West Coast architect of an old-age pension scheme, was an early backer of the septuagenarian senator, William Borah, for the Republican nomination. Born in Illinois, educated mainly in Kansas, and elected in Idaho, Borah went to the Senate in 1907 (after only five years in Idaho), and was still there thirty years later. A superb orator, fiercely independent, scrupulously honest and sublimely inconsistent, Borah espoused the causes close to the hearts of struggling pioneers — inflation, silver, prohibition, anti-Big Business, humanitarianism, and international isolation. Nor did he disdain Townsend support until Townsend, despairing of Borah's chances for the nomination, urged him to head a third-party movement which he and Gerald L. K. Smith would support. Borah, failing to get the Republican nomination, supported the national ticket only lukewarmly; as late as October 12, he was principal speaker at a Lemke rally in Boise.

Since usurping the Share-Our-Wealth Society after the assassination of Long, Gerald Smith had done considerable political hedge-hopping. In January he was elbowing Eugene Talmadge for the spotlight at the Macon convention. When it became clear that the Talmadge boom was getting nowhere, the handsome, florid politician-preacher pledged his support to Al Smith if Smith would "take a walk" and lead a third party. Meanwhile, his courtship of the Townsend people bore fruit. Standing beneath the historic arch at Valley Forge late in May, Smith and Townsend closed ranks with a handshake. When their importuning of Borah bore no results the Smith-Townsend alliance was left without a candidate.

But there was still Lemke.[2]

III

With the slogan "Anybody but Roosevelt," the Townsend, Coughlin, and Smith forces gathered in Cleveland in mid-July at what was originally scheduled as a Townsend convention. The two men of the cloth stole the show from their bewildered host; and the endorsement of Lemke had the air of an afterthought.

Another Smith injected the only discordant note in an otherwise harmonious meeting. Gomer Smith, an Oklahoma City attorney (and later congressman), was a member of the board of the Townsend organization but had, on occasion, defended Roosevelt vigorously against attacks by Coughlin. Midway in the convention, Smith got the floor and delivered a short impassioned speech attacking both Coughlin and Gerald Smith, claiming that Smith and his lieutenants were "paid agents of the American Liberty League," a charge which Shouse promptly denied as "a baseless falsehood." Of course it was untrue, but the fact that the charge was made shows what uninformed people might be expected to believe about the League by this date.

Lemke faced the improbable task of welding together the Townsendites, Coughlin's Union of Social Justice, and Share-Our-Wealth with radical agrarian groups like the Farmers' Union and the Farmer-Labor party behind a platform of farm relief and novel currency proposals. "Lemke money" was the centripetal force holding the nebulous mass together; but any success of the new party was dependent upon the ability of the four men involved to deliver the votes of their followers.

Coughlin was boasting that he could deliver 10,000,000 votes to Lemke. If he could they would be mostly Democratic votes from eastern states where Coughlin was particularly popular. The Democrats had already had a scare from the Long organization. It was not to be expected that Gerald Smith would wield the same influence as the late senator; but if he could deliver a substantial part of the Share-Our-Wealth Society votes — say even half — the effect could be very damaging. The Townsend group was entirely unpredictable. And Democratic leaders were uneasy over Minnesota, North and South Dakota, Montana, and possibly other western states where Lemke was popular in his own right.

The Lemke candidacy, while unexpected, seemed an inviting opportunity to do Roosevelt harm. The *New Republic*, for one, claimed that Lemke got support from Liberty Leaguers, despite his denials that he was receiving money and encouragement from Hearst, the Republican party, or the American Liberty League. Certainly the Union party was not, as Earl Browder, the Communist leader, charged, a "Hearst-Landon-Liberty League intrigue."

The Townsend, Smith, and Coughlin coalition was a limited threat to the Democratic cause, if it was a threat at all. When the Union party succeeded in getting on the ballot in only thirty-five states, Smith and Townsend urged their supporters to vote for Landon in those states where Lemke was not a candidate. Considering the close relationship of the Liberty League to the Republican campaign, which stood to gain by the Lemke candidacy, it may well be that League members gave aid and comfort to the prairie reformer with unorthodox views on abundant money even if he did advocate confiscating all income over $500,000.[3]

IV

Al Smith's "walk in absentia" from the Democratic National Convention was not without its effect. Encouraged by his example and with the kind of help from Liberty Leaguers that counted — money — two other anti-New Deal groups were formed.

One was the Independent Coalition of American Women. Formed in July at Toledo, Ohio, the Coalition adopted a resolution endorsing Landon and Knox and went to work to reach its goal of "1,000,000 anti-New Deal or inactive Republican women for the Kansas governor."

The national director, Mrs. Mabel Jacques Eichel of Wilton, Connecticut, was an old friend of Shouse, Raskob, Smith, and the du Ponts from the days of the fight against the prohibition amendment, and had served as an officer of the Women's Organization for National Prohibition Reform. In 1934 she was prominently identified with the campaign of Colonel Henry Breckinridge for the United States Senate. The national chairman, Mrs. Edwin T. Meredith of Des Moines, was wife of the Secretary of Agriculture in the Wilson Administration. Other officers included Mrs. Christian R. Holmes, heiress to the Fleischmann fortune, and Mrs. William T. Healey of Atlanta, both members of the Liberty League Advisory Council, and Mrs. James A. Reed and Mrs. Joseph B. Ely, wives of two prominent Liberty Leaguers who had signed the Smith telegram. To make it entirely a family affair, Mrs. Ely's son was in charge of Liberty League headquarters in Massachusetts.

The Coalition had the blessing of the Republican party; Republican National Chairman John D. M. Hamilton had suggested Mrs. Meredith for national chairman. Within the month the Coalition (which the redoubtable Molly Dewson of the Democratic National Committee described as "a sort of ladies' auxiliary of the Liberty League") had divided the country into six regions and had active organizations in twelve states. In less than four months some $80,000 was raised by the ladies, most of it from members of the Liberty League, including John Raskob, E. T. Weir, and J. Howard Pew. On the eve of the election the Coalition claimed active members in about twenty-five states.

The other organization inspired by Smith's defection was the National Jeffersonian Democrats. The initiative for organizing the group came from ex-Senator James A. Reed of Missouri. At the invitation of Sterling Edmunds, a St. Louis attorney and a director of Kirby's Southern Committee to Uphold the Constitution, forty prominent anti-New Deal Democrats from twenty-two states gathered in Detroit early in August.

Among those attending were such bitter foes of the Administration as Reed, Colonel Henry Breckinridge, Bainbridge Colby,

Joseph B. Ely, John Henry Kirby, Graham Wright of Georgia, R. Contee Rose of Maryland, Joseph W. Bailey, Jr., son of the former Texas senator and himself an ex-member of Congress, and J. Evetts Haley, western Texas rancher-historian. Reed was unanimously elected national chairman, Edmunds was named secretary, and Ely headed the finance committee. The others present automatically became the national committee.

All agreed that a third-party movement was out of the question: with the election little more than three months away it was too late for that. Governor Ely favored a formal endorsement of Landon as the Independent Coalition of American Women had done; but there was strong opposition to this, especially from the Southerners. Remembering what had happened to Democrats who bolted in 1928, and arguing that an endorsement of Landon would impair the effectiveness of their support of Democrats at the local and state level, Joe Bailey led the fight against Ely's proposal. It was agreed that instead of openly endorsing the Republican ticket the organization would attempt to coordinate into a national crusade the efforts of all the various anti-New Deal movements; but the methods for opposing the Democrats would be left entirely to the states.

The two-day conference adjourned with the adoption of a "Declaration of Purposes and Intent" (a declaration that read Roosevelt out of the Democratic party) and an emotion-packed speech by Reed which moved the speaker to tears as he pleaded for a "disciplinary defeat of Franklin Roosevelt" to "return the party to its rightful heirs."

With ample funds (which included generous contributions from wealthy Liberty Leaguers like E. T. Weir, Alfred P. Sloan, the du Ponts, John Raskob, who alone gave $50,000, and from David K. E. Bruce, a son-in-law of Andrew Mellon whose father, William Cabell Bruce, former Democratic senator of Maryland, was already campaigning for Landon), the National Jeffersonian Democrats boasted from their St. Louis headquarters that they could divert from Roosevelt at least three million Democratic votes.[4]

v

Despite efforts to disrupt the Democratic party and its third-party and quasi-third-party activities, "there was never any doubt," wrote Farley, "that the League would eventually support whatever Republican candidate was nominated . . ."

But the strategy at first was to deny an open alignment with the Republicans. Instead, the League pleaded innocently that it would not take sides. A week before the public announcement, Jouett Shouse had gone to the White House to assure the President that the League would be "absolutely non-partisan in character"; at his first press conference Shouse had continued to stress the nonpartisan nature of the new organization; and in the days that followed, other League representatives spoke similarly reassuring words. Fictitious as it was, neutrality was the official position of the Liberty League throughout 1934 and 1935, a position that became untenable in the election year.

Early in February 1936, Hamilton's predecessor, Republican National Chairman Fletcher, denied that there would be any cooperation with the League. ("We will confine our efforts to the Republican cause and there will be no combination with the League.") In answer to the many criticisms that its individual members were hardly observing neutrality, the League's Executive Committee issued a formal statement from the offices of Al Smith, insisting the League was pursuing "a non-partisan opposition to Franklin D. Roosevelt," a *non sequitur* peculiar to politics. Again in August, persistent rumors that the League was about to announce for Landon provoked from Shouse this emphatic denial: "It will endorse no party. It will endorse no candidate. It has not contributed and will not contribute to any campaign fund."

The relation between the Republican party and the Liberty League was a strange one indeed, with some of the characteristics of an illicit love affair. The League supported the Republican ticket in every way short of an open endorsement; the Republican party accepted that support; yet both sides vehemently denied it.

The Executive Committee of the League met at its National Press Building headquarters the afternoon of the Liberty League dinner. Out of that meeting came the decision to wait until July, after the national conventions, before deciding on a policy for the campaign. But one unnamed member of the committee was quoted immediately afterward as saying, "If the Republicans behave well at Cleveland and give us somewhere to go as to a candidate and platform, we will solidly support the Republicans as the only hope of restoring the government to sound methods," a statement that Republican National Chairman Fletcher countered with his "no combination with the League" comment.

In February, Senator Arthur Vandenberg of Michigan let the cat out of the bag. Speaking at the Lincoln Day dinner of the National Republican Club in New York's Waldorf-Astoria Hotel, Vandenberg called for the support of anti-New Deal Democrats. ("For myself, I welcome Jeffersonian cooperation – not only in the battle line, but subsequently in the council chamber after next November's victory is won.") The next morning, Fletcher confessed that some thought had been given to the idea of offering Cabinet spots in exchange for the support of anti-New Deal Democrats. The names most often mentioned were those of Lewis Douglas, former Director of the Budget, and Governor Ely. Both Vandenberg and Senator David Reed of Pennsylvania, said Fletcher, were willing to go so far as to name a Democrat to the second place on the Republican ticket, an idea that raised the hackles of at least one proud member of the Grand Old Party. (Senator Dickinson of Iowa: "They must be mad!")

In April, Ogden Mills and Bainbridge Colby told a luncheon meeting of the Republican Women of Philadelphia that Democrats "across the land" would vote Republican if they nominated a strong candidate on a platform "committed to the principles of the American system of government." "Democrats," said Shouse in a radio speech in June, "left without a party in present circumstances, must decide the course they will pursue. They owe no duty of loyalty to the New Deal . . . masking under the name of the Democratic party, the machinery of which it has momentarily seized . . ." The New Deal, Shouse continued, "faces almost certain defeat in November" because "some two million Democrats will take a walk to vote Republican," a walk with Al Smith at the head of the column.[5]

VI

June 9, 1936. Republicans converged on Cleveland. The gloom that had enveloped the proceedings four years earlier had turned to cautious optimism; and hope, that eternal nourishment of young lovers and politicians, was the theme of Chairman Fletcher's opening remarks and the remarks of Senator Frederick Steiwer of Oregon, who was convention keynoter. But all the fun and excitement of a national convention with its intoxicating effect upon one's sense of reality — the crowds, the bands, the demonstrations, the eloquent perorations — could not hide the glaring weakness. The routs of 1932 and 1934 had left the Republican party leaderless.

Five men (Borah, Knox, Hoover, Vandenberg, and Landon) figured in the preconvention skirmishing, with the usual number of favorite sons and dark horses waiting in the background for the front runners to finish off each other.

Borah began running for the Presidency in 1912. Always too erratic for the party leaders, and now too old as well, the Idaho senator had a hardcore of support that might influence the platform and maybe be decisive in determining the outcome of a close contest.

Herbert Hoover might have wished for a second chance to redeem himself; but he did not openly declare himself a candidate, and seemed more intent upon the nomination of Vandenberg on a strong anti-New Deal platform. The convention listened politely to Hoover's halting, stilted animadversions against the New Deal without any serious thought of renominating him. Ever the ultraconservative, temperamentally as well as politically, his strictures against social and economic experimentation, his insistence that a balanced budget, a gold standard, and a stabilized currency were the cure for every malady, were like a voice out of the past, a past which the Republican party was trying to forget.

Arthur Vandenberg and Frank Knox were old friends as well as rivals. Fifty-two years old in 1936, Vandenberg had never held public office until appointed in 1928 to fill the vacancy created by the death of Senator Woodbridge N. Ferris. Active in local politics, editor and publisher of one of Michigan's more influential papers, Vandenberg's star rose rapidly in the Senate as leader of the Republican Young Turks — a group of "enlightened conservatives" he called them — who supported the World Court, strict control of munitions makers (he was on the Nye Committee), the Securities Act of 1933, and the Securities Exchange Act of 1934, and vigorous enforcement of the antitrust laws. But Vandenberg did not appear anxious for the prize; his eyes were on 1940.

Knox was the first avowed Republican candidate in 1936. Born in Boston, he had grown up in Michigan, fought with Teddy Roosevelt at San Juan Hill, and, after the Cuban adventure, worked with Vandenberg on the Grand Rapids *Herald* before buying a paper of his own in Sault Sainte Marie. His newspaper career eventually took him to Manchester, New

Hampshire, where he later sought unsuccessfully the Republican nomination for governor. Retaining his interest in the Manchester paper, Knox went to Boston as a top executive with the Hearst chain. In 1931 he bought controlling interest in the Chicago *Daily News*. Able, popular, the picture of health, Knox had two liabilities: lack of vote-getting credentials, since he had never held public office; and Hearst.

The front runner at Cleveland was, as Farley called him in one of his few *faux pas* of the campaign, "an inexperienced governor of a typical prairie state." Hearstman John Lambert had spent less than twenty-four hours in Topeka in October 1935. "Any ringbones on your pony that would show up in dry weather?" asked Landon, as Lambert stood waiting for his train. "You could have been more definitely against the League of Nations," Lambert replied. With a handshake the two men parted. Alfred Mossman Landon, twice governor of Kansas, had been "discovered."

Landon was only forty-eight years old at convention time in 1936. Born in Pennsylvania and reared in Ohio, he had moved to Kansas in his early teens, earned a law degree at the University of Kansas, but had never practiced. Bored by the banking business he turned to wildcatting for oil, and made money. Lots of it. A skilled fisherman, hunter, horseman, inveterate card player, chainsmoker, and political independent, Landon supported Roosevelt and the Bull Moosers in 1912. (His father was among the Roosevelt delegates who bolted the Republican convention in 1912.) When Bull Mooser Henry J. Allen was elected governor in 1916, Landon became his secretary briefly before donning lieutenant bars in World War I. A variety of political jobs after the war led to the governorship (he was the only Republican governor elected west of the Mississippi River in 1932) and re-election in 1934.

The Landon buildup had begun quietly. As early as September 1935 the name began to appear with increasing regularity in Hearst papers, and late that month Dick Berlin of *Good House-*

keeping sent Adela Rogers St. Johns to interview Mrs. Landon.

In October, after the Lambert visit, Hearst pulled all the stops. If Landon was an unknown to politicians, he soon became the darling of the newspaper owners. Oscar S. Stauffer, owner of a string of Kansas newspapers, joined the crusade and opened Landon-for-President headquarters in Kansas City's Muehlebach Hotel late in October. In the weeks that followed, others joined the boom: Fred Seaton of the Young Republicans (whose father owned the newspaper in Hutchinson, Kansas); Arthur Capper, senator and publisher of *Capper's Weekly;* the editor of the Emporia *Gazette* and friend of Presidents, William Allen White; and Roy W. Roberts of the potent Kansas City *Star.*

Landon lay low. In the eight months before the convention he made only three major speeches, and only one of these (at Cleveland) was east of the Mississippi. The reason was a matter of strategy, not reticence. For one thing, Landon was not a good speaker, which accounted for the attempt to pass him off as a "Kansas Coolidge." He was articulate enough, and spoke a crusty plains idiom all his own; but the Midwestern nasal twang was unmistakable, and the voice headed for the upper register when he became excited. In the campaign Landon supporters tried to turn this defect into virtue, as Harry Truman did in 1948. His was the voice of common sense, of honesty, of the unaffected people, the melliferous voice of Franklin Roosevelt was the voice of the brain-truster, the radical reformer, the hypocrite, the waster and spender. But it never came off.

Another reason for the strategy of silence was that Landon went along with much of the New Deal. In correspondence with the President, Landon expressed approval of the AAA, the public works program and drought relief, but was caustically critical of deficit spending and bureaucratic inefficiency, particularly in handling relief. He was to base his campaign on these two issues: failure to balance the budget and administrative waste.

Landon steadfastly refused to expose himself in the primaries.

He foresaw correctly that his best hope for the nomination lay in letting the "favorite son" vote be cast on the first ballot and then pushing for victory on the second ballot, when the votes of the uninstructed delegations were released. The outcome of the primary in California confirmed the wisdom of this strategy. Governor Frank Merriam supported Landon over the protests of Hoover, who wanted an uninstructed delegation. To complicate matters, C. A. Sunderlin, Borah's campaign manager in California, shifted to Landon on the eve of the primary. Even so, Landon was beaten in California by more than 100,000 votes, a result that was interpreted as a protest against Hearst rather than an endorsement of Hoover. The blessing of Hearst, who had paved the way for Roosevelt's nomination four years earlier, had thorns as well as roses.

As Landon's preconvention strength increased there developed the inevitable "Stop Landon" movement among the other candidates. Center of the opposition was Hoover and Borah, both of whom were not unfriendly to Vandenberg. Landon was too liberal for Hoover and had too many connections with the eastern corporations and "interests" to suit Borah. But the opposition evaporated when the New York and Pennsylvania delegations announced for Landon on the afternoon before the first roll call. Realizing that further opposition could not stop the Kansas governor but might split the party, Hoover and Borah gave up the fight. Vandenberg, Knox, Dickinson, and Robert A. Taft seconded Landon's nomination; only Borah flatly refused.

On the first roll call, one vote went to Borah from West Virginia and eighteen from Wisconsin. Landon had all the rest. Wisconsin moved to make the nomination unanimous and it was done.

With the nomination as Vice-President of the Chicago publisher and editor, the country was prepared to "Get off the rocks with Landon and Knox." [6]

VII

Liberty League influence upon the Republican campaign was probably considerable; but the full extent of that influence can only be guessed. The record is gone, gone with the quiet conversations, the long-distance telephone calls, the random letters buried in obscure and dusty files, the hurried memos wadded up and thrown into wastebaskets. All that is left is the obvious, the superficial, the surface evidences.

Jouett Shouse has said that strong pressure was brought to have the League endorse the Republican ticket even before the convention met or a candidate was nominated, pressure brought, among others, by Henry Fletcher, chairman of the Republican National Committee, and this despite Fletcher's statements that there would be no combination with the League. The choice of Fletcher's successor implied that the strange relationship between the League and the party would continue into the campaign.

John Daniel Miller Hamilton was forty-four years old when he inherited Fletcher's job after the Republican convention. A Topeka lawyer, Hamilton rose rapidly through the ranks: assistant city attorney, probate judge, speaker of the state House of Representatives, unsuccessful candidate for governor, chairman of the state Republican Central Committee, general counsel of the Republican National Committee, and, finally, national chairman.

Hamilton, who had been directing the Landon campaign since March, was handpicked by the new Republican candidate. But it had not always been so; once they had been enemies. In 1928, Landon managed the campaign of the liberal Clyde Reed against Hamilton, who was the candidate of the conservative Mulvane forces. Reed won. In 1930, the struggle between the two wings of the party in Kansas continued, which permitted the Democrat, Harry Woodring, to slip into the governorship.

Events in the election of 1932 cemented the friendship of the erstwhile enemies. The remarkable Dr. Brinkley, who had gained a fortune from spent males with a goat-gland cure, polled more than 100,000 votes for governor in 1930 as a write-in candidate. When Landon opposed Woodring two years later, both men feared him. On election day the Democrats pulled an old-fashioned political trick. Buying up radio time, they broadcast slanted returns that had Woodring beating Brinkley and Landon running third. Sensing the effect this might have on late voters, Hamilton (on his own initiative and at his own expense) also bought time, although according to his figures Landon was leading and Woodring was trailing Brinkley. Landon won. Convinced that Hamilton had made the victory possible, the two became fast friends. When Dave Mulvane died, Landon named Hamilton to the vacancy on the Republican National Committee.

The platform adopted at Cleveland was everything that the League could have hoped for; indeed, the amazing similarity between the Republican platform adopted at Cleveland and Liberty League Document No. 83, *A Program for Congress*, suggested something more than coincidence. Of the fifty-three-member platform committee, four were Liberty Leaguers, and there may have been more. In any case, the membership was drawn from recommendations made by the state organizations, where League influence was certain to be considerable. They did not have to be on the committee to influence the ones who were; for example, Andrew Mellon and Ernest Weir would have had "terrific influence" on Senator David Reed. "I haven't the slightest doubt," said Hamilton, "that these men who formed the Liberty League had tremendous influence on the platform."

Of the twenty-one-man Republican national finance committee, one third were conspicuously identified with the Liberty League: Sewell L. Avery and Herbert L. Pratt were members of the League Executive Committee; Joseph M. Pew was brother of another Executive Committee member, J. Howard Pew, Jr.; Hal H. Smith of Detroit was a prominent member of the League Lawyers' Committee; William B. Bell, the finance committee chairman, Ernest T. Weir, and Silas Strawn were League members; and Strawn's Chicago law partner, Ralph Shaw, was director of the Illinois branch of the League. The Republican campaign was made possible largely with Liberty League money (not from the League itself, of course — this was part of the nonpartisan charade — but from Liberty Leaguers who paid tremendous sums for the dubious honor of backing a loser): R. R. M. Carpenter, $23,500; A. Felix du Pont, $34,000; Archibald du Pont, $1000; Mrs. Coleman du Pont, $5250; Eugene du Pont, $3600; Henry B. du Pont, $26,000; Irénée du Pont, $121,530; Lammot du Pont, $190,500; Pierre du Pont, $111,990; Pierre du Pont III, $3000; S. Halleck du Pont, $5500; William du Pont, Jr., $21,000; Lammot du Pont Copeland, $7000; Edward S. Harkness, $15,000; Arthur E. Pew, Jr., $15,775; Miss Ethel Pew, $109,125; J. Howard Pew, $125,638; J. Howard Pew, Jr., $125,314; Mrs. Mabel Pew Myrin, $110,125; Alfred P. Sloan, $51,600; Mrs. Alfred P. Sloan, $32,500; Ernest T. Weir, $52,800.

This was by no means a complete list, not even of the largest contributors from Liberty League ranks. At least two score could be added. It is perhaps noteworthy that the du Pont and Pew families alone contributed more than one million dollars, and this in addition to their Liberty League contributions. "Without Liberty League money," Hamilton later admitted candidly, "we couldn't have had a national headquarters."

Some of the most prominent figures among the League's Democratic members, notably Al Smith, Joseph B. Ely, and James A. Reed, actively supported the Republican campaign. After a breakfast conference with Hamilton in Springfield, Massachusetts, Ely told the press that he intended to campaign for Landon ("I'll do anything I can to help him"). The same day, July 17, Colonel Frank Knox disclosed that he had received several letters from Smith and expected to see him in New York sometime after July 30. Shortly afterward, J. Fred Essary, chief of the Washington bureau of the Baltimore *Sun*, revealed that Smith and Hamilton had met on July 20 and that Hamilton had "begged" Smith to campaign for Landon as Ely had promised to do. Neither man denied the story. "All I've got to say," said Smith, "is that I met Hamilton." Hamilton would say only that he would be "tickled to death" to have Smith campaign for Landon. Smith did not publicly announce that he would campaign for Landon until September 20, although his decision was known in Landon's Topeka headquarters as early as August 30.

Ely and Reed each made six speeches for Landon in which they hammered away at the leftist tendencies of the New Deal: "What he [Roosevelt] stands for and what he says constitute a great stride toward actual communism" (Ely); ". . . radical and revolutionary left-wing ties" (Reed), by which he meant specifically support from the La Follette and La Guardia groups.

The efforts of Al Smith were particularly noteworthy. On September 20, Smith announced that on October 1 he would begin a series of anti-New Deal speeches. He spoke five times — at New York, Boston, Chicago, Philadelphia, and Albany; the Philadelphia speech was sponsored by the National Jeffersonian Democrats, the others by the Independent Coalition of American Women.

The setting for the first speech was New York's Carnegie Hall. Still protesting that he cherished no personal grievance against Franklin Roosevelt and that he was acting only from what he conceived to be his political duty, Smith, before a capacity house and a nationwide radio audience, uttered the fateful words that made complete his repudiation of the Democratic party: "I firmly believe that the remedy for all the ills that we are suffering from today is the election of Alfred M. Landon." From New York to Philadelphia, then on to Chicago (accompanied by John Hamilton) and back to Boston, Smith carried his new gospel of Landon the Deliverer.

In Albany, on October 31, Smith's crusade ended. And it ended right where it had begun nine months earlier at the Liberty League dinner — on the Communist issue.

> Now we are hearing a whole lot about Communism [said Smith]. Let me deal with that for a minute, and let me start off by saying . . . don't let anyone tell you that President Roosevelt is a Communist. That is not so. Or don't let anyone tell you that he is a Socialist. That is not so. He is neither a Communist nor a Socialist — any more than I am — but something has taken place in this country — there is some certain kind of foreign "ism" crawling over this country. What it is I don't know. What its first name will be when it is christened I haven't the slightest idea. But I know that it is here, and the sin about it is that he [Roosevelt] doesn't seem to know it.

As in his earlier speeches, so it was at Harmanus Bleecker Hall, in the shadow of the capitol where he had made political history as Democratic governor of New York, Smith faded into political obscurity pleading hoarsely that "there is nothing you can do if you love America except change from the present administration to Governor Landon of Kansas." [7]

VIII

After Smith's Liberty League speech in January, Arthur Krock had observed editorially: "Historians of this political year may unanimously conclude that its contribution was a rich one to the President."

Krock was prophetic. Roosevelt and his associates were

quick to capitalize on the alignment suggested by the dinner. "It [the Liberty League] seemed to be one of the most vulnerable ever to appear in politics," said Farley, "and our campaign was developed on that theory." The vulnerability of the League was in the wealth of its backers, a fact that the dinner only served to highlight. Men and women whose names, rightly or wrongly, were synonymous in the public mind with social and economic privilege had cheered Smith's assault on the New Deal. The Administration was delighted with the possibilities of branding the Liberty League the tool of organized wealth to further the political interests of the rich regardless of what happened to others. Here was the "gaping hole in the battlelines of the opposition" of which Farley spoke. "Wishing to take advantage of that," the national chairman wrote later, "the Democratic National Committee's first 'battle-order' was to ignore the Republican Party and to concentrate fire on the Liberty League."

Concentrate fire it did. Senator Pat Harrison of Mississippi branded it the "American 'Lobby' League," "a group of griping and disgruntled politicians . . . masquerading as patriots but in reality apostles of greed." A Liberty Leaguer, said Virginia state senator Charles E. Burks, is "a man who is a Republican but ashamed of it, [or] a man raised as a Democrat who's become able to buy flour by the barrel and sugar by the sack, made one trip to New York and bought a forked-tail coat and a stove-pipe hat." "Just who are the people," asked the Indiana governor, Paul V. McNutt, "to whom he [Landon] is willing to be obligated in the unlikely event of his election? Can they be other than the group of which the du Pont Liberty League is characteristic . . .?"

Others exploited what Michelson called "the gold-coast complexion" of the organization. Speaking to the John Dewey Society in St. Louis, Dr. George S. Counts of Columbia University observed acidly: "They have appropriated the Liberty

Bell as their symbol, but they apparently think the [American] Revolution was fought to make Long Island safe for polo players." The Long Island Conference of the United Lutheran Synod questioned the sincerity of "so-called liberty leagues dedicated to protect the Constitution" when actually they are working "to hinder any movement to regulate business and are all set to bring back the good old days of rugged individualism." In Washington at its annual convention, the United Mine Workers adopted a resolution castigating millionaires "who have piled up huge fortunes while denying their employees the right to organize," and condemned "the so-called American Liberty League as wholly selfish in its aims, un-American in its methods and policies and inimical to the interests of the people of the United States." If the Liberty League is the champion "of laissez-faire, of unregulated individualism, of economic liberalism," declared Fordham University professor of ethics, the Reverend Ignatius W. Cox, S.J., "no Catholic who knows Catholic social doctrine can approve this phase of the league. All Catholic ethics, all Catholic doctrine, all Catholic tradition, the utterances of Popes and Bishops, the voices of Leo XIII and Pius XI are raised trumpet-tongued in damnation of this indefensible doctrine."

Among Administration members Farley himself led the assault. Epithets rolled from his lips in a torrent of abuse: The American Liberty League is "the center and soul of the predatory powers," "the ally of the Republican National Committee," "those Bourbons who learn nothing and forget nothing," "speaks as conclusively for the reactionaries and their party as does Mr. Hoover, the United States Chamber of Commerce and the National Manufacturers' Association," "would squeeze the worker dry in his old age and cast him like an orange rind into the refuse pail." In St. Louis he told a Democratic rally: "The Republican National Committee has a little cry baby brother called the American Liberty League. The brothers are always together. They pal around together, they think the same thoughts, they echo the same phrases, and they seek the same end. . . ." At a Washington Day banquet in Wichita for the Kansas Democratic Clubs, he remarked that it "ought to be called the American Cellophane League" because "first, it's a du Pont product and second, you can see right through it."

More than any other person, it was a little-known newspaperman who was responsible for coordinating the wrecking job on the American Liberty League in 1936. Edward L. Roddan, a former Hearst writer, had covered the Albany beat while Roosevelt was governor of New York. In 1933 he moved on to Washington as White House correspondent for International News Service. When early in 1936 Farley was looking for someone to devote full time to the League, Charlie Michelson recommended Roddan. In his early forties, slight, wiry, sandy hair tinged with gray, Roddan was a tough, likable Irishman who smoked hard, drank hard, and swore the same way.

A confirmed New Dealer and totally dedicated to Franklin Roosevelt, Roddan did a superb job on the League. "I am tired of defensive tactics," the President told him when he went over to the National Committee as Michelson's assistant. Once he was there, the campaign picked up speed. Farley and Roddan quickly became fast friends, and between them (and Michelson) the two sons of the Old Sod planned the strategy that put the League on the run. Some of Farley's most effective verbal blasts came from Roddan, who later helped Farley write his first book, *Behind the Ballots*. It was Roddan who planted stories, saw to it that friends of the Administration — farm and labor leaders and businessmen — missed no opportunity to be quoted in criticism of the League, and who developed the plan of attacking the Republican party by attacking the Liberty League. "Millionaires' Union," a name that dogged the League throughout the campaign, was a piece of Roddan imagery.

"It was simple," Roddan explained afterward. All we did was "parade their directorate before the people" at every opportunity and "blame them for everything." [8]

IX

The strategy of "concentrating fire" on the League was a spectacular success. The League had been a sensation in January; by midsummer it was on the defensive; in September it was asking itself whether it should try to continue after the election.

Routing the League was only part of the victory. By exaggerating the connections between the League and the Republican party the Administration could charge "guilt by association," the very pleasant game of killing two birds with the same political stone. That the Liberty League did support the Republican party was obvious. (There is no record that any of its claimed membership supported Roosevelt.) Nor was there any reason why it should not have supported the Republicans except that the Democratic campaign was making the League a political liability the Republican party could not bear.

So the strange entente continued as the months wore on, the Democrats passing no opportunity to link the League with the Republican opposition (Farley, New York State committee dinner, Albany: "And so the Liberty League is making it more embarrassing for the Republicans every day. They can't repudiate it because they need the money; they can't absorb it, otherwise they make the American Liberty League out a liar; they can't ignore it, because they need American Liberty League ideas and brains"). In his speech opening the Democratic convention, Farley continued to press the point: "Behind the Republican ticket is the crew of the du Pont Liberty League and their allies. . . ." The acceptance speech by Governor Landon, said New York Representative John J. O'Connor, "was written by the National Manufacturers' Association and edited by Jouett Shouse, head of the American Liberty League." Not so gross, but with the same thought in mind, were the remarks of Farley: "Undoubtedly the Governor's effort was satisfactory to the du Pont Liberty League, for it rather skillfully avoids criticising anything for which that organization stands, which is really as far as the du Ponts and Mr. William Randolph Hearst had any right to expect him to go."

The League meanwhile continued to protest that no such link existed. In July it issued its "nonpartisan opposition" statement; and in early August, Shouse said, "The League is neither an adjunct nor an ally of the Republican party."

These denials of any association with the Republican party were technical facts; but the reason for it was because Landon leaders were urging the League to refrain from too close an association with the Republican campaign. "Republicans," wrote Arthur Krock, "feeling that its [the Liberty League's] implied endorsement and support are very hurtful, have made plain their wish that the League as a unit take a position outside the party breastworks." The political liability of the League, Krock continued, "was so great by June that, at Cleveland, Chairman Hamilton . . . would have walked a mile out of his way rather than be seen in the company of a leaguer." The *New York Times* correspondent concluded that for the League to disband "would probably have been the only way to have repaired some of the damage it has dealt the Republicans." All of which so nettled James Wadsworth that he posted a letter to the *Times* denying that Landon, Knox, or Hamilton "have shied away" from Liberty League support.

Was Krock correct? Would Hamilton have walked a mile out of his way to avoid being seen with a Liberty Leaguer? The answer was yes. Not because he had any quarrel with the League or with what it stood for. It was because, according to

Hamilton, "nothing is more stupid" than for an organization of big businessmen to get out and "carry a flag in a political parade." What he meant was that the Republican party wanted and needed help from these people, but as individuals, not as a flag-waving organization that the Democrats could readily discredit. And here lay the entire political error of the League from beginning to end.

Hamilton saw "a lot of those men"; saw "a lot" of Jouett Shouse during the campaign; and, according to his appointment book, so did the presidential candidate (Colonel Breckinridge in New York, Judge Proskauer at Lake Placid, and so on). But it was a painful association, the "kiss of death" Landon called it. By the time Krock suggested in August that the League should disband to spare the Republicans further embarrassment, others, who had been sympathetic toward the League at the outset, shared that sentiment. Frank Kent, the caustically anti-New Deal writer of the Baltimore *Sun*, accused the League of "glaring ineptitude," and Walter Lippmann said that it was "manna from Heaven" for the Democrats. They and David Lawrence, who had once enthusiastically described it as a "call to arms," repeatedly urged that the League dissolve.

By insisting that its role in the campaign was neutral and nonpartisan the League was being forced into an untenable position, a position that left it no place to go and made it appear absurd in the process. Sinking Landon by aiming at Shouse was a political billiard shot of championship caliber. "Their names were on our stationery," said Hamilton wryly. "There was nothing we could do." [9]

X

Behind its massive propaganda campaign, which daily became more damaging to the Republicans, the League was a study in futility. On May 14, the Executive Committee sent out a letter to its membership launching a "Get Out the Vote" crusade. The plan promised about as much success as the chain-letter idea after which it was modeled. The plan was for each League member to send in to national headquarters a pledge to vote, accompanied by the names of at least ten other voters (non-League members) who would also promise to vote. The headquarters would then write to these people, soliciting them to forward ten more names of voters who would take the pledge. And so on, ad infinitum. With the letters from the Executive Committee went solemn reminders that the League was not seeking pledges for votes "to support any individual candidate or any particular party." Even in this kind of undertaking the problem inherent in its neutral posture was evident when, a month later, the League announced optimistically that returns coming in indicated the plan would be instrumental in turning out "several millions of aroused citizens" at the polls in November. It was clear to anyone that it was not the League's intention that they be aroused in favor of Roosevelt.

The League employed other equally unproductive vote-getting techniques. The Executive Committee accepted the offer of Irénée du Pont to finance the printing and distribution of a 1936 calendar, "patriotic" in theme and "in color." Liberty Leaguers cooperated with the Eastern Division of Landon Volunteers in circulating *A Declaration of Independence by Democrats*. Conceived by disgruntled Democrats Eugene W. Stetson and Robert L. Garner, both former vice-presidents of New York's Guaranty Trust Company, the *Declaration* bore the endorsement of both Alfred E. Smith and John W. Davis. By September, the League was promoting automobile emblems for twenty-five cents each to be attached to license plates. Made of metal with white-enameled background and blue embossed lettering, the emblem bore the legend "Uphold the Constitution." [10]

XI

The President, hitting the campaign trail late in September, completed the rout of the Liberty League. His opening speech was at the Democratic state convention at Syracuse, September 29. Landon, who had begun his campaign as a "practical progressive" in sympathy with the general aims of the New Deal but critical of its waste and inefficiency, had gradually joined Hoover, Hearst, and the Liberty League in depicting a choice between the "American way of life" and the New Deal program, an alien "ism" subverting the Constitution, poisoning the economy, endangering freedom and liberty, the road toward some kind of European dictatorship — possibly the forerunner of communism if not communism itself.

Roosevelt's Syracuse speech challenged the truth of this set of alternatives. "I have not sought, I do not seek, I repudiate the support of any advocate of communism or of any other alien 'ism'. . . . That is my position. It always has been my position. It always will be my position." Mr. Roosevelt recalled how, in 1933, banking and industrial leaders "came to me in Washington . . . pleading to be saved." This reminded him of the story about the old gentleman who, having fallen off the pier, and having been fished out, berated his friend for not also saving his old silk hat. The point was that the New Deal had saved the United States from communism by eradicating conditions "congenial to communism." (Nevertheless, the Communist party was urging its people to vote for Roosevelt in those states where they could not vote for the Communist candidate, Earl Browder.)

From Syracuse on to St. Paul, Omaha, Denver, Wichita, and Kansas City Roosevelt carried the fight against his critics who claimed his program was a foreign one undermining the American system. At Chicago, in mid-October, Roosevelt unleashed his most effective attack of the campaign upon his Liberty League critics in this withering sarcasm:

> Some of these people really forget how sick they were. But I know how sick they were. I have their fever charts. I know how the knees of all of our rugged individualists were trembling four years ago and how their hearts fluttered. They came to Washington in great numbers. Washington did not look like a dangerous bureaucracy to them then. Oh, no! It looked like an emergency hospital. All of the distinguished patients wanted two things — a quick hypodermic to end the pain and a course of treatment to cure the disease. They wanted them in a hurry; we gave them both. And now most of the patients seem to be doing very nicely. Some of them are even well enough to throw their crutches at the doctor.

In a more serious vein at Chicago the President reiterated his faith in the free enterprise system ("I believe, I have always believed, and I will always believe in private enterprise as the backbone of economic well-being in the United States . . .") and in the belief that the New Deal had saved that system ("You have heard about how antagonistic to business this Administration is supposed to be. . . . The answer to that is the record of what we have done. It was this Administration which saved the system of private profit and free enterprise after it had been dragged to the brink of ruin by these same leaders who now try to scare you").

In his radio address to the businessmen's dinners a week later, the President returned to the theme of the New Deal as savior of the private enterprise system: "If the Administration had had the slightest inclination to change that system, all that it would have had to do was to fold its hands and wait — let the system continue to default to itself and to the public."

After a quick trip through Pennsylvania the last week in October, "a last whirl" in Maryland, and a look in on Wilmington ("just to assure myself that the du Ponts are not broke," he wrote Senator Robinson), the President ended his campaign at Madison Square Garden. This last speech before the election was a "gloves off, no holds barred" speech, the mocking, teasing, ridiculing speech of a Roosevelt confident of victory, a defiant challenge, a gauge of battle that he knew the enemy could not pick up.

"For twelve years this Nation was afflicted with hearnothing, see-nothing, do-nothing Government," the President charged. "The Nation looked to Government but the Government looked away." And then in words of feigned reproach: "Nine mocking years with the golden calf and three long years of the scourge! Nine crazy years at the ticker and three long years in the breadlines! Nine mad years of mirage and three long years of despair!" And finally the bold defiance: "Powerful influences strive today to restore that kind of government with its doctrine that that Government is best which is most indifferent. . . . Never before in all history have these forces been so united against one candidate as they stand today. They are unanimous in their hatred for me — and I welcome their hatred." [11]

XII

In September, League support of the Republican candidate appeared to bear fruit.

For many years political mythology had it that "as Maine goes, so goes the nation." That the voters of Maine, unlike the voters of the rest of the country, went to the polls in September rather than November made the myth possible; chance had taken care of the rest. Victory in Maine, then, was a thing to be cherished for its psychological advantage if nothing else. Although there was little doubt on either side that the Republicans would carry Maine, the leadership went all out to make the victory as impressive as possible. To satisfy appeals for help from local Republicans, Landon made a major speech at Portland on the Saturday before the election, as though the outcome hung in the balance.

Liberty Leaguers poured thousands of dollars into the Maine campaign, and others worked tirelessly on behalf of the Republican ticket in a victory the impressiveness of which was somewhat lessened by a Senate investigation of campaign expenditures there. In a preliminary report the committee chairman, Senator Augustine Lonergan of Connecticut, revealed that the heaviest individual contributors appeared to be: Pierre du Pont, $5000; Lammot du Pont, $5000; Irénée du Pont, $5000; A. Felix du Pont, $5000; Henry B. du Pont, $2500; Alfred P. Sloan, $5000; J. P. Morgan, $5000; A. Atwater Kent, $1000; John D. Archbold, $2500; and Ann Archbold, $2500. As the investigation went on it was learned that the du Ponts had even spent considerably more in Maine.

Joseph B. Ely and James A. Reed campaigned vigorously, their noteworthy efforts moving Landon to write them identical letters: "Millions of American citizens are grateful for the help you gave in the Maine campaign. . . . Not only were your speeches helpful, but more important perhaps was the personal participation of a man of your national reputation."

Democrats gloated that the election in Maine definitely linked Landon with the American Liberty League. "It is . . . interesting to note," said Farley, "the generous contributions made by the backers of the American Liberty League, in view of the fact that a statement was recently issued by that organization indicating their neutrality in this campaign." [12]

XIII

The realization that Roosevelt would win re-election in 1936 dawned at different times on those who opposed him. Soon after the Cleveland convention Benjamin F. Anderson of the Chase National Bank and Colonel Leonard P. Ayres of the Cleveland Trust Company called on Landon in Topeka. Business was getting better every month, they told him in answer to his questions. "I knew then," said Landon, "that I was beaten. I always had my feet on the ground the rest of the campaign."

Late in September, National Chairman Hamilton was having lunch with David Lawrence and Albert Lasker in Chicago. Hamilton threw cold water on their faint enthusiasm by predicting that Landon would carry "only six or seven states." In his last report the Sunday before the election, Hamilton realistically told the Kansas governor he would win five states (Maine, Vermont, South Dakota, Nebraska, Kansas) at the most.

Shortly after the election Jouett Shouse and Robert J. Cuddihy, editor of the *Literary Digest*, were aboard a revenue cutter headed out to meet the *Roma* on its return voyage from Europe. Their conversation turned to the presidential poll conducted by the *Literary Digest*, a poll so disastrously inaccurate (it predicted a Landon victory) that it was usually cited as the cause for suspending publication of the weekly news magazine. Cuddihy insisted that the poll was correct at the time that it was made, in mid-August. As a precaution, Cuddihy ran a recheck in normally Democratic strongholds, notably the Scranton-Wilkes-Barre area, but the results were the same. Landon was in the lead. Despite the eventual outcome, said Cuddihy, Roosevelt was trailing Landon at least until late in the summer.

Later, Shouse had occasion to mention his encounter with Cuddihy to Emil Hurja. An editor and politician of some experience, Hurja had come to the Chicago Democratic convention in 1932 as head of the Alaskan delegation pledged to Roosevelt. After the convention Hurja joined the team as statistician and executive director of the Democratic National Committee, a job he filled until 1937. Hurja partially corroborated Cuddihy's findings. The polls Hurja made, he told Shouse, had also shown the President to be in trouble. (In July Hurja had said privately: ". . . the situation is very serious . . . the President receiving slightly more than fifty per cent, but with Landon leading on electoral votes.")

Whether Roosevelt was ever in danger of defeat is the kind of question that starts fights in barrooms; one may have strong opinions on the matter but there is probably no accurate way of proving them. At least the Liberty League began the year believing that Roosevelt could be beaten. But certainty gradually changed to uncertainty, then to doubt, and by late September the League too was convinced that theirs was a lost cause.

On September 24, Raoul Desvernine read to the Executive Committee a resolution of the Lawyers' Committee urging that the Liberty League continue after the election "regardless of the outcome." The Executive Committee agreed unanimously that the League should continue, and a committee was appointed (Irénée du Pont, Grayson M.-P. Murphy, Raoul Desvernine) to bring back recommendations concerning its future activities. The meaning of this move was perfectly clear — the League was beaten; Roosevelt would be re-elected.

And re-elected he was. On November 11, Farley and Roddan (and Ambrose O'Connell, First Assistant Postmaster General) left New York harbor for a vacation trip to Ireland. They had earned it. Just ten days earlier, Farley had sat down at the New York Democratic headquarters and written his prediction for the headquarters pool: "Landon will only carry Maine and Vermont. 7 electoral votes." What did it matter that Maine and Vermont had eight electoral votes between them? The incredible had happened. Polling over eleven million votes more than the opposition, Roosevelt had overwhelmed Landon by 523 to 8.

It was over. All over. Landon, Knox, the Republican party had failed. The Liberty League, Al Smith, John W. Davis, Joseph Ely, Jim Reed, the du Ponts, the anti-New Deal forces had failed. Everything — money, propaganda, hatred — had failed. The symbol of that failure came on election day. Al Smith passed on his way to the polls, jaunty as ever, the over-sized cigar at a defiant angle. Smith passed by. And the people booed.[13]

9

WHEELS WITHIN WHEELS

What was the connection between these organizations
whose business it was to attack the New Deal?
New York Times

But looking back on the results achieved, they must now
find very little satisfaction in what they got for their money.
New York Times

As an organization, the American Liberty League under the
leadership of Jouett Shouse had fought Roosevelt and the New
Deal relentlessly and, for the most part, fairly. It was the behavior of a few individual members that reflected unfavorably
upon the League, that gave it an undeserved black eye. Of the
many anti-New Deal organizations which they chose to support, some members of the Liberty League showed a dismaying
lack of judgment and discrimination, a fault the Administration
was quick to exploit.

In June 1936, in his opening remarks to the Democratic National Convention in Philadelphia, Democratic National Chairman, James Farley, had charged: "Behind the Republican ticket
is the crew of the du Pont Liberty League and their allies,
which have so far financed every undercover agency that has
disgraced American politics with their appeals to race prejudice,
religious intolerance and personalities so gross that they had to

be repudiated by the regular Republican organization." The same day the League's Executive Committee had answered Farley with a formal statement: "Such false and defamatory language goes beyond the limit of self-respect and cannot remain unnoticed. It is incredible that any man, no matter what his background, occupying high official position would in any circumstance make such representation without convincing evidence."

Despite the League's disclaimer, Farley's meaning was lost on no one except those who never read the newspapers. For weeks before the convention the Black Committee had been making headlines, headlines that went a long way toward explaining the sudden deflation of the Liberty League in the spring and summer of 1936.[1]

II

The committee headed by the Alabama senator Hugo L. Black was created in July 1935 to investigate lobbying activities in connection with the Public Utility Holding Company Act, better known as the Wheeler-Rayburn Act.

The Wheeler-Rayburn Act had resulted from extensive studies by the Federal Trade Commission, a special investigation conducted by the House Committee on Interstate and Foreign Commerce, and the survey by the National Power Policy Committee appointed by Roosevelt in 1934.

The findings of these separate studies showed that the holding company idea had spread rapidly during the decade of normalcy. By 1925, holding companies controlled nearly two thirds of the electric utility industry. Seven years later, thirteen holding companies controlled 75 per cent of the industry and the "big three" — United Corporation, Electric Bond and Share Company, and the Insull interests — controlled 40 per cent.

With their interests in natural gas pipelines, coal mines, construction companies, banks, and related affiliations, the holding companies had long since ceased to be a device that could be controlled by the states.

Enacting the Wheeler-Rayburn bill fulfilled a pledge in the Democratic platform of 1932; but it was not accomplished without a struggle. The opposition centered on that provision of the bill — the "death sentence," it was called — which required holding companies to dissolve if within a five-year period they could not demonstrate that they had effected economies in the businesses they controlled. The Senate passed the bill in June 1935 without serious trouble, but the House refused to accept the "death sentence" provision. Only a neatly timed special message from the President, the psychological pressure of his first Fireside Chat in 1935 ("I consider this legislation a positive recovery measure"), and two trips to conference produced the desired results. The "death clause" stayed and the Supreme Court subsequently upheld its constitutionality.

The holding companies lobbied relentlessly against the bill, pouring more than three and a half million dollars into the fight to defeat it — more than was normally spent by a political party in a presidential campaign. In July a House committee (the O'Connor Committee) began an investigation into lobbying, an investigation brought on by Ralph Brewster of Maine, who claimed that Tom Corcoran, co-author of the bill with Benjamin Cohen, had threatened to have construction stopped on the Passamaquoddy Dam if Brewster voted against the death-sentence provision. The lobbying apparently was not all one-sided.

The same day (July 2) that Brewster made his charge in the House, Senator Black introduced a resolution asking for a Senate investigation into lobbying activities. What had brought the matter to a head was the publishing in the Washington *Daily News* of the House vote on the "death sentence" the previous day. This was the first time on record that names of congress-men participating in a teller vote had been published. Black wanted to know why. With an investigation of the same thing being conducted simultaneously by both Houses (and these before final action had been taken on the bill), it was little wonder that Representative Samuel Pettengill felt led to say what everyone else was thinking: "It is all very confusing. One feels as bewildered as a pup with a flea on each ear." [2]

III

The Black investigation, which lasted from July 1935 to June 1936, unfolded an incredible tale of lobbying, pressure politics, and intrigue.

The American Liberty League entered the picture in January 1936. All but lost amid the ballyhoo of the Smith Liberty League speech was an announcement by Black that his committee had sent questionnaires to business leaders inquiring about their contributions to the League, a seemingly natural move since members of the League, by writing to congressmen, had displayed no little interest in the Wheeler-Rayburn Act. One of the recipients of these letters, Scott Lucas of Illinois, made a speech in the House protesting the letter he had received, which congratulated him for his vote against the death-sentence clause and commended him for asserting his independence from executive domination ("defying the most ruthless pressure"). Said Lucas: "The League revels in our independence and gratitude if we see eye to eye with its members upon legislative matters in which they as individuals are vitally interested."

It was clear to most observers that the Black Committee had more in mind than asking questions about lobbying against the utilities bill; the timing was a little too pat. The *New York Times* predicted that the committee would attempt to discredit the League by probing its organizational relatives: "What was the connection between these organizations whose business it was to attack the New Deal?" The League also sensed what was coming. At its regular meeting in New York the Executive Committee advised its members that they did not have to answer the Black Committee's questionnaires.

Between March and June 1936 more than a dozen organizations were invited to Room 357 of the Old Senate Office Building to squirm under the publicity spotlight. The list included: the Crusaders, Sentinels of the Republic, American Taxpayers' League, Farmers' Independence Council, the Southern Committee to Uphold the Constitution, American Federation of Utility Investors, National Committee on Monetary Policy, League for Industrial Rights, Minute Men and Women of Today, National Economy League, New York State Economic Council, Repeal Associates, and Women Investors of America. The American Liberty League was itself never called. It did not have to be. Tried in absentia, it was declared guilty by association.[3]

IV

If the Black Committee seemed to prove anything, it was that this galaxy of anti-Administration organizations derived most of its membership, its support, and its economic nourishment from the same source, a small, closely knit group of wealthy citizens, banks, and corporations. During the eighteen months preceding the investigation these organizations (including the Liberty League) received more than a million dollars. These were only the contributions of which the committee could find record; the actual total was probably higher. Of the amounts collected by the various organizations roughly 90 per cent came from the same people, which need not have implied anything wrong any more than that the same people contribute to a number of different charities. What made the picture unwholesome were the questionable activities of some of these organizations.

The Crusaders were fairly typical. Like the Liberty League, the organization had been founded (in 1929) to fight prohibition; or, as the charter put it, "to investigate, study and analyze the effect of sumptuary laws upon the people." After repeal, it had become a pressure group agitating for constitutionalism, a balanced budget, sound money, and waging war against "forces destroying liberty and individual freedom."

Its program, although on a more modest scale, was quite like that of the Liberty League. This duplication of effort led to discussion of a merger. A merger with the Liberty League "would be no surprise," said Edgar Allan Poe, Jr., commander of the Maryland battalion of the Crusaders, late in August 1934. The national commander, Fred G. Clark, talked with Shouse on several occasions about joining forces, and Shouse took up the matter with the League Executive Committee. At one of the meetings late in September a three-member committee (Shouse, Raskob, and Mrs. Sabin) was empowered to negotiate with the Crusaders and "fix the relations between the two organizations."

The merger never came off and the two groups operated independently, although with a closely interlocking leadership. Serving on the national advisory council of the Crusaders were Colby M. Chester, John W. Davis, Sewell L. Avery, and William L. Clayton, all of whom were members of the Executive Committee of the Liberty League. Other advisory council members were Edwin Kemmerer, Alfred P. Sloan, Robert L. Lund, George M. Moffett, and Elton Hoyt II, who were also members of the Liberty League's National Advisory Council.

Liberty Leaguers likewise provided much of the financial support of the Crusaders, the Black Committee listing the following Leaguers who had given from five to ten thousand dollars each to the Crusaders: Edward F. Hutton, General Foods Corporation; George M. Moffett, president of Corn Products Refining Company; J. Howard Pew, president of the Sun Oil Company; Ernest T. Weir, Weirton Steel Company; and Alfred P. Sloan of General Motors. Du Pont contributions, from Irénée and Lammot, exceeded all others in size. The Liberty League became directly involved in the financing of the Crusaders in 1934, when Jouett Shouse revealed that his organization had given the Crusaders nine thousand dollars.

Principally through its radio program, "The Radio Voice of the Crusaders," the organization fought the Wheeler-Rayburn Act, TVA, AAA, and other New Deal measures. As the "voice," National Commander Clark made nearly ninety radio speeches that cost the Crusaders some $148,000. James F. Bell, president of General Mills, figured most prominently in raising the radio fund, a job made easier by the generous contributions of Liberty Leaguers, of whom seven (Sewell Avery, Irénée du Pont, Edward F. Hutton, Ernest T. Weir, George M. Moffett, H. B. Earhart, and Howard Heinz) contributed a fourth of the total.

The Crusaders seemed to operate on the assumption that "to inform, educate, and instruct" included propagandizing against Administration legislation that was inimicable to backers of the organization, although they stressed the effect of these measures on the "average citizen." "I am with you on your opposition to the utility, banking, and AAA bills," wrote Fred W. Blaisdell, director of the central division, to Clark in May 1935, "but that opposition . . . should be based primarily on what these bills are going to do . . . to the pocketbooks of the average man who is holding a job. We have got to make Jim Smith in Wichita understand that what these 'birds' in Washington are doing is affecting his pocketbook, otherwise he won't stir his stumps in opposition." The same correspondent inquired about another issue on which the people needed educating. "What about taking a crack at the Wagner Bill?" he asked. "Our friends in Detroit are after me hot and heavy for the Crusaders to get on the Wagner Bill." He was aware, he said, of the risk of opposition from organized labor; but he believed that "a sound argument can be developed" proving that the Wagner Act was "the most dangerous measure to labor itself of any bill now pending in Congress." [4]

v

Born during the Red scare after World War I, the Sentinels of the Republic were a group composed largely of wealthy and near-wealthy ardent patriots dedicated to stopping the spread of communism and the increasing centralization of power in the federal government, and to promoting "the preservation of the fundamental principles of the Constitution," and "a return to American principles." Their motto: "Every citizen a Sentinel! Every home a sentry-box!"

Up to 1935, the Sentinels had fought the Child Labor Amendment, the Sheppard-Towner Maternity Act, and creation of a federal Department of Education. Meanwhile, they had "card indexed more than 2000 radical propagandists, making it comparatively easy to check their movements and counteract their activities."

In 1935, Raymond Pitcairn of the Pittsburgh Plate Glass Company became national chairman and active head of the Sentinels. Under his leadership the organization lobbied against social security, the Wagner Act, the Guffey-Snyder Bituminous Coal Conservation Act, and the Wheeler-Rayburn Act. Its greatest success was in winning repeal of the "pink slip" clause of the income tax laws, which had provided for publicity of personal incomes. A spokesman for the organization also suggested repeal of the Sixteenth Amendment and the "general welfare clause" through its syndicated editorial service to more than 1300 small newspapers. "The American ideal would be achieved," argued the Sentinel W. A. Wilson of the Yale University faculty, by deleting one phrase from the Constitution. "My own proposal would be to strike out the general welfare clause in Article I, Section 8."

At the time that the organization came under the investigation of the Black Committee they were vigorously supporting the candidacy of Colonel Henry Breckinridge in the presidential primaries, largely through the showing of an animated cartoon, *The Amateur Fire Brigade*. In February 1936 the Ohio State Division of Film Censorship barred it on grounds that it "encourages disrespect" for the office of the President. In it Roosevelt was depicted as a boy astride the Democratic donkey and as the engineer of the broken-down New Deal train. At another point the Administration was pictured as a house built of alphabet blocks. The house was in flames and the amateur brigade, the New Deal administrators, rushed to save it, but too late.

It developed that finances for the showing of *The Amateur Fire Brigade* (the Sentinels were trying to raise $360,000 for the purpose) were discussed at a meeting of Liberty Leaguers in New York in December 1935, a meeting presided over by John Raskob. The film received a private showing at the Palm Beach home of William F. Kenny, where Al Smith was a guest for about a month after his Liberty League speech. Smith, Thomas L. Chadbourne, former senator James A. Reed, Edward T. Stotesbury, Jay Cooke II, and other Liberty Leaguers "were delighted" and "most sympathetic." Chadbourne, who strongly urged League financing for the film, met later with C. A. Berry, representative of the Sentinels, in New York to discuss the matter further. There was no concrete evidence that the League ever contributed toward the showing of the cartoon, but there were some other interesting by-products of the investigation into the Sentinels' activities.

Correspondence between Chadbourne and Berry subpoenaed by the committee from the files of the Sentinels revealed that it was Chadbourne who had extended the original invitation to Governor Smith to speak at the Liberty League dinner in January 1936. Smith had at first declined, but later accepted with the comment that the League needed him "to clear it of its financial taint." Besides, said Smith, he felt that he was well enough known so that he could "use any board from which to spring back into the public eye."

Letters exchanged by W. Cleveland Runyon of Plainfield, New Jersey, and the Sentinel president, Alexander Lincoln, a Boston attorney and Republican member of the Massachusetts State Board of Tax Appeals, suggested a darker aspect of the Sentinels' interest. Runyon wrote Lincoln in pessimistic tones complaining of the Jewish influence in the New Deal Administration and declaring that "the old-line Americans of $1200 a year want a Hitler." To this Lincoln replied that the "Jewish threat" was "a real one." Lincoln later denounced all forms of autocratic government, "whether they be communism, bolshevism, fascism, or Hitlerism," and the commander-in-chief of the Jewish War Veterans wrote to Lincoln that after investigation his organization had concluded that Lincoln did not "entertain any antipathy against the Jewish people or any other racial minority," but the harm had been done to the League by the attitudes and association suggested by the Black investigation.

Shouse denied that the Liberty League had any connection with the Sentinels of the Republic: "The description of the Sentinels of the Republic as 'one of the interlocking branches of the Liberty League' is equally untrue and its falsity is equally well known." But the denial could not change certain facts about League members. Among the financial supporters of the Sentinels were such Liberty Leaguers as Irénée du Pont, A. B. Echols, a du Pont vice-president, Alfred P. Sloan, J. Howard Pew, and Edward T. Stotesbury. In October 1935 the Sentinels sponsored a rally in New York, where a crowd of more than five thousand heard Representative James W. Wadsworth, a director of the Liberty League, score the planned economy of the New Deal. And buried in the mass of correspondence subpoenaed by the Black Committee was the exchange of letters between Lincoln and Liberty League treasurer, William F. Stayton, in which Stayton proposed that the two groups merge their efforts, a proposal, however, that never got beyond the suggestion stage. The connection had been established in the public mind, if not in fact.[5]

VI

The American Taxpayers' League, using a variety of names, had a history that antedated World War I. At the time of the Black inquiry it had approximately 3000 members, paying annual dues of $10 a year. The brain behind the Taxpayers' League was the veteran conservative, James A. Arnold, whose activities had come under the scrutiny of the Senate as early as 1918. In those days Arnold was associated with John Henry Kirby and Vance Muse (of whom more shall be heard presently) in raising a quarter of a million dollars to fight Wilson's New Freedom legislation, notably the Adamson Act. During the 1920's Arnold was manager of the Taxpayers' League and a group of related organizations numbering the Southern Tariff Association and National Council of State Legislators.

In 1929 Arnold was again investigated, this time by the Caraway Committee. The record showed that Arnold had raised nearly a million dollars since 1926, most of it from a small group of utility and industrial concerns and persons prominent in them, including W. L. Mellon of Pittsburgh, the Van Sweringen brothers, the Insull interests, William Wrigley, Jr., and the P. A. B. Widener estate. Caraway was not impressed with Arnold's activities, describing them as "all aliases, under which one J. A. Arnold operates ostensibly to influence Congressional legislation, but in fact for the purpose of making a living for himself. . . ." How businessmen "of ordinary sagacity" could be hoodwinked into contributing to Arnold's organizations was "entirely inexplicable to your committee," Caraway wrote in the final report.

Caraway's appraisal of Arnold's activities may have been correct then, but not later. Actually, Arnold had unusual success in representing the views of his small group of financial backers. The purpose of the Taxpayers' League, he testified, was to make "the nation tax-conscious." Specifically, the program was to encourage state sales taxes, while agitating for reduction of income and corporation taxes and elimination of gift taxes. The object in making the country tax conscious, he told the committee, was to get the government to "stop spending and stop taxing." The Taxpayers' League claimed credit for the passage of sales taxes in Illinois and Mississippi, and was campaigning against the AAA and its processing taxes at the time of the Black hearings.

Black found that Arnold had collected $45,000 in 1935, mostly from Andrew Mellon, Irénée du Pont, other du Ponts, Charles A. Munroe, president of Columbia Oil and Gas Corporation, Herbert L. Pratt, and Parmalee Prentice, a son-in-law of John D. Rockefeller, Sr. This was in addition to free press and radio time. The Taxpayers' League was on radio for seventy-seven weeks, using Hearst's New York station, WINS, and the National Broadcasting Company facilities.

When questioned about his connections with Hearst through Bainbridge Colby, Arnold at first denied receiving help from either one. The committee refreshed his faulty memory by reading into the record a telegram sent by him to Colby in March 1935: "Will be in New York Monday. Think it important that we enroll at least 10,000 members within a very few days. The support you are giving it demands that sort of a base."

Once again, to those who read the newspapers the Liberty League, through prominent members, was associated with the rich, who seemed to be organized against the interests of the common man, who in the long run had the votes.[6]

VII

The subject of telegrams gave the Liberty League a limited opportunity to salvage something from the Black investigation. On March 6 it was learned that agents of the Federal Communications Commission had made copies of some 13,000 messages in the Washington offices of Western Union which they turned over to the committee. In addition, the committee had issued blanket subpoenas for the telegrams of certain individuals, business firms, and organizations, including the American Liberty League.

That same evening Shouse took to the air. The Black Committee could have any information it wanted from the Liberty League, provided that it asked properly, said Shouse, because "there are no skeletons in its closet." But the committee had not proceeded properly. Its action, he contended, violated the constitutional guarantee against illegal search and seizure. To be valid the subpoena must specify the nature of the documents required in such manner that "it is apparent that the documents seized have a bearing on the subject Congress is investigating." Shouse, conjecturing that President Roosevelt must have been personally involved (since the FCC was used to get the telegrams for Black), called upon his audience to combat the committee's "terrorism" by "mounting a mammoth petition of protest against this monstrous invasion of our fundamental rights." Lewis Schwellenbach, a member of the committee, answered Shouse in a radio speech on April 2. Only certain telegrams received between February 1 and December 1, 1935, were being checked, some 22,000 in all, explained Schwellenbach, not every telegram (which would have numbered about 14,000,000). The sensitivity about telegrams was understandable, said the Democratic senator from Washington, since the committee had unearthed evidence showing that lobbyists had used names from telephone and city directories to sign some 100,000 unauthorized telegrams trying to influence congressional action on the Wheeler-Rayburn bill.

Shouse's plea did not fall on deaf ears. In May, the Liberty League sent to Vice-President Garner petitions bearing 55,000 signatures protesting the telegram seizures. The figure was probably higher, because an indeterminate number of petitions was sent directly to individual senators without first going to Liberty League headquarters. Signatures were obtained from every state, 13,600 being from New York City.

Meanwhile, William Randolph Hearst filed suit in the District of Columbia Supreme Court for an injunction to prevent further seizures. Hearst, in fact, brought two suits. The first, against Western Union, became a moot case when the company decided not to contest it. Hearst then sued the Black Committee. Handling the case for the offended publisher was the Chicago firm of Winston, Strawn and Shaw, old allies of the AAPA and more recently associated with the League. Ralph Shaw, one of the firm's partners, headed the Illinois branch of the Liberty League, and was a member of the National Lawyers' Committee. His partner, Silas Strawn, one-time president of the United States Chamber of Commerce, retained Frank J. Hogan (also a member of the National Lawyers' Committee) to seek the injunction from the Washington court.

Confiscating the messages was not done lightly. On three separate occasions the Senate discussed the matter, the past practices of Senate committees, the form of subpoenas, the propriety of the seizures, and other aspects of the problem. "If I had any idea," said Senator Black, upon hearing of Hearst's suit, "that any judge would issue an injunction against this body, the Senate, getting certain evidence, I would long ago have introduced a bill taking away the power to do so."

For those who brought the suit Black had only words of contempt. When the question of a name came up for "a certain widespread organization in America" it had been suggested that it be called the League to Protect Property, said Black, and "straightway came back the reply, 'That will never do.'" They had to have a name that would "deceive the people," so they called it the Liberty League.

Black, who was soon to be a judge himself, was not of one mind with Justice Alfred Wheat. On March 11, Wheat granted a temporary injunction, enjoining Western Union from handing over telegraphic correspondence to the committee. In invalidating the committee's earlier action Judge Wheat upheld Hearst's claim to protection under the Fourth Amendment, ruling that the blanket subpoenas went "way beyond any legitimate exercise of the right of the subpoena *duces tecum.*" Hearst made front-page headlines of his victory over the "Blackguard Committee." Shouse, in a radio address, congratulated the court for blocking "the opening wedge to censorship of the press," and suggested that the Senate investigate the activities of the Black Committee. Former senator James A. Reed of Missouri thought the ruling was a delightful embarrassment of Roosevelt: "That seizure is the high point among the infamies of the New Deal. It is so contemptible a thing as naturally to suggest its author."

The court decision brought immediate congressional reprisals. The Senate, by appropriating an additional $12,500 to continue the investigation, in effect endorsed the committee's activities. On March 27, to curb the kind of practices uncovered by the Black inquiry, the House passed the Lobbyist Registration Act, requiring regular and detailed reports of contributions and expenditures by persons and organizations engaged in lobbying activities.

The court injunction had little effect on the course of the Black investigation; but as a diversion it did provide some satisfaction to the ones being investigated.[7]

VIII

In the wide variety of anti-New Deal organizations receiving their support the Liberty Leaguers did not overlook the farmer. The leaders of the Farmers' Independence Council of America celebrated the first anniversary of their organization by appearing before the Black Committee. Organized in April 1935, in the agricultural environment of Washington's Raleigh Hotel, the Council set out to protect "the freedom of every farmer to operate his farm according to his own best judgment." To its twelve-point Declaration of Principles a thirteenth was added when Stanley F. Morse, an original founder of the Council, admitted that one objective was "to get rid of the New Deal." This, it developed, meant financing a few radio addresses and trying to influence leaders of Young Republican Clubs in the farm states against the "tyranny of the AAA."

As the investigation got under way Shouse emphatically denied any connection between the Council and the Liberty League. "Whatever may be the attempt of the Black Committee to connect the American Liberty League with the Farmers' Independence Council," insisted Shouse, "the league had no hand in the organization of the council; no part in the financing of the council; and neither has had nor now has any connection of any kind with council."

The facts seemed to suggest otherwise. The president of the Farmers' Independence Council was Daniel D. Casement, Kansas cattleman and member of the Liberty League Advisory Council. Stanley Morse, who described himself as an agricultural engineering consultant for the Liberty League, was first vice-president and general manager.

During its brief history the Council maintained headquarters first in Washington, later in Chicago. In Washington it had shared office space with the Liberty League on the tenth floor of the National Press Building and received its mail and telegrams in care of the League. When Morse moved on to Chicago he again used Liberty League headquarters there.

Morse swore that Shouse was not consulted about the organization of the Council; but that before moving to Chicago, he talked it over with Shouse and "told him what we were proposing to do." He also admitted that, in planning the Council's activities, Council officials conferred regularly with Shouse, Lammot du Pont, "and other officials of du Pont and General Motors." In the important matter of money, Liberty Leaguers contributing to the Farmers' Independence Council included such dirt farmers as Lammot du Pont, Winthrop W. Aldrich, Alfred P. Sloan, Cornelius Bliss, A. B. Echols, C. H. Haskell, and others.[8]

IX

"Fat, freckled, old" was the way *Time* Magazine described John Henry Kirby, chairman of the Southern Committee to Uphold the Constitution and inveterate organizer of patriotic causes. *Time* might have added that Kirby, onetime president of the National Association of Manufacturers, was also broke. Once wealthy (oil and lumber) even by Texas standards, Kirby was ruined by the depression. In 1933 he declared himself bankrupt.

His penchant for organizations with a patriotic flavor had first gained him national attention in 1929 when the Caraway Committee investigated two organizations of which he was president, the Southern Tariff Association and the National Council of State Legislators. Through them, said the committee's report, Kirby "heads a lobby operating in every state of the union."

Kirby admitted that his organizations paid all of the expenses of state and municipal officials to meetings (six of which were held in 1929) for the purpose of creating the proper sentiment toward tariff and tax legislation. With his associate James A. Arnold, Kirby had tried to influence President Hoover — "stiffening the backbone of the President," Arnold had called it — in favor of higher tariff rates by getting "interested parties from widely scattered parts of the country" to bring pressure.

At the time of the Black investigation, Kirby, besides being chairman of the Southern Committee to Uphold the Constitution, was on the executive committee of the Sentinels of the Republic, the Texas Tax Relief Committee, and the Order of American Patriots. The Southern Committee, Texas Taxpayers' League, Texas Tax Relief Committee, Texas Election Managers' Association, and the Order of American Patriots all occupied office space in the Kirby Building in Houston. (Built and owned by Reconstruction Finance Corporation chairman Jesse Jones, the building was named in honor of Kirby.)

In September 1935, in a letter sent out from its branch office in Washington to the more than five thousand members, the Southern Committee to Uphold the Constitution stated its purpose thus: ". . . has been formed to combat encroachment against American liberties by the New Deal. . . . Every informed American knows that if Mr. Roosevelt is re-elected in 1936, the sovereign rights of the states will be completely demolished and power over all their affairs little and big will be consolidated in Washington. . . . We are organizing the Southern states as rapidly as we can." Less than a month before it was called before the Black Committee, the Southern Committee bought full-page advertising space in the New York *Herald Tribune* and other newspapers. Under the caption "Liberty must bow her head when such pledges are evaded," the Southern Committee berated Roosevelt and accused him of violating his oath of office for advising the Congress to pass the Bituminous Coal Conservation

Act even though it might have misgivings about its constitutionality.

It was Kirby and the Southern Committee along with Gerald L. K. Smith, who were, said Senator Black, "the guiding spirits" of Eugene Talmadge's Grass Roots Convention in Macon, Georgia, late in January 1936. Much of the financial backing for this abortive anti-Roosevelt movement, as already mentioned, came from prominent Liberty Leaguers, notably John Raskob, Alfred P. Sloan, and the du Ponts. Kirby's assistant, Vance Muse, a tall, loose-jointed Texan, testified that he explained to Raskob, Pierre du Pont, and others the purpose of the Macon meeting and that "they approved."

The committee inquired whether their approval included circulation of the "nigger pictures." Muse admitted that the pictures slandering Mrs. Roosevelt were printed at his direction, that they were distributed to the delegates at the Macon meeting, and were later mailed throughout the South by the Texas Election Managers' Association from lists provided by the Southern Committee to Uphold the Constitution. When asked if Raskob or any of the others had objected to the pictures, Muse said they did not know about them. Senator Schwellenbach, reminding Muse that the pictures had appeared in most newspapers at the time of the Macon meeting, observed dryly: "It is apparent they did not disapprove, for I note that since the convention Mr. Sloan gave you $1000 and Henry du Pont $500." Once again, prominent Liberty Leaguers were put in an unenviable light through association and contribution.[9]

X

The Liberty League had additional justification for being annoyed with Senator Black. Late in March 1936, Senator Robert M. La Follette, Jr., proposed an investigation of alleged violations of the Wagner Act. The Senate approved his resolution and Black appointed La Follette, along with Murphy of Iowa and Thomas of Utah, to a permanent subcommittee of Black's own Committee on Education and Labor, with La Follette as chairman. Thus began an investigation that eventually took the committee from coast to coast and lasted until 1940.

On April 15, La Follette's committee gathered in Room 412 of the Old Senate Office Building to interrogate Heber Blankenhorn, an industrial economist for the National Labor Relations Board. (On the floor below, the Black Committee was plying officers of the Farmers' Independence Council with embarrassing questions.) Blankenhorn had an ugly story to tell, a shocking story, but one that was not new.

It was the story of an industry without stocks or bonds, without inventories, without annual reports, or dividends, an industry without known employers or employees. It was a secret industry to spy on unions, propagandize company-dominated unions, betray unions to employers, supply strikebreakers and *provocateurs*, and infiltrate unions with traitors — all of which meant that, despite whatever protection labor thought it had from Section 7a of the National Industrial Recovery Act and the Wagner Act, management had espionage and violence with which to combat them.

Blankenhorn produced a chart listing nearly two hundred agencies whose exclusive or primary business was industrial strikebreaking and espionage. Some of these operated independently, but most were organized into about a dozen national or regional systems with branch offices in every major city and industrial area. These agencies, according to Blankenhorn, employed no less than 40,000 agents and did a business of at least $80,000,000 annually.

The $80,000,000 paid for more than strong-armed strikebreakers. Some two hundred firms purchased through these agencies more than 60 per cent of all the tear gas, vomiting gas, submachine guns, revolvers, gas grenade guns, billy clubs, and armored cars sold in the United States — more than was bought by the United States Army.

Union espionage and strikebreaking, agreed officials of the National Labor Relations Board, were "the principal method of frustration" of the Wagner Act. The evidence seemed to bear that out, prompting the La Follette Committee to write in its preliminary report: "Wage-earners, attempting to take advantage of their legal rights to organize, find that to do so imperils their right to peaceable assembly, to freedom of speech, and to vote, no less than to keep their jobs. . . ." "Public records," the report continued, "show the close organizational connections between professional spy and strikebreaking agencies, plant munitioning concerns and a league of lawyers sponsoring concerted obstructiveness in the courts. . . ." The practice of not mentioning names, an occupational disease shared by government officials and Broadway columnists, was here followed, but many concluded that the committee was talking about the National Lawyers' Committee of the American Liberty League.

Again without mentioning names (complete details were, of course, contained in the printed records of the hearings), the report related how the third-largest shoe manufacturer in the United States hired the largest strikebreaker in the Midwest. When called in for questioning by the National Labor Relations Board, the strikebreaker defied the board, and was defended in doing so by the legal counsel of the shoe company, a member of the Liberty League Lawyers' Committee. A large trucking company hired a detective agency and was defended in doing so in hearings before the NLRB by another eminent member of the Liberty League Lawyers' Committee. ("We see no reflection in any way in the employment of detectives.") In Blankenhorn's words, another member of the Liberty League Lawyers' Committee appeared before the NLRB "defending a steel company which is buying tear gas from [a] chemical company and spies from [a] detective agency, whose offices interlock with the Liberty League lawyer."

Certainly the Liberty League and its Lawyers' Committee did not advocate labor violence and espionage or endorse the questionable motives of some of the anti-Administration organizations flourishing in 1936. Their public statements were always dignified, but were properly indignant and alarmed at the treachery of the New Deal; they worshiped the Constitution and law and order. But the Black and La Follette Committees were saying, and saying eloquently, what the League dared not: that in the period covered by the Black investigation more than a million dollars were contributed to the League and thirteen other organizations; that over 90 per cent of this sum came from a small group of rich men closely identified with the Liberty League; that some of this money was used to finance the most reprehensible kind of activities; that not a few of the League's members were powerful in companies that employed vicious tactics ("a dirty business," the NLRB called it) in fighting unionism; that prominent attorneys from the Liberty League Lawyers' Committee not only supported them in it but devised arguments to show that it was unconstitutional for government to do anything about it.

The investigations would have been embarrassing at any time. In an election year they proved devastating; ". . . looking back on the results achieved," wrote the *New York Times*, speaking of those who financed these undertakings, "they must now find very little satisfaction in what they got for their money."[10]

IO

. . . AND THEN THERE WERE NONE

The vast, deep, unwonted hush from the direction of the American Liberty League nowadays prompts the inquiry, "What has become of the league, anyway?"

New York Times

Washington observers predict that after a decent interval has demonstrated that the league's career was not coeval with the campaign against President Roosevelt, sustenance will be withdrawn and the league will disappear.

New York Times

THE LIBERTY LEAGUE conceded the re-election of Roosevelt but it was hardly prepared for a Roosevelt victory of such magnitude. This was implicit in the report of the committee appointed in late September to consider its future course. The consensus was that the League "should and must" continue after the election. To admit defeat by disbanding would virtually preclude the possibility of creating a similar organization in the future, not to mention the loss of publicity already achieved by the League and its Lawyers' Committee, however unfavorable it frequently proved.

There was still the chance of a miracle, of course. He had assurances, Desvernine told Shouse ("from members of the Republican high command whose names I do not want to give for obvious reasons") that in the event of a Landon victory the labors of the League would be most welcome in the "cultivation of public opinion along the lines of sound constitutional government." If Roosevelt were re-elected the need for continuing, Desvernine added, "is obvious."

Had Landon made a strong bid in 1936, chances are that the Liberty League would have continued after the election much as before, perhaps on a more modest scale. But the magnitude of the Roosevelt sweep required a substantial change of plans. Immediately after the election, the Administrative and Executive Committees held hurried consultations with available members of the Advisory Council. The decision was to close down completely the public activities of the League ("go into winter quarters at Valley Forge") and concentrate on analyzing proposed New Deal legislation "for the benefit of legislators."

Accordingly, the office staff was trimmed to a minimum. Only Shouse, Captain Stayton, statistician Arthur W. Crawford, Shouse's competent assistant, Ewing Laporte, and a few stenographers remained. The du Ponts, Irénée and Pierre, became almost the sole financial support of the stricken organization. The salary of Shouse, who began spending more time with his private law practice, was cut from a handsome $54,000 to $12,-500; after 1937, he served without pay. All branch offices and state divisions were closed down; the Executive Committee held no meetings between December 9, 1936, and September 3, 1940.

Laporte busied himself auditing the League's books; Stayton, proud of the punishment they had absorbed ("our heads are bloody but unbowed"), did what he could to hold the League together. Writing hundreds of letters, soliciting contributions, and urging patience until "our hour comes," Stayton importuned the membership to wait until destructive taxation brought about a change in popular sentiment; then the League could "strike when the iron is hot." According to Shouse, the aged Captain tried, without success, to give the records of the organization to the Library of Congress. Eventually the files were taken to Stayton's home in Smyrna, Delaware, and burned. Crawford continued work on the monthly bulletin series (until early 1938) and on the analyses of New Deal legislation which were distributed to members of Congress.

Friend and foe of the League knew that it was dead. This was no breathing spell, no minute between rounds. This was a wake. For two years the Liberty League had been one of the most widely publicized, most lavishly financed, most articulate, and potentially one of the most powerful pressure groups ever to appear in American history. For two years the League had done much, threatened to do more; and much was being done in its name. As a barometer of its fame one historian has observed that between August 1934 and November 1936 the League made the front-page of the *New York Times* thirty-five times, the back pages almost daily. During the next four years the *Times* mentioned the League only fifteen times, and five of those were brief statements of its financial reports to the Congress.

The last occasion the *Times* made note of the League was on September 24, 1940. A news item — three short paragraphs, just twenty lines buried on page twenty — announced that the American Liberty League had closed its offices in the National Press Building. Jouett Shouse, who had been on the cover of *Time* Magazine's election issue in November 1930, passed from the political scene a decade later with the simple statement that he had been "the only president" of the organization. Joined by Laporte, he returned to private law practice; Crawford went to work for the United States Chamber of Commerce; Stayton, ever the crusader, founded the Association for Interstate Tax Agreement.

The immediate reason for dissolving the American Liberty League in the fall of 1940 appeared to be the passage of the second Hatch Act limiting contributions to political campaigns. The du Ponts, who by this time were virtually the sole support of the League, were not sure whether contributions to it came within the meaning of the law. Desirous of giving Willkie the maximum financial support in the 1940 campaign, they thought it wise to disband the League.[1]

II

Only once in the four years after the election of 1936 did the League display a momentary flash of its old form.

Roosevelt called a Cabinet meeting for Friday, February 5, 1937, the purpose being to discuss the message he was about to send to Congress. The President was ready to spring on the country his proposals for a reorganization of the judiciary, the famous "court-packing" plan as the anti-New Deal press called it with semantic shrewdness.

By 1936 the estrangement between the executive and judicial branches had become intolerable. After the mandate given him by the people, the President must have decided that a showdown with the court could no longer be postponed. Working closely with his Attorney General, Homer Cummings, but without consulting other intimate advisers, Roosevelt developed a plan. What he asked was that whenever a federal judge reached the age of seventy and failed to retire, another judge be appointed. The appointee was not to replace but to supplement the older judge and the number of such appointees for the entire federal court system could not exceed fifty. According to the plan the membership of the Supreme Court would be held to fifteen. Since six of the nine justices were past seventy in 1937 Roosevelt would, under the plan, have been entitled to appoint six new justices forthwith.

Considering the recent vote of confidence at the polls and the huge Democratic majorities in each house, Roosevelt must have been stunned by the violent reaction to his proposal. But the fight over the reorganization bill was still to come, tomorrow, next week, next month. Today, February 5, the President sat with his Cabinet discussing the plan. Revising the court system was the only way, he told them. Secrecy was imperative. Passage of the bill depended upon surprise, before the opposition could crystallize. Admittedly there were any number of ways to achieve the same end by constitutional amendment; but, explained Roosevelt, the obstacles to the passage of an amendment were insurmountable.

Not the least of these was the Liberty League. He had it on good authority, said the President, that the League had earmarked "a large sum of money in New York" to be used to beat down any constitutional amendment if it reached the state level. What he did not know was that his plan had already been leaked to the opposition. Shouse, aware that Roosevelt's special message would contain the court proposal, tried to get Turner Catledge of the *New York Times* to do a feature story that would deflate the plan in advance. We can "beat Roosevelt to the punch," Shouse told him. Catledge missed a scoop when he refused to believe the League president.

For a consummate politican like Roosevelt the court plan was poorly staged. Emphasizing crowded dockets, the delay and confusion caused by insufficient and infirm judges, the need for new blood, the President's accompanying message lacked the candor that he usually displayed in dealing with Congress and the public. Opposition was instantaneous. The spearhead of that opposition, men like Carter Glass, Walter F. George, Burton K. Wheeler, and Edward Burke, were of his own party; for the first time Roosevelt lost control of the Congress.

Many explanations, all of them at least partly valid, could be given for the defeat of the reorganization plan. Roosevelt had failed to take Democratic leaders into his confidence; he had created a fog of suspicion by not stating boldly that his purpose was creation of a liberal court; he permitted Farley to wield the patronage club with too heavy a hand after the controversy began; fate intervened to remove his chief spokesman, Joseph T.

Robinson of Arkansas, at the height of the controversy. Not to be discounted was the general reluctance to play fast and loose with that which was regarded as sacred. Chief Justice Hughes tossed the weight of his prestige against the plan with an open letter to Senator Wheeler in which he refuted Roosevelt's chief arguments. While the controversy was in progress Senator Burke, collaborating with Merlo Pusey, rushed from the presses their book, *The Supreme Court Crisis*, a bitter denunciation of the plan. Each of these had its effect; but it may be, as has so often been conjectured, that the decisive factor was the court itself, its adroit shift to the judicial portside while the fight raged, that saved it from debasement.

Whatever caused Roosevelt to give up the fight and settle for a compromise, one thing is certain: the defeat was inflicted by Democrats. Republicans wisely stayed out of the family quarrel. The Liberty League stayed out too, after a fashion. Less than two weeks after Roosevelt presented the plan to Congress, William Allen White wrote to James E. Watson:

> I hope that the more evident representatives of his [Roosevelt's] economic opponents will not be too prominent in this political fight; by which I mean the Liberty League and the Du Ponts and that whole crowd. They are black beasts in the popular imagination and if they rally against the President, they are liable to make him friends instead of enemies.

White put his finger on the weakness of the League. As a result of the indiscretion of some of its prominent members, the temper of the times, and the efforts of the Administration, the League had certainly acquired the kiss of death.

No one knew this better than Jouett Shouse. Not only did he keep the League silent; quietly he worked with James Wadsworth, Arthur Vandenberg, Burton K. Wheeler, and Edward Burke to prevent Republican opposition from breaking into the open. As it turned out, no Republican speeches were made in

Congress against the plan. The real triumph of this strategy of silence came just before Republicans assembled to pay homage to Lincoln. Alf Landon was to deliver the Lincoln Day address at the Waldorf-Astoria Hotel, and advance press notices indicated that the recent Republican standard-bearer intended to maul the court plan in his speech. Landon was already en route to New York by train when Shouse called Roy Roberts, editor of the powerful Republican Kansas City *Star* and close friend of the Kansas governor. After talking to Shouse, Roberts put through a call to Chicago. When Landon arrived to change trains for New York, Colonel McCormick, publisher of the Chicago *Tribune*, was there to meet him.

A few minutes with McCormick convinced Landon that Shouse was right: between Chicago and New York the speech was rewritten with deletion of all but one oblique reference to the court plan ("events have occurred . . . which make it out of place for me to talk on a party basis"). Much later, Landon agreed that one word from him, the titular head of the party, and the lid would have been off Pandora's box. The president of the Liberty League, he conceded, had kept him from "sticking my foot in my mouth." At least one newspaper, the Newark *Evening News*, learned of the part Shouse had played, headlining its edition of February 27 "Jouett Shouse, Liberty League Head, Set Forces in Motion that Got Landon to Pull Punches on Supreme Court Plan."

Hearings on the bill were dragged out for weeks and it was mid-June before the Senate Judiciary Committee was ready with its report, a report wholly unfavorable to the President's court plan. Liberty Leaguers were jubilant. With unconcealed delight Raoul Desvernine wrote to Shouse:

> I never was optimistic enough to hope that such an indictment would be handed down against President Roosevelt. . . . It is a complete vindication of the teachings of the American Liberty

League. I am certain if it was not that we all fought so valiantly for the Constitution under your leadership, there never would have been the foundation upon which such a report could be issued. As each day goes by I am proud of my contribution to the League in spite of the damage it has done me.

When Senator Logan of Kentucky recommitted the bill he thought he knew where to place the blame for the failure. The bill, he said, would have passed the Senate "even without the formality of a roll call" but for all the "tumult and shouting brought about by the Liberty League. . . ." "The Liberty League lost the election last November," said Barkley's junior colleague glumly, "but it appears that it is in a fair way to win it in the Congress."

Ten days later the substitute compromise passed the Senate without a contest, a substitute that contained badly needed reforms in judicial procedure while denying to the President power to enlarge the courts. On August 26, Roosevelt signed the Judicial Procedure Reform Act, and the court fight was over. Friends of the President might laugh off the victory of the opposition. The fact remained that the Liberty League had played a major role in inflicting the most singular legislative rebuke of Roosevelt's long tenure. Had it earlier learned the techniques it used on this occasion, its history might have been far different.[u]

III

It is much easier to exult in victory than to explain defeat. But the defeat of the Liberty League in 1936 was so total, so humiliatingly total, that it imperiously demanded an explanation. What had happened?

From the outset the American Liberty League represented something novel in politics. Here was political protest of a new kind. Traditionally the role of protester was a monopoly of the down-at-the-heel, the out-at-the-elbow, the farmer, the laborer, the dreamer, the intellectual, not the summer-in-Newport and winter-in-Florida crowd. It was an unaccustomed role, one for which they were ill fitted and ill prepared, particularly when it meant absorbing the rabbit punches, elbows in the ribs, and eye-gouging that went with roughhouse politics.

Theirs was the lofty approach. The continual insistence on nonpartisanship was supposed to mean that the League was above the sordidness of party politics; critics charged that the Liberty Leaguers meant to solve their problems by buying off both parties. In any case, they were rudely shocked and offended to learn what any veteran political crusader could have told them, that the role of the protester, the political gadfly, was one fraught with indignities and abuses.

The nonpartisan approach betrayed the frequent obtuseness of businessmen in politics. The League conceived the campaign of 1936 as a huge advertising stunt. Selling the country politically was like selling motor oil and razor blades. Tell your story, keep it simple, tell it often; the public will buy. This had been the technique in fighting the prohibition amendment; it would work again. What the Liberty Leaguers did not understand was that in the fight over liquor they were not leading the parade, they were running along in front. The steelworker in Pittsburgh who wanted a cold mug of fermented grass seeds was for them in that fight, not because of who they were but because of what they advocated. But he would not kick Roosevelt in the shins in 1936; he was against them then because of what they stood for in the popular mind.

Talk about a new party after the election emphasized this lack of understanding of what politics was really about. National campaigns are exciting and stimulating, but political victories are a combination of many little things — ringing doorbells, stuffing envelopes, buttonholing voters, volunteering transportation — a thousand things that cannot be accomplished by network radio speeches or slick paper pamphlets. Elections are won in the precincts, not in the dining room of the Metropolitan Club. That is the reason local Republican leaders laughed Hamilton out of town when he came to them with the third-party proposal. Although Landon had taken quite a beating, at the local levels the Republican party was in surprisingly good shape. But to hear the Liberty Leaguers tell it, the Republican party was finished.

The failure to grasp elementary politics led the League into a series of lesser blunders. The Smith speech at the Liberty League dinner was considered the most effective thing the organization had done up to then. Later Shouse confessed it was the worst mistake of the campaign, because of the setting in which he had said it rather than what Smith had said. When Liberty Leaguers thought of a political rally it was a formal dinner attended by millionaires at the Mayflower Hotel. It would never occur to them to have Smith speak among his cronies in one of his familiar haunts, say at Madison Square Garden, with a stamping, clapping, singing, sweating crowd whooping it up. Except for a meeting in 1935 for members in the Chicago area (at the Drake Hotel, naturally) and one at Charlotte a week after the NIRA decision, the Washington dinner was the only thing the League did that could pass for a mass rally.

The League counted too much on the popularity of Smith. The Smith of 1928 and before was one thing; the Liberty League Smith was something quite different. But they could not see the difference. The Smith of 1928 could say in his acceptance speech at Houston:

> It is our new world theory that government exists for the people as against the old world conception that the people exist for the government. A sharp line separates those who believe that an elect class should be the special object of the government's concern and those who believe that the government is

the agent and servant of the people who create it. Dominant in the Republican Party today is the element which proclaims and executes the political theorics against which the party liberals like Roosevelt and La Follette and their party insurgents have rebelled. This reactionary element seeks to vindicate the theory of benevolent oligarchy. It assumes that a material prosperity, the very existence of which is challenged, is an excuse for political inequality. It makes the concern of the government, not people, but material things.

By 1936 he seemed to the vast majority of Americans to have allied himself with those for whom he had such harsh words in 1928.

With Smith's reputation as a fighter, there was something ignoble, almost cowardly, certainly less than courageous about using an impersonal telegram to take his stand at the Democratic convention of 1936. As a delegate (which he was) he would have had every right to repudiate Roosevelt publicly before the convention. Leaving the party seriously impaired whatever influence he might have had, for he was now a man without a party, which meant that he was a man without a respectful and sympathetic forum. No matter what the provocation, his support of Landon lacked conviction and carried with it the taint that goes with changing sides. Whatever may have been his personal feelings and however disparate may have been his views from those of the New Deal, Smith should have stayed in the Democratic party as its elder statesman, as its conscience.

The election revealed the extent of his alienation. Even the eastern cities that had once looked to him for leadership decisively shifted their allegiance to Roosevelt. Smith took his walk from the Democratic party unaware that no one was following, and he could find no explanation for it except "You can't lick Santa Claus."

The assumption that Smith would clear the League of its big business stigma was part of the general ineptitude of its campaign against the New Deal. "I would have paid good money," said Molly Dewson of the Democratic National Committee, "to have him make that speech." What she meant was that Smith's performance, rather than removing or minimizing the big money aspects of the League, only served to exaggerate them. In the long run the effect was to ruin Smith rather than help the League.[3]

IV

The League erred in that it never understood that to the enormous majority of Americans the enemy was not Franklin Roosevelt but poverty, misery, and want. It adamantly refused to see that Roosevelt might, in fact, be its best insurance against substantial change, perhaps even armed revolution, or that his concessions to a mounting radicalism in the country would save rather than destroy the capitalist structure.

This is what Hamilton Basso was saying when he wrote for the *New Republic* a whimsical tongue-in-cheek piece, "The Liberty League Writes," in which he had a Future Historian trying to explain the League to his unsophisticated spouse. "The climax of the career of the American Liberty League," the Future Historian explained patiently, "was the dinner on January 25. That was the occasion, you will remember, my dear, when Al Smith went out gunning for Roosevelt II and shot himself in the foot — wounding himself so badly that he couldn't even take a walk." But his good wife did not understand. In exasperation the Future Historian put it as simply and bluntly as he knew how: "It is as if a band of men joined together to assassinate their best friend."

No Liberty Leaguer would have assassinated Roosevelt if he had had the chance; but to rid the country of Roosevelt politically was not the answer to their problems any more than shooting Lincoln was in 1865 to the cause of the South. What if he had been defeated? Was it to be supposed that the New Deal would have evanesced over the weekend? New administrations inherit what has come before; they are often obligated to finish what has been started, to build where others leave off. The break is never as final and irrevocable as a divorce. Landon has expressed one regret over the loss in 1936: he would like "to have seen the faces of some who supported me after I had been in office for a year." Landon meant that he would have done some new dealing of his own, with more moderation perhaps, with less waste and inefficiency, he hoped, but something comparable to the New Deal nonetheless. Given the times and circumstances, the alternatives for both Roosevelt and Landon were a *modus vivendi* of experimentation or the hand-wringing of Hoover, the cowering hope that, like an air raid, sooner or later the ordeal is bound to end. Mistakenly, the League believed Roosevelt was the New Deal, that he and he alone was personally responsible; to be rid of him was to solve everything. The League was betrayed by the same kind of mentality that believed communism would go away if Stalin would die.

Just as the League wasted too much energy on Roosevelt the man, so did it do too much worrying about what the New Deal would become rather than about what it was. Motivated by a negative conservatism that was more the result of habit than of thought, the League seldom looked for merit in the ideas of the opposition or for possible grounds for compromise. Seeking only to discredit, discount, or denounce the New Deal as some foreign "ism" the League cried "Wolf!" until the country was stone-deaf to its alarms.

If the New Deal was, as the League claimed, some dangerous, alien thing, then what the League stood for must be American and patriotic. It sought to identify itself with the national interest by exaggerating and overdramatizing the conflict between philosophies of government. One was supposed to believe that the League stood alone in defending the Constitution, the Amer-

ican way of life, freedom, liberty, patriotism. Certainly these
are things worthy of defending, of preserving at any cost. But
they are things about which most Americans, then and now, have
a feeling of shyness, modesty, self-consciousness. They are
warm and intimate things like bathing and love-making which
should not be put on public display. That is why Americans are
awkward, never know what to do with their hats when the flag
passes and glance about stupidly like retarded children when they
stand before the symbols of their great heritage in the nation's
capital. Americans are instinctively suspicious of him who
flaunts his patriotism; they may never have heard of Samuel
Johnson but they know intuitively what he meant when he wrote
"Patriotism is the last refuge of a scoundrel." The public eventually acquired this feeling about the League; it was not trying
to sell patriotism, it was trying to peddle the Brooklyn Bridge.

Overt patriotism runs another serious risk: it readily becomes
farce. Take that which is always a delicately balanced emotion
and add to it the ultraseriousness of the Liberty League, the
humorless sense of its own crucial significance, and the result is
the low comedy of Flute the Bellows-mender and Bottom the
Weaver. The League was never aware that it was being laughed
at. When Michelson and Roddan would call League pronounce-
ments "dupontifical" propaganda, the League thought they were
just being sarcastic. It was this "strangely honest faith in its
sanctity," wrote Charles W. Ferguson of the *Reader's Digest,*
that kept it "from dying of embarrassment over the anomaly
of its own existence." The Liberty Leaguers in the knee breeches
and cocked hats of 1776 were as ludicrous as a mummers' parade
to everyone but themselves.[4]

v

In 1936 the Liberty League failed, not because of what it did
("It was not for any incompetence on the part of those who man-

aged the show," wrote Michelson) but because of what it seemed to represent. To the country it stood for a system that had apparently failed, a system that, as Stuart Chase so aptly put it, "disappeared under a memorial wreath of ticker tape on a certain October morning in 1929."

There appeared ample justification for making business the prime suspect for what had happened to the economy. Where else should the blame fall? The land had not been raped by a foreign invader, there had been no catastrophic acts of nature, no disease, no pestilence. Yet hunger and despair stalked the land in the midst of plenty. And desperate men were drawing their own conclusion, assuming they were not half-witted; the country was in one hell of a shape because business had failed.

It was little comfort to have the League explaining that the depression was nobody's fault, that it was global not local. It appeased few appetites to hear that economic disaster was a natural thing, a good thing that would eventually make man and system stronger in mind and body like giving up cigarettes during Lent. It was particularly grim humor to have the League blaming foreign "isms" for the discontent with tradition as though freezing, starving men seeking sanctuary in the warmth of the public library needed to read dangerous books to start them thinking.

Business had failed. No incantations about individualism, initiative, supply and demand, free enterprise, or any of the other spook words in the witchcraft of the conservative would bring it back. Why not scrap it, then; try something else? That was what was happening in Germany, in Italy, in country after country.

But that did not happen here, and for a very good reason. Roosevelt offered what seemed a reasonable alternative. The economic system needed some adjustments, perhaps in some cases a major overhaul, but basically it was sound. Here was a logical place to start, with what we already had, with what was familiar, recognizable, known. If the economic system was unable to right itself, heal its own wounds, get out of its troubles the same way it got in, then let government try its hand at reviving and revitalizing the free enterprise system — not some strange and terrifying machinery of coercion with fascist or Communist trumpery but the existing government, the old Republic, the Uncle Sam that everyone knew and trusted.

If this was un-American then so were its spiritual antecedents, the New Nationalism and the New Freedom. If this was alien and subversive then Theodore Roosevelt and Woodrow Wilson deserved a place alongside Benedict Arnold and James Wilkinson. The people did not think it was; to them it made good sense. They approved the New Deal, voted for it, worked with it, cheered it on even when the news was bad. And all the while they shrugged off the League's cries of alarm with the same bland indifference with which their Jeffersonian and Jacksonian forebears had shrugged off the Federalist and Whig prophets of doom.

Here was one major explanation for the League's dismal failure. The people trusted Roosevelt, he was their friend, he took them into his confidence (who does not remember the Fireside Chats?). Had all the League's indictments against him been true it probably would have made little difference, so complete was the infatuation.

The casual observer saw the League as an instrument of uncomplicated selfishness, or of suicidal stupidity, or both. How could men who prided themselves on being practical, hardheaded, up-to-date in their business affairs be so archaic, so paleolithic in their approach to politics? Unless it was because they were so enchanted by a system that had sufficed in the crude, decentralized individualistic capitalism of the nineteenth century. Then competition had been very much on a man-to-man basis; the League's analogy of life's being a footrace was not entirely unrealistic. In the centralized, corporate, monopolistic style capitalism of the twentieth century, a system more like a prizefight than a footrace, the virtues of traditional individualism had less meaning. The disaster of 1929 left the defenders of the status quo without their most effective argument. So long as the country appeared prosperous, who could refute the validity of the conservative position? In the face of depression that position was nakedly vulnerable; reiterating the creed neither convinced nor satisfied anyone except conservatives. To the majority, the suggestion that the only proper relation of government to business was one of nonintervention by government — the right to do business "in the old ways" — the only logical conclusion was that American businessmen were determined upon a "business-as-usual and the public-be-damned" approach to the depression. This the public would not listen to, much less accept.

The League could never understand why no one listened. The farther it went the more futile, the more disillusioned it became. It could only conclude that Roosevelt and the New Deal had completely debauched the people, bought them off with bread and circuses, sown the seeds of class consciousness, lulled and beguiled them into a passive servitude with promises of security from crib to crypt.

This was hardly the case. The League failed because the people, rightly or wrongly, regarded it as the executor of a bankrupted estate, the medicine man selling worthless stump water. The League failed because it represented economic and political conservatism at a time when both were out of style.

In the 1930's the political pendulum was swinging, had swung, and the arc it was describing was toward the Left. It remained to be seen whether in time the pendulum would ever swing far enough back to the Right to satisfy the Liberty Leaguers. Meanwhile, they took what comfort they could in the thought that they had forced some restraint and temperance on the Administration; that without the Liberty League the New Deal would have been far more radical than it was. "This was its great contribution," said Jouett Shouse.[5]

VI

The Democrats also had some explanations for the failure of the Liberty League. The country, said Michelson, was in no mood in 1936 to "accept the mandate of big business. . . ." Looking back on the election, the Democratic publicity director con-cluded that about all the League got for its efforts was "the con-version of America's favorite family — the Du Ponts — into political enemy number one." In Farley's estimation, the most serious blunder of the campaign of 1936 was in letting the Liberty League "direct the firing during the preliminary skir-mishing." Actually, it probably made little difference; the Liberty League, said the bald, florid Democratic national chair-man, was "licked to a standstill by the overpowering personality of one individual." In this analysis his Republican counterpart concurred. Said Hamilton, "The Lord couldn't have beaten Roosevelt in 1936, much less the Liberty League."

Friend and foe alike were willing to leave it at that.[6]

NOTES

APPENDIX

INDEX

NOTES

CHAPTER I (*pages 20–36*)

1. Jouett Shouse interview,* September 4, 1958; *New York Times,* August 23, 1934.
2. Special Senate Committee Investigating the Munitions Industry, *Munitions Industry: Hearings,* 73 Cong. Recess (1934), 4424-27; Senate Committee to Investigate Lobbying Activities, *Investigation of Lobbying Activities: Hearings,* 74 Cong., 2 Sess. (1936), 2059.
3. Shouse interview, September 4, 1958.
4. American Liberty League, "Underwriters' Agreement," Shouse File, no pagination; Shouse interview, September 4-5, 1958.
5. Jouett Shouse, "Personal Memorandum Relating to the Substance of Conversation Had with President Roosevelt at the White House Wednesday Afternoon, August 15, 1934," August 16, 1934, Shouse File.
6. *Commonweal,* XX, No. 19 (September 7, 1914), 415; *Collier's,* XCIV, No. 14 (October 6, 1934), 58; *Christian Century,* LI, No. 36 (September 5, 1934), 1107; *Newsweek,* VI, No. 23 (December 7, 1935), 12; *New York Times,* August 23, 24, 25, 28, 29, 1934.
7. *New York Times,* August 24, 25, 28, 1934; *Newsweek,* VIII, No. 10 (September 1, 1934), 5; *New York Times,* August 30, 1934; Spreckels to Roosevelt, August 31, 1934, OF File 1150, Box 1, Roosevelt Papers; Giannini to Roosevelt, September 2, 1934, *ibid.;* Herbert Hoover, *The Memoirs . . . The Great Depression, 1929-1941* (New York, 1952), III, 454; *Time,* XXIV, No. 10 (September 3, 1934), 19.
8. Shouse interview, September 4, 1958; *New York Times,* August 25, 1934; Basil Rauch (ed.), *The Roosevelt Reader* (New York, 1957),

---

* All interviews cited were between the author and persons mentioned.

127-28; Elliott Roosevelt (ed.), *F.D.R.: His Personal Letters, 1928-1945* (New York, 1950), I, 417.
9. *Time*, XXIV, No. 10 (September 3, 1934), 18.

CHAPTER 2 (*pages 37–55*)

1. *New York Times*, December 31, 1933, Section IV, 1.
2. *Congressional Record*, 68 Cong., 1 Sess. (January 21, 1924), 1213.
3. Senate Judiciary Committee, *Lobbying Activities: Hearings*, 71 Cong., 1 and 2 Sess. (1929-30), hereafter cited as Caraway Committee; *Annual Report of the President of the Association Against the Prohibition Amendment for 1931* (Washington, 1932), 17; Caraway Committee, 4096-98, 3895; *Annual Report of the President of the Association Against the Prohibition Amendment for 1933* (Washington, 1934), 37; *Annual Report of the President of the Association Against the Prohibition Amendment for 1930* (Washington, 1931), 14-15.
4. Caraway Committee, 3914-15, 4177-78.
5. Shouse to author, October 29, 1958; Fletcher Dobyns, *The Amazing Story of Repeal* (Chicago, 1940), ix; Caraway Committee, 4164-66, 3991-92.
6. *New York Times*, January 23, 1929, November 9, 1933; *Literary Digest* (November 25, 1933), 8.
7. Senate Committee to Investigate Lobbying Activities, *Investigation of Lobbying Activities: Hearings*, 74 Cong., 2 Sess. (1936), 2059; quoted in Dobyns, *Amazing Story*, 405-6; William H. Stayton, *Confidential Memorandum for Former Members of the Board of Directors of the Association Against the Prohibition Amendment*, quoted in James C. Pitney, "American Liberty League, Inc." (unpublished master's thesis, Princeton University, May 1947), 33.

CHAPTER 3 (*pages 56–79*)

1. Shouse interview, September 5, 1958; Shouse to author, October 29, 1958; Charles Michelson, *The Ghost Talks* (New York, 1944), 141.
2. American Liberty League, *Minutes*, Book I, September 1934, no pagination, Shouse File (the *Minutes* are of meetings of the Administrative Committee contained in three books and running until early 1937); Jouett Shouse, *Seventeen Months of the American Liberty League*, ALL Document No. 96 (January 25, 1936), 8; *Facts about*

the American Liberty League, ALL Document No. 38 (May 1935), 12-14.

3. Shouse, *Seventeen Months*, 7-8; *New York Times*, January 26, 1936; ALL, *Minutes*, Book II, July 1935, Shouse File; *Exhibits to Accompany Memorandum Concerning the Activities of the American Liberty League from Its Organization, August, 1934, to June, 1938*, 53, Shouse File.

4. *New York Times*, January 11, 1935, January 3, 1936, January 8, September 11, 1937, March 11, 1938; ALL, *Monetary Pledges and Loan Agreements*, Shouse File; Shouse interview, September 5, 1958.

5. *New York Times*, January 26, March 17, 1936; ALL, *Minutes*, Book I, May 1935, Book II, January 1936; *Newsweek*, VI, No. 23 (December 7, 1935), 12; *Facts about the American Liberty League*, ALL Document No. 38 (May 1935), 10; Shouse, *Seventeen Months*, 8-10; Shouse interview, September 4, 1958; for list of ALL publications, see Appendix.

6. *New York Times*, August 23, 1934; Shouse, *Seventeen Months*, 7; ALL, *Minutes*, Book II, April 1936; *Professors and the New Deal*, ALL Document No. 91 (January 1936), 23.

7. *New York Times*, July 21, 1935; Nicholas Roosevelt, *Two Amazing Years*, ALL Document No. 49 (July 8, 1935); Demarest Lloyd, *Fabian Socialism in the New Deal*, ALL Document No. 50 (July 9, 1935); Walter E. Spahr, *The People's Money*, ALL Document No. 51 (July 10, 1935); Raoul E. Desvernine, *The Principles of Constitutional Democracy and the New Deal*, ALL Document No. 52 (July 11, 1935); J. Howard Pew, *Which Road to Take?* ALL Document No. 53 (July 12, 1935); Neil Carothers, *Recovery by Statute*, ALL Document No. 56 (July 9, 1935); William H. Stayton, *Today's Lessons for Tomorrow*, ALL Document No. 62 (July 13, 1935); James W. Wadsworth, Jr., *The Blessings of Stability*, ALL Document No. 54 (July 12, 1935).

8. ALL, *Minutes*, Book I, September, 1934; *New York Times*, June 10, August 22, 24, 1935, February 1, 1936; James M. Beck, *The Duty of the Lawyer in the Present Crisis*, ALL Document No. 69 (October 1935); Ethan A. H. Shepley, *The National Lawyers' Committee of the American Liberty League*, ALL Document No. 74 (November 1935); Shouse, *Seventeen Months*; ALL, *Minutes*, Book I, June 1935.

9. ALL National Lawyers' Committee, *Report on the Constitutionality of the National Labor Relations Act*, September 5, 1935; *New York Times*, September 20, 1935; "A Conspiracy by Lawyers," *Nation*,

CXLI, No. 3665 (October 2, 1935), 369; "Liberty League Lawyers," *New Republic*, LXXXIV, No. 1087 (October 2, 1935), 203; *United States Law Review*, LXIX (October 1935), 506, LXIX (November 1935), 615, LXX (January 1936), 24.

10. *New York Times*, October 17, November 1, 11, 1935; Beck, *Duty of the Lawyer*, 9; *Opinion 148 of the Standing Committee on Professional Ethics and Grievances of the American Bar Association*, ALL Document No. 79 (November 1935), 5; James C. Pitney, "American Liberty League, Inc." (unpublished master's thesis, Princeton University, 1947), 65.

11. *New York Times*, October 20, November 1, 1935; Benjamin R. Twiss, *Lawyers and the Constitution: How Laissez-Faire Came to the Supreme Court* (Princeton, 1942); Michelson, *Ghost Talks*, 143.

12. *New York Times*, November 10, 1934.

CHAPTER 4 (*pages 80–101*)

1. *New York Times*, August 13, 1948; *Biographical Directory of the American Congress, 1774-1949* (Washington, 1950), 1086; Dorothy Waring, *American Defender* (New York, 1935), Chaps. 1-2.

2. *National Cyclopaedia of American Biography* (New York, 1953), XXXVIII, 536-37.

3. Harold Lavine, *Fifth Column in America* (New York, 1940); Nathaniel Weyl, *Treason* (Washington, 1950); Morris Schonbach, "Native Fascism During the 1930's and 1940's" (unpublished doctoral dissertation, University of California at Los Angeles, 1958); Special House Committee on Un-American Activities, *Investigation of Nazi Propaganda Activities and Investigation of Certain Other Propaganda Activities: Hearings*, 73 Cong., 2 Sess. (1934), 8-15, hereafter cited as McCormack-Dickstein Committee.

4. McCormack-Dickstein Committee, 8-15.

5. *Ibid.*, 15-23.

6. *Ibid.*, 23-87, 99-162; *New York Times*, November 22, 1934.

7. McCormack-Dickstein Committee, 128; George Seldes, *Facts and Fascism* (New York, 1943), 113; George Seldes, *One Thousand Americans* (New York, 1947), 209; New York *Evening Post*, November 20, 1934; Waring, *American Defender*, 234-39; *New York Times*, November 23, 26, 1934.

8. *New York Times*, November 21, 22, 23, 24, 1934; *Time*, XXIV, No. 23 (December 3, 1934), 14; Seldes, *One Thousand Americans*, 79-80, 208-12, 287.

9. Frederick A. Ogg, "Does America Need a Dictator?" *Current History*, XXXVI (September 1932), 641-48; Demarest Lloyd, "Let Congress Abdicate," *Affairs*, VI, No. 4 (January 27, 1933); *Congressional Record*, 72 Cong., 1 Sess. (May 5, 1932), 9644; Ernest K. Lindley, *Half Way With Roosevelt* (New York, 1937), 6; Weyl, *Treason*, 334; Charles W. Ferguson, *Fifty Million Brothers* (New York, 1937), 129; Lavine, *Fifth Column*, 44-54; Van Horn Moseley, "Our Enemies, Foreign and Domestic," *Vital Speeches*, V, No. 7 (January 15, 1939), 199-201; Cornelius Vanderbilt, *Man of the World* (New York, 1959), Chap. 25; McCormack-Dickstein Committee, *Final Report*, February 15, 1935.

CHAPTER 5 (*pages 102–141*)

1. James A. Farley, *Jim Farley's Story: The Roosevelt Years* (New York, 1948), 16-18; James A. Farley, *Behind the Ballots* (New York, 1938), 103-4; Shouse interview, September 4, 1958.
2. Alfred E. Smith, *Up to Now* (New York, 1929); Emily Smith Warner, *The Happy Warrior* (Garden City, 1956); Charles Michelson, *The Ghost Talks* (New York, 1944), 140.
3. Marquis W. Childs, "They Hate Roosevelt," *Harper's*, Vol. 172 (May 1936), 634-42; *Time*, XXVII, No. 17 (April 27, 1936); Albert Samuel Karr, "The Roosevelt Haters" (unpublished doctoral dissertation, University of California at Los Angeles, 1956); Fitzgerald Hall, *The Imperilment of Democracy*, ALL Document No. 58 (July 18, 1935), 5; ALL Leaflets *The President Wants More Power, Will It Be Ave Caesar? New Labels for Old Poisons, The Way Dictatorships Start;* Jouett Shouse, *The New Deal vs. Democracy*, ALL Document No. 128 (June 21, 1936), 5; James A. Reed, *Shall We Have Constitutional Liberty or Dictatorship?* ALL Document No. 120 (April 14, 1936), 14; William H. Rogers, *Should We Amend the Constitution to Grant the National Government General Welfare Powers?* ALL Document No. 113 (April 2, 1936), 29; *Economic Planning — Mistaken But Not New*, ALL Document No. 75 (November 1935), 4-5; Jouett Shouse, *The Return to Democracy*, ALL Document No. 46 (July 1, 1935), 10; *New Work Relief Funds*, ALL Document No. 117 (April 2, 1936), 7; *The AAA Amendments*, ALL Document No. 30 (April 1935), 1; ALL Leaflet *Gratitude in Politics;* James M. Beck, *What Is the Constitution between Friends?* ALL Document No. 22 (March 27, 1935), 3-10; Forney Johnston, *The Economic Necessity in the Southern States for a Return to the Constitution*, ALL Document No. 73 (October 29, 1935), 7; Walter E. Spahr, *Political Bank-*

ing, ALL Document No. 31 (April 26, 1935), 6; Demarest Lloyd, *Fabian Socialism in the New Deal*, ALL Document No. 50 (July 9, 1935), 13, 22; J. Howard Pew, *Which Road to Take?* ALL Document No. 53 (July 12, 1935), 15; Charles I. Dawson, *The President Has Made the Issue*, ALL Document No. 95 (January 25, 1936), 1; James A. Reed, *The Constitution: The Fortress of Liberty*, ALL Document No. 105 (February 11, 1936), 11; Alfred E. Smith, *The Facts in the Case*, ALL Document No. 97 (January 25, 1936), 18; Dixon Wecter, *The Age of the Great Depression* (New York, 1948), 89; Raoul E. Desvernine, *Democratic Despotism* (New York, 1936); Ralph M. Shaw, *The New Deal: Its Unsound Theories and Irreconcilable Policies*, ALL Document No. 39 (May 31, 1935), 16-17; *Alternatives to the American Form of Government*, ALL Document No. 81 (December 1935), preface.

4. ALL *Bulletin*, I, No. 12 (July 15, 1936); William H. Stayton, *Confidential Memorandum . . . Prohibition Amendment*, quoted in James C. Pitney, "American Liberty League, Inc." (unpublished master's thesis, Princeton University, May 1947), 39-40; *Newsweek*, IV, No. 10 (September 1, 1934), 5; James A. Reed, "The Constitution of the United States," *Vital Speeches*, I (October 8, 1934), 9-10; Ogden Mills, "Constitutional Liberty," *Vital Speeches*, I (May 6, 1935), 492; *Time*, XXVI, No. 14 (September 30, 1935), 14; ALL Leaflet *New Labels for Old Poisons;* Johnston, *Economic Necessity*, 6; Dawson, *President Has Made*, 7, 8, 10; Samuel I. Rosenman (comp.), *The Public Papers and Addresses of Franklin D. Roosevelt* (New York, 1938-50), IV, 297-98.

5. William H. Stayton, *Is the Constitution for Sale?* ALL Document No. 40 (May 30, 1935), 4; *The Supreme Court and the New Deal*, ALL Document No. 42 (June 1935), 3; Albert C. Ritchie, *The American Bar*, ALL Document No. 48 (June 29, 1935), 7; Borden Burr, *The Constitution and the Supreme Court*, ALL Document No. 70 (September 19, 1935), 18; Jouett Shouse, *Shall We Plow under the Supreme Court?* ALL Document No. 101 (February 6, 1936), 14; G. B. Cutten, *Entrenched Greed*, ALL Document No. 109 (February 8, 1936), 8-9; Irving Brant, *Storm over the Constitution* (Indianapolis, 1936), xiv; Henry A. Wallace, *Whose Constitution?* (New York, 1936); Raoul E. Desvernine, *A Reply to Secretary Wallace's Question — Whose Constitution? The Dominant Issue of the Campaign*, ALL Document No. 131 (August 1936); Dawson, *President Has Made*, 13-14.

6. *Delegation of Legislative Power to the Executive under the New Deal,* ALL Document No. 132 (August 1936), 4; Shouse, *Shall We Plow under the Supreme Court?* 14; Jouett Shouse, *Democracy or Bureaucracy,* ALL Document No. 14 (February 4, 1935), 7, 10; Jouett Shouse, *The Legislative Situation,* ALL Document No. 20 (March 7, 1935), 14; *Lawmaking by Executive Order,* ALL Document No. 60 (August 1935), 22; James A. Reed, *Shall We Have Constitutional Liberty or Dictatorship?* ALL Document No. 120 (April 14, 1936), 6; Fitzgerald Hall, *A Federal Union: National and State Responsibilities,* ALL Document No. 123 (April 20, 1936), 14; *Delegation of Legislative Power,* 3; Albert C. Ritchie, *The American Form of Government — Let Us Preserve It,* ALL Document No. 92 (January 18, 1936), 9; John W. Davis, *The Redistribution of Power,* ALL Document No. 93 (January 24, 1936), 13, 18-19; ALL Leaflet, *Abolishing the States; The Dual Form of Government and the New Deal,* ALL Document No. 134 (September 1936), 1; *New York Times,* September 17, December 28, 1935; Hall, *Federal Union,* 15.

7. Stuart Chase, "Ode to the Liberty League," *Nation,* CXLI, No. 3673 (November 27, 1935), 615; Drew Pearson and Robert S. Allen, *The Nine Old Men* (Garden City, 1937), 21-22.

8. Shaw, *New Deal,* 27; ALL *Bulletin,* II, No. 2 (September 15, 1936); Shouse, *Democracy or Bureaucracy,* 20; Johnston, *Economic Necessity,* 6; Jouett Shouse, *Arousing Class Prejudices,* ALL Document No. 84 (December 23, 1935), 2; William R. Perkins, *Rising or a Setting Sun?* ALL Document No. 135 (September 1936), 20; Ernest T. Weir, "Present Relations of Business to Government," *Vital Speeches,* I (April 22, 1935), 476-78; Demarest Lloyd, "The American Liberty League Makes History," *Awakener* (February 1, 1936), 3; S. Wells Utley, *The Duty of the Church to the Social Order,* ALL Document No. 43 (May 21, 1935), 2-3; Shaw, *New Deal,* 13; *Professors and the New Deal,* ALL Document No. 91 (January 20, 1936), 15; Perkins, *Rising or a Setting Sun?* 10.

9. Neil Carothers, *Government by Experiment,* ALL Document No. 28 (April 17, 1935), 6; Utley, *Duty of the Church,* 2-3; Rosenman (comp.), *Public Papers,* I, 657; *ibid.,* II, 453; Neil Carothers, *Recovery by Statute,* ALL Document No. 56 (July 9, 1935), 10; Walter E. Spahr, *The People's Money,* ALL Document No. 51 (July 10, 1935), 19.

10. *$4,880,000,000: Emergency Relief Appropriation Act of 1935,* ALL Document No. 12 (January 28, 1935), 1; *The Dual Form of Government and the New Deal,* ALL Document No. 134 (September 1936),

20; J. Howard Pew, *Which Road to Take?* ALL Document No. 53 (July 12, 1935), 3-4, 8, 10; *Economic Planning — Mistaken But Not New*, ALL Document No. 75 (November 1935), 6.

11. Ralph D. Casey, "Republican Propaganda in the 1936 Campaign," *Public Opinion Quarterly*, I (April 1937), 28; Stayton, *Confidential Memorandum*, quoted in Pitney, "American Liberty League, Inc." (unpublished master's thesis, Princeton University, May 1947), 34-35; *ibid.*, 36; *New Deal Budget Policies*, ALL Document No. 130 (July 1936), 7, 12; *New York Times*, October 31, 1935; *Budget Prospects*, ALL Document No. 71 (October 1935), 3; Jouett Shouse, *You Owe Thirty-one Billion Dollars*, ALL Document No. 125 (May 19, 1936), 4-5; *The President's 1936 Tax Proposals*, ALL Document No. 112 (April 1936); *Social and Economic Experimentation under the Guise of Taxation*, ALL Document No. 129 (July 1936); *Yesterday, Today and Tomorrow*, ALL Document No. 26 (April 1935), 5; *New York Times*, January 28, 1935; Jouett Shouse, *Recovery, Relief and the Constitution*, ALL Document No. 7 (December 8, 1934), 6; *Dangerous Experimentation*, ALL Document No. 72 (October 1935); *New York Times*, March 11, 1936; *Congressional Record*, 74 Cong., 2 Sess. (March 10, 1936), 3494.

12. *The Pending Bank Bill*, ALL Document No. 19 (March 1935), 2; Walter E. Spahr, *Political Banking*, ALL Document No. 31 (April 26, 1935), 3-4; Carothers, *Recovery by Statute*, 9; Jouett Shouse, *Breathing Spells*, ALL Document No. 65 (September 16, 1935), 4; Ray Bert Westerfield, *How Inflation Affects the Average Family*, ALL Document No. 29 (April 18, 1935); Spahr, *People's Money*, 13; E. W. Kemmerer, *Our Growing National Debt and Inflation*, ALL Document No. 76 (November 1935), 6; Neil Carothers, *Inflation Is Bad Business*, ALL Document No. 77 (November 1935), 6-7.

13. *Economic Security*, ALL Document No. 13 (February 4, 1935); Shouse, *Legislative Situation*, 13; *The Farmers' Home Bill*, ALL Document No. 36 (May 1935), 8; James W. Wadsworth, Jr., *Where Are We Going?* ALL Document No. 23 (March 29, 1935), 6; G. W. Dyer, *Regimenting the Farmers*, ALL Document No. 33 (May 5, 1935), 11; *Consumers and the AAA*, ALL Document No. 67 (October 1935), 10; *Potato Control*, ALL Document No. 64 (September 1935), 11; Jouett Shouse, *American Liberty League*, ALL Document No. 2 (September 7, 1934); *New York Times*, September 8, 1934; *Professors and the New Deal*, 2.

14. Jouett Shouse, *Progress vs. Change*, ALL Document No. 6 (Novem-

ber 20, 1934), 1; *A Program for Congress*, ALL Document No. 83 (December 1935).

15. Ogden Mills, "A Revolutionary Proposal," *Vital Speeches*, II (July 15, 1936), 656-60; *New York Times*, July 18, 1935; Shaw, *New Deal*, 29-30.

CHAPTER 6 *(pages 142–162)*

1. *New York Times*, January 17, 26, 1936; Harold L. Ickes, *The Secret Diary of Harold L. Ickes* (New York, 1953-54), I, 516.
2. *New York Times*, December 29, 31, 1935; *Time*, XXVII, No. 1 (January 6, 1936), 1.
3. U.S. Board of Tax Appeals, *Reports*, XXXVII, 1228-29, 1266; Charles Michelson, *The Ghost Talks* (New York, 1944), 27; *Congressional Record*, 74 Cong., 2 Sess. (January 30, 1936), 1227; *New York Times*, January 13, 1936.
4. *New York Times*, January 2, 4, 1936; Samuel I. Rosenman (comp.), *The Public Papers and Addresses of Franklin D. Roosevelt* (New York, 1938-50), V, 8-18.
5. *The 1937 Budget*, ALL Document No. 86 (January 1936), 3; *New York Times*, January 5, 6, 10, 1936; *Congressional Record*, 74 Cong., 2 Sess. (January 30, 1936), 926.
6. *New York Times*, January 8, 9, 1936; Rosenman (comp.), *Public Papers*, V, 38-44.
7. *New York Times*, January 26, 27, 29, 1936; Emily Smith Warner, *The Happy Warrior* (Garden City, 1956), 276-78.
8. Charles I. Dawson, *The President Has Made the Issue*, ALL Document No. 95 (January 25, 1936); Neil Carothers, *Time to Stop*, ALL Document No. 94 (January 25, 1936); Eleanor Roosevelt to author, February 21, 1958; *New York Times*, January 26, 1936; *Time*, XXVII, No. 5 (February 3, 1936), 14; Alfred E. Smith, *The Facts in the Case*, ALL Document No. 97 (January 25, 1936).
9. John W. Davis, *The Redistribution of Power*, ALL Document No. 93 (January 24, 1936); Warner, *Happy Warrior*, 282; *New York Times*, January 25, 26, 27, February 1, 1936; *Congressional Record*, 74 Cong., 2 Sess. (January 27, 1936), 1048-49; *ibid.* (January 31, 1936), 1305-7.
10. Ickes, *Secret Diary*, I, 517; *Congressional Record*, 74 Cong., 2 Sess. (January 23, 1936), 925-30; Ickes, *Secret Diary*, I, 517-18; Arthur M. Schlesinger, Jr., *The Coming of the New Deal* (Boston, 1958), 516.

11. Ickes, *Secret Diary*, I, 526-27, 664; *New York Times*, February 8, 1933; *ibid.*, January 26, 1936.
12. Joseph T. Robinson, "Jacob's Voice," *Vital Speeches*, II (February 10, 1936); *New York Times*, January 30, 1936; Elliott Roosevelt (ed.), *F.D.R.: His Personal Letters, 1928-1945* (New York, 1950), I, 559.
13. *New York Times*, January 30, February 2, 1936; Shouse interview, September 4, 1958.
14. Shouse interview, September 4, 1958; *New York Times*, December 24, 1935; *ibid.*, March 22, 1936; James A. Farley, *Behind the Ballots* (New York, 1938), 293-94; Ernest K. Lindley, *Half Way with Roosevelt* (New York, 1937), 10.

CHAPTER 7 (*pages 163–188*)

1. Samuel I. Rosenman, *Working with Roosevelt* (New York, 1952), 98; James A. Farley, *Jim Farley's Story: The Roosevelt Years* (New York, 1948), 54; Elliott Roosevelt (ed.), *F.D.R.: His Personal Letters, 1928-1945* (New York, 1950), I, 453-54; *Work Relief*, ALL Document No. 78 (November 1935), 8; *Dangerous Experimentation*, ALL Document No. 72 (October 1935), 3; *The TVA Amendments*, ALL Document No. 37 (May 1935), 1; *The National Labor Relations Act*, ALL Document No. 66 (September 1935), 8; *Potato Control*, ALL Document No. 64 (September 1935), 1; *The Pending Bank Bill*, ALL Document No. 19 (March 1935), 1; *The AAA Amendments*, ALL Document No. 30 (April 1935), 1; *The Holding Company Bill*, ALL Document No. 21 (March 1935), 3; *Bituminous Coal Bill*, ALL Document No. 32 (April 1935), 7; *The President's Tax Program*, ALL Document No. 47 (July 1935), 1; Ernest T. Weir, "A Challenge to Businessmen," *Nation's Business*, Vol. 23, No. 73 (June 1935); *New York Times*, January 1, 5, 19, 1936.
2. Roosevelt (ed.), *F.D.R.*, I, 560; Arthur M. Schlesinger, Jr., *The Coming of the New Deal* (Boston, 1958), 242-43; *New York Times*, January 19, 1936; *ibid.*, February 22, 1936; Farley, *Jim Farley's Story*, 207.
3. Jouett Shouse, *Shall We Plow under the Supreme Court?* ALL Document No. 101 (February 1936), 10; *New York Times*, February 7, 1936; *ibid.*, February 2, 1936; James A. Farley, *Behind the Ballots* (New York, 1938), 292; Charles Michelson, *The Ghost Talks* (New York, 1944), 142; *New York Times*, July 23, 1936; Shouse interview, September 4, 1958.

4. Shouse interview, September 5, 1958; *New York Times*, February 7, 1936; Farley, *Behind the Ballots*, 291-92, 250; Kenneth G. Crawford, *The Pressure Boys* (New York, 1939), 168; Farley, *Jim Farley's Story*, 50-51; Harnett T. Kane, *Louisiana Hayride* (New York, 1941), 95, 101, 117, 120-34; Raymond Moley, *After Seven Years* (New York, 1939), 305; Harold L. Ickes, *The Secret Diary of Harold L. Ickes* (New York, 1953-54), I, 346; Lela Stiles, *The Man behind Roosevelt* (New York, 1954), 285; *New York Times*, April 10, 1936; *ibid.*, May 3, 1936.

5. Huey P. Long, *My First Days in the White House* (Harrisburg, Pa., 1935), 6-8, 86-90; Kane, *Louisiana Hayride*, 139; Farley, *Behind the Ballots*, 293-94; *New York Times*, February 7, March 1, 12, 15, 1936; Roosevelt (ed.), *F.D.R.*, I, 452-53; Shouse interview, September 4, 1958; Farley to author, August 14, 1958.

6. Houston *Chronicle*, September 15, 1935; *New York Times*, January 5, 19, 25, 30, 31, 1936; *Time*, XXVII, No. 17 (April 27, 1936), 10-11; Senate Committee to Investigate Lobbying Activities, *Investigation of Lobbying Activities: Hearings*, 74 Cong., 2 Sess. (1936), 1877-78.

7. *New York Times*, March 1, April 10, May 3, 1936; Shouse interview, September 4, 1958; Sen. Com. to Invest. Lobbying Activities, *Invest. of Lobbying Activities: Hearings*, 1877-78.

8. Farley, *Behind the Ballots*, 292-304; *New York Times*, March 1, 12, 15, May 17, June 18, 1936; Shouse interview, September 4, 1958; James A. Farley interview, December 17, 1959.

9. *New York Times*, June 18, 22, 23, 26, 28, 1936; Emily Smith Warner, *The Happy Warrior* (Garden City, 1956), 285; Joseph Proskauer interview, September 5, 1958.

10. *New York Times*, June 22, 24, 1936; Stiles, *Man behind Roosevelt*, 33.

11. *New York Times*, June 28, 1936; Rosenman, *Working with Roosevelt*, 106; Samuel I. Rosenman (comp.), *The Public Papers and Addresses of Franklin D. Roosevelt* (New York, 1938-50), IV, 283-85.

CHAPTER 8 *(pages 189-223)*

1. Shouse interview, September 4, 1958; Alfred M. Landon interview, February 14, 1959; Shouse to author, July 1, 1959; Joseph Proskauer interview, September 7, 1958; John D. M. Hamilton interview, December 18, 1959; *New York Times*, January 2, 1936.

2. *New York Times*, May 28, July 16, August 5, 1936; *Biographical Directory of the American Congress, 1774-1949* (Washington, 1950),

1454; Russel B. Nye, *Midwestern Progressive Politics, 1870-1950* (East Lansing, Mich., 1951); Bruce Mason, "American Political Protest, 1932-1936" (unpublished doctoral dissertation, University of Texas, 1953); *New York Times*, May 3, July 7, 1936; Donald McCoy, *Angry Voices* (Lawrence, Kans., 1959); *Biog. Dir. of the Amer. Cong.*, 868; *New York Times*, January 27, May 23, June 2, 1936.

3. *New York Times*, July 7, 17, 18, 26, 31, 1936; Mason, "American Political Protest"; McCoy, *Angry Voices*, 146-47; T.R.B., "Washington Notes," *New Republic*, LXXXVII, No. 1127 (July 8, 1936), 265-66; Earl Browder, *The People's Front* (New York, 1938), 34.

4. *New York Times*, February 2, July 2, 28, August 9, October 2, 27, 1936; Hamilton interview, December 18, 1959; Shouse interview, September 4, 1958; *New York Times*, August 6, October 17, 22, 1936.

5. James A. Farley, *Behind the Ballots* (New York, 1938), 292; Shouse interview, September 4, 1958; *New York Times*, February 14, July 1, August 6, 1936; *New York Times*, February 13, 14, April 24, 1936; Jouett Shouse, *The New Deal vs. Democracy*, ALL Document No. 128 (June 21, 1936).

6. *Biog. Dir. of the Amer. Cong.*, 868; *ibid.*, 1948; *Encyclopedia Americana* (New York, 1956), XVI, 495; *ibid.*, 703; W. S. Myers and W. H. Newton, *The Hoover Administration* (New York, 1936); James A. Farley, *Jim Farley's Story: The Roosevelt Years* (New York, 1948), 62; Harold L. Ickes, *The Secret Diary of Harold L. Ickes* (New York, 1953-54), I, 639; Landon interview, February 14, 1959; Frederick Palmer, *This Man Landon* (New York, 1936); Ickes, *Secret Diary*, 633, 641ff.; Landon-Roosevelt correspondence is in the Landon Papers, Kansas State Historical Society, Topeka, Kansas; *New York Times*, May 3, 10, June 14, 1936; Hamilton interview, December 18, 1959; *New York Times*, June 12, 14, 1936.

7. Shouse interview, September 5, 1958; Landon interview, February 14, 1959; Hamilton interview, December 18, 1959; *A Program for Congress*, ALL Document No. 83 (December 1935); *New York Times*, June 24, July 17, 1936; Louise Overacker, "Campaign Funds in the Presidential Election of 1936," *American Political Science Review*, XXXI (June 1937); *New York Times*, September 20, 26, October 1, 2, 18, November 1, 1936; Emily Smith Warner, *The Happy Warrior* (Garden City, 1956), 285-86.

8. *New York Times*, March 22, 1936; Farley, *Behind the Ballots*, 294; *New York Times*, December 27, 1935, February 6, 8, 22, 23, 24, 26, 27, 1936; *Literary Digest* (February 15, 1936), 6; Elliott Roosevelt

(ed.), *F.D.R.: His Personal Letters, 1928-1945* (New York, 1950), I, 566; James A. Farley interview, December 21, 1959; Edward L. Roddan interview, September 5, 1958.

9. *New York Times,* April 16, June 24, July 25, August 6, 7, 8, 1936; Hamilton interview, December 18, 1959; Appointment Book (1936), Landon Papers; Landon interview, February 14, 1959.

10. ALL *Bulletin,* I, No. 10 (May 15, 1936), 1; *ibid.,* I, No. 11 (June 15, 1936), 2; ALL, *Minutes,* Book II, October 1, 1935; *A Declaration of Independence by Democrats,* Landon Papers; ALL *Bulletin,* II, No. 2 (September 15, 1936), 4.

11. Ernest K. Lindley, *Half Way with Roosevelt* (New York, 1937), 11; Samuel I. Rosenman, *Working with Roosevelt* (New York, 1952), 109-12, 117-19, 130-35; Roosevelt (ed.), *F.D.R.,* I, 623-24; *New York Times,* November 4, 1936; *Newsweek,* VIII, No. 19 (November 7, 1936), 7.

12. Ickes, *Secret Diary,* I, 675; Senate Committee on Campaign Expenditures, *Hearings,* 74 Cong., 2 Sess. (1936); *New York Times,* September 10, 18, 1936.

13. Landon interview, February 14, 1959; Hamilton interview, December 18, 1959; Shouse interview, September 4, 1958; Ickes, *Secret Diary,* I, 641; ALL, *Minutes,* Book III, September 24, 1936; *Newsweek,* VIII, No. 19 (November 7, 1936), 7.

CHAPTER 9 *(pages 224-245)*

1. *New York Times,* June 24, 1936.

2. Samuel I. Rosenman (comp.), *The Public Papers and Addresses of Franklin D. Roosevelt* (New York, 1938-50), V, 101-2; Karl Schriftgiesser, *The Lobbyists* (Boston, 1951), 64-67; Walter Lippman, *Interpretations, 1933-1935* (New York, 1936), 280; Kenneth G. Crawford, *The Pressure Boys* (New York, 1939), 56; *Congressional Record,* 74 Cong., 1 Sess. (July 2, 1935), 10659; *ibid.,* 10589-90; *ibid.* (August 14, 1935), 13190-91; *New Republic,* LXXXVII, No. 1134 (August 26, 1936), 64.

3. *New York Times,* January 26, 1936; *Congressional Record,* 74 Cong., 1 Sess. (July 11, 1935), 11056; *New York Times,* February 15, 1936; Senate Committee to Investigate Lobbying Activities, *Investigation of Lobbying Activities: Hearings,* 74 Cong., 2 Sess. (1936), 1751-1877, hereafter cited as the Black Committee.

4. Black Committee, *Digest of Data,* 74 Cong., 2 Sess. (1936), 1; *New*

York Times, August 25, 1934; Shouse interview, September 5, 1958; ALL, *Minutes,* Book I, September 24, 1934, Shouse File; Black Committee, 1751-1877; *Time,* "Mutual Friends," XXVII, No. 16 (April 20, 1936), 17; *New York Times,* January 11, 1935, April 9, 1936; Wayne Cole, *America First* (Madison, Wisc., 1953); Black Committee, 1748-50.

5. Norman Hapgood (ed.), *Professional Patriots* (New York, 1927), 170; Charles W. Ferguson, *Fifty Million Brothers* (New York, 1937), 329-30; Crawford, *Pressure Boys,* 166-68; *New York Times,* February 12, April 18, 1936; Black Committee, 2047-95; *New York Times,* October 20, 1935; Shouse interview, September 5, 1958.

6. Black Committee, 1653-1729.

7. Jouett Shouse, *The Right of Petition,* ALL Document No. 111 (March 6, 1936), 3; *New York Times,* May 11, 1936; *Congressional Record,* 74 Cong., 2 Sess. (March 20, 1936), 4104-5; *ibid.* (April 3, 1936), 4892-93; *New York Times,* March 6, 1936; Schriftgiesser, *Lobbyists,* 69; *Congressional Record,* 74 Cong., 2 Sess. (March 20, 1936), 4101; Jouett Shouse, *The New Inquisition,* ALL Document No. 114 (March 27, 1936); *Congressional Record,* 74 Cong., 2 Sess. (March 27, 1936), 4461.

8. Black Committee, 1835-1957; *New York Times,* April 11, 1936.

9. *Time,* XXVII, No. 17 (April 27, 1936), 11; *Congressional Record,* 74 Cong., 2 Sess. (April 1, 1936), 4706; Crawford, *Pressure Boys,* 163-64; Black Committee, 1955-2075.

10. *Congressional Record,* 74 Cong., 2 Sess. (March 23, 1936), 4151; *ibid.* (June 6, 1936), 9186; *ibid.* (June 20, 1936), 10495; *ibid.,* 76 Cong., 3 Sess. (May 16, 1940), 6213-28; George Soule, "Liberty League Liberty," *New Republic,* LXXXVIII, No. 1136 (September 9, 1936), 122; Crawford, *Pressure Boys,* 125; Senate Committee on Education and Labor, *To Investigate Violations of the Right of Free Speech and Assembly and Interference with the Right of Labor to Organize and Bargain Collectively: Hearings,* 74 Cong., 2 Sess. (1936), 1-344, cited in text as La Follette Committee; *New York Times,* September 20, 1935; Black Committee, *Digest of Data,* 74 Cong., 2 Sess. (1936), 1; *New York Times,* April 17, 1936.

CHAPTER 10 *(pages 246-263)*

1. *New York Times,* December 20, 1936; ALL, *Minutes,* Book III, September 24, 1936, Shouse File; Memorandum, Desvernine to Shouse,

September 21, 1936, Shouse File; Shouse interview, September 4, 1958; William R. Stayton, "Memorandum Concerning the Activities of the American Liberty League . . ." quoted in James C. Pitney, "American Liberty League, Inc." (unpublished master's thesis, Princeton University, May 1947), 100; Frederick Rudolph, "The American Liberty League, 1934-1940," *American Historical Review*, LVI, No. 1 (October 1950), 19-33; *New York Times*, September 24, 1940; *Time*, XVI, No. 19 (November 10, 1930); Pitney, 108.

2. Harold L. Ickes, *The Secret Diary of Harold L. Ickes* (New York, 1953-54), II, 66; Merlo J. Pusey, *The Supreme Court Crisis* (New York, 1937); Edward S. Corwin, *Court over Constitution* (Princeton, 1938); Robert H. Jackson, *The Struggle for Judicial Supremacy* (New York, 1941); Shouse interview, September 4, 1958; Walter Johnson, *William Allen White's America* (New York, 1947), 465; Alfred M. Landon interview, February 14, 1959; quoted in Pitney, 103; Joseph Alsop and Turner Catledge, *The 168 Days* (Garden City, 1938); *New York Times*, February 13, 1937; quoted in Pitney, 104-5; *Congressional Record*, 75 Cong., 1 Sess. (July 22, 1937), 7381.

3. Shouse interview, September 5, 1958; Democratic National Committee, *What Everybody Wants to Know about Alfred E. Smith* (Albany, N. Y., 1928), 47; Oscar Handlin, *Al Smith and His America* (Boston, 1958), 181; *New York Times*, March 27, 1936.

4. Hamilton Basso, "The Liberty League Writes," *New Republic* LXXXVII, No. 1129 (July 22, 1936), 320; Landon interview, February 14, 1959; Charles W. Ferguson, *Fifty Million Brothers* (New York, 1937), 331; Charles Michelson, *The Ghost Talks* (New York, 1944), 144; "Are Conservatives Naturally Stupid?" *American Mercury*, XLVI (February 1939), 129-35.

5. Michelson, *Ghost Talks*, 144; Stuart Chase, *A New Deal* (New York, 1932); Ernest Weir, "Present Relations of Business to Government," *Vital Speeches*, I (April 22, 1935), 476-78; Shouse interview, September 4, 1958.

6. Michelson, *Ghost Talks*, 144; James A. Farley, *Behind the Ballots* (New York, 1938), 290, 295; Hamilton interview, December 17, 1959.

APPENDIX: AMERICAN LIBERTY
LEAGUE PUBLICATIONS

DOCUMENTS*

* The first eight documents were unnumbered; the reason for assigning 10 instead of 9 to the first numbered document is not known.

LEAFLETS

8. The Magi and the Show Down
9. Government by Busybodies
10. Gratitude in Politics
11. Twenty-eight Facts about the New Deal
12. New Labels for Old Poisons by Representative C. G. Fenerty
13. New Deal Boondoggling Circus
14. Government by Law Still Forced to Fight against the New Deal
15. Who Are the Economic Royalists?
16. Danger Signals
17. And Satan Came Also
18. An Open Letter to the President by Dr. G. W. Dyer
19. The Campaign Is On; Let the People Take Heed by John E. Edgerton
20. Self-styled Liberals
21. Only One Main Issue by J. Ben Wand
22. Tax Facts
23. The Way Dictatorships Start
24. Abolishing the States

BULLETINS

Bulletins were published beginning in August 1935 (Vol. 1, No. 1) and one issued each month up to and including October 1936 (Vol. 2, No. 3).

1937 Bulletin Series

1. The President's Budget Message	1/15/37
2. Government Reorganization	1/25/37
3. The O'Mahoney Federal Licensing Bill	2/5/37
4. Revised Budget Estimates	4/24/37
5. Federal Control and Subsidizing of Agriculture	5/26/37
6. Control of Wages and Hours	6/4/37
7. Extending the TVA Idea	6/21/37
8. Regimentation of Agriculture	6/29/37
9. Taxation for Experimentation	7/9/37
10. Continuance of Emergency Powers	7/21/37
11. Another Budget Fiasco	10/25/37
12. Administration Labor Policies	11/1/37
13. Executive Powers under Reorganization Proposals	11/10/37

1938 Bulletin Series

1. Agricultural Adjustment Act of 1938   2/25/38

LAWYERS' COMMITTEE REPORTS

Report on Constitutionality of National Labor Relations Act (9/5/35)

Report on Constitutionality of Bituminous Coal Conservation Act of 1935 (12/9/35)

Report on Constitutionality of the Potato Act of 1935 (12/30/35)

Welfare Clause in the Light of the AAA Decision (1/6/36)

Discussion of the Constitutionality of the Social Security Act (This report not made public; a few copies printed 11/30/36)

INDEX